P9-CQK-830
LINCOLN CHRISTIAN COLLEGE AND SEMINARY

YOU SHALL NOT ABHOR AN EDOMITE FOR HE IS YOUR BROTHER

EDOM AND SEIR IN HISTORY AND TRADITION

ARCHAEOLOGY AND BIBLICAL STUDIES

published jointly by

The Society of Biblical Literature
and
The American Schools of Oriental Research

Series Editor:
L. Michael White

Number 3

YOU SHALL NOT ABHOR AN EDOMITE
FOR HE IS YOUR BROTHER:
EDOM AND SEIR IN HISTORY AND TRADITION

edited by
Diana Vikander Edelman

YOU SHALL NOT ABHOR AN EDOMITE FOR HE IS YOUR BROTHER

EDOM AND SEIR IN HISTORY AND TRADITION

edited by
Diana Vikander Edelman

Scholars Press
Atlanta, Georgia

YOU SHALL NOT ABHOR AND EDOMITE FOR HE IS YOUR BROTHER
Edom and Seir in History and Tradition

edited by
Diana Vikander Edelman

© 1995
The Society of Biblical Literature
The American Schools of Oriental Research

Library of Congress Cataloging in Publication Data

You shall not abhor and Edomite for he is your brother : Edom and Seir in history and tradition / edited by Diana Vikander Edelman.
p. cm. — (Archaeology and biblical studies ; no. 3)
Includes bibliographical references and index.
ISBN 0-7885-0063-5 (alk. paper)
1. Edomites. 2. Jordan—History. 3. Jordan—Antiquities.
I. Edelman, Diana Vikander, 1954– . II. Series.
DS154.2.Y68 1994
939'.46—dc20 94-40041
CIP

Printed in the United States of America
on acid-free paper

TABLE OF CONTENTS

96745

EDITOR'S NOTE

For the sake of consistency within the volume, I have changed British English to American English in the few instances where there are differences. I have also corrected all the manuscripts to use the term Judahite to refer to the monarchic kingdom of Judah from its rise to its demise in 587 BCE, in contrast to the term Judean, which is to be reserved for reference to the Persian province of Yehud and its successor under the Greek and Roman empires, Judaea. This distinction appears to have been introduced into the historian's vocabulary by Max Miller and John Hayes in their 1986 volume, *A History of Ancient Israel and Judah.* I have a vivid recollection of wondering what the distinction meant when I first saw it in their volume and asking Max for clarification. While at least one colleague has complained that "Judahite" is an "ugly-sounding" term and most non-American historians have not yet adopted this terminological distinction, I feel its usefulness outweighs any lack of melodiousness. Finally, I have not enforced a uniform use of dating terminology—BCE or BC, CE or AD—because I feel that this is very much a personal choice that needs to be respected on an individual basis.

LIST OF ABBREVIATIONS

AASOR	Annual of the American Schools of Oriental Research
ABD	*Anchor Bible Dictionary.* 6 volumes; ed. D. N. Freedman; New York: Doubleday, 1992.
ADAJ	*Annual of the Department of Antiquities of Jordan*
AfO	*Archiv für Orientforschung*
ANET	*Ancient Near Eastern Texts Relating to the Old Testament.* 3d edition with supplement; ed. J. B. Pritchard; Princeton, NJ: Princeton University, 1969.
AOS	American Oriental Series
AS	Assyriological Studies
AUSS	*Andrews University Seminary Studies*
BA	*Biblical Archaeologist*
BAR	British Archaeological Reports
BASOR	*Bulletin of the American Schools of Oriental Research*
BN	*Biblische Notizen*
BTAVO	Beihefte zum Tübinger Atlas des Vorderen Orients
BZ	*Biblische Zeitschrift*
ConBOT	Coniectanea biblica, Old Testament
DMOA	Documenta et Monumenta Orientis Antiqui
EAEHL	*Encyclopedia of Archaeological Excavations in the Holy Land.* 4 volumes; ed. M. Avi-Yonah; Jerusalem: Israel Exploration Society and Massada Press, 1975.
EI	*Eretz Israel*
GM	*Göttinger Miszellen*
Had Arkh	*Hadashot Arkheologiyot*
HSM	Harvard Semitic Monographs
HUCA	*Hebrew Union College Annual*
ICC	International Critical Commentary
IDB	*Interpreter's Dictionary of the Bible.* 4 volumes; ed. G. A. Buttrick; New York: Abingdon, 1964.
IEJ	*Israel Exploration Journal*

JBL	*Journal of Biblical Literature*
JEOL	*Jaarbericht . . . ex oriente lux*
JESHO	*Journal of the Economic and Social History of the Orient*
JNES	*Journal of Near Eastern Studies*
JNSL	*Journal of Northwest Semitic Languages*
JPhil	*Journal of Philology*
JSOT	*Journal for the Study of the Old Testament*
JSOTSup	Journal for the Study of the Old Testament Supplement Series
JTS	*Journal of Theological Studies*
NTOA	Novum Testamentum et Orbis Antiquus
OBO	Orbis biblicus et orientalis
OLA	Orientalia Lovaniensia Analecta
OTS	*Oudtestamentische Studiën*
PEQ	*Palestine Exploration Quarterly*
QDAP	*Quarterly of the Department of Antiquities in Palestine*
RB	*Revue biblique*
RHR	*Revue de l'histoire des religions*
SAM	Sheffield Archaeological Monographs
SBLDS	Society of Biblical Literature Dissertation Series
SEL	*Studi epigrafici e linguistici*
SWBAS	The Social World of Biblical Antiquity Series
TA	*Tel Aviv*
UF	*Ugarit Forschungen*
VT	*Vetus Testamentum*
VTSup	Vetus Testamentum Supplements
WO	*Die Welt des Orients*
ZAW	*Zeitschrift für die alttestamentliche Wissenschaft*
ZDPV	*Zeitschrift des deutschen Palästina-Vereins*

LIST OF CONTRIBUTORS

Diana Vikander Edelman
Department of Philosophy and Religion
James Madison University

John R. Bartlett
Principal
The Church of Ireland Theological College

Beth Glazier-MacDonald
Department of Religion
Centre College

Itzhaq Beit-Arieh
Department of Archaeology
Tel Aviv University

Piotr Bienkowski
Curator of Egyptian and Near Eastern Antiquities
National Museums and Galleries on Merseyside, Liverpool

Ernst Axel Knauf-Belleri
Faculté Autonome de Théologie Protestante
Université de Genève

J. Andrew Dearman
Associate Professor of Old Testament
Austin Presbyterian Theological Seminary

David S. Vanderhooft
Department of Near Eastern Languages
Harvard University

INTRODUCTION

The Edomites have finally come into their own in the last decade and a half, after almost a century of obscurity and extremely low profile. They received an initial burst of attention in the 1890s with the publication of Frants Buhl's *Geschichte der Edomiter* (1893) and Joseph Lury's *Geschichte der Edomiter im biblischen Zeitalter* (1896). The two books became the standard references for articles on Edom, Seir, and Idumaea in encyclopedias and dictionaries written thereafter. Meanwhile, the Edomites received only sporadic attention during the first seven decades of this century, much of which came from John Bartlett. From 1965-1983, he wrote a series of articles placing the Edomites in literary and historical perspective. His efforts culminated in the volume, *Edom and the Edomites,* which appeared in 1989. For years John was a lonely voice crying in the literary wilderness. Then, in the 1980s and continuing through the 1990s, E. Axel Knauf-Belleri began to examine literary, linguistic, geographical, archaeological, and historical issues relating to Edom.

Archaeological exploration of the Edomite homeland in modern Jordan has followed a more steady and frequent course than the literary exploration. A few brave European adventurers visited the region of Edom beginning with John Burckhart in 1812, but the first expeditions with scientific objectives only began to explore the region in the second half of the nineteenth century. After a brief hiatus caused by World War I, the first systematic archaeological survey of Edom using pottery typology to date sites was undertaken by Nelson Glueck, a student of W. F. Albright, in 1933 and 1934. He excavated the site of Jebel et-Tannur in northern Edom, just south of the Wadi el-Ḥasa, in 1937 and Tell el-Kheleifeh in the southern ghor from 1938-1940.

After another dry spell during World War II, archaeological survey and excavation resumed and grew at an unprecedented rate. Crystal Bennett directed excavations at Umm el-Biyara in 1960, 1963 and 1965, at Tawilan from 1968-1970 and again in 1982, and at Buseirah from 1971-1974 and in 1984, while Walter Rast and Thomas Schaub surveyed the southeastern plain of the Dead Sea in 1973. Manfred Weippert surveyed territory south of the Wadi el-Ḥasa in 1974 and 1978 while William Jobling conducted a survey in the ʿAqaba-Maʿan region in 1980 and 1982. From 1979-1983, Burton MacDonald surveyed the area south of the Wadi el-Ḥasa from the road going between at-Ṭafila and Aima in the west eastwards across the plateau to the village of Qalat el-Ḥasa, just west of the modern desert highway. The southern border lay ca. 15 km from the Wadi el-Ḥasa in the west to less than 1 km in the eastern extremity. Meanwhile, Alastair Killick excavated at Udhruḥ and surveyed the surrounding region from 1980-1982. Burton then continued his survey work in the southern ghor and northeast ʿArabah from just north of al-Safi south to Wadi Fidan, ca. 40 km, in 1985 and 1986. Manfred Lindner conducted surveys of the Petra region in 1987 and 1988, and at Selaʿ near Buseirah also in the 1980s. During this period, Andreas Hauptmann and Gerd Weisberger conducted archaeometallurgical investigations in Feinan in 1984, 1986, and 1988, while Stephen Hart undertook an Edom Survey Project between Ṭafila and Ras en-Naqb in 1984-1985 and excavated Grareh in 1986.

The results of the archaeological field work and surveys is still being processed in many instances, and many of the projects still await final publication. Nevertheless, the material remains provide a new set of data to be used in the reconstruction of the history of Edom that was not available to the pioneers in Edomite research, Frants Buhl and Joseph Lury, and not fully available to the most recent Edomite champion, John Bartlett. As a result, John's historical reconstruction in 1989 was primarily a political one, relying almost exclusively on textual material. In the present volume, E. Axel Knauf-Belleri has undertaken a social and economic reconstruction of Edomite history that relies primarily on the new body of archaeological data, supplementing John's earlier work and providing new and exciting dimensions to our knowledge of the Edomites.

The archaeological testimony is not problem-free, however, as evidenced by the recent volume edited by Piotr Bienkowski, *Early Edom and Moab: The Beginning of the Iron Age in Southern Jordan* (1992). Here the issue of how to place material remains in an interpretive chronological framework is addressed by focusing on the most problematic period of evidence, the Iron I. At the core of the dispute is the reliability of dating Transjordanian sites by using pottery typologies and dating sequences based upon them that have been developed on the basis of excavations at Cisjordanian sites. The recognition of the importance of regionalism has strongly influenced this questioning. Since to date, no site has been excavated in Edom that has yielded a continuous and clear stratigraphic sequence from the Late Bronze through the Iron II period that could serve as a standard for developing a local, Edomite chronology, the identification of Iron I and pre-8th century Iron II diagnostic pottery forms remains a debated issue and will preclude the resolution of historical debates about the status and location of any possible Edomite kingdom during the reigns of Saul, David and Solomon. The observant reader will note a range of opinions on the historicity of the biblical references to Edom during the reigns of these three kings within the present volume.

Neither John Bartlett's book nor Piotr Bienkowski's volume of collected essays includes in the discussion a consideration of the Edomite-style pottery and material remains that have been discovered in the Negeb. This important body of evidence opens up a whole set of issues concerning Edom's relationship to Judah in the mid-7th-early 6th centuries BCE, its role in manning or controlling trade routes west of the ʿArabah, and its possible political expansion into the Negeb. Itzhaq Beit Arieh's essay on Edomites in Cisjordan in the present volume fills this crucial gap by providing a summary of archaeological evidence currently available from the Negeb, with accompanying bibliography.

The first six essays were initially presented at the 1990 Annual Meeting of the Society of Biblical Literature and the American Schools of Oriental Research in Kansas City, MO, in a session of the Hebrew Bible, History and Archaeology Section. They have been revised and in some cases, expanded, for final publication. The last two essays have been solicited for inclusion in the volume in order to deal with the religious and linguistic dimensions of Edomite culture. The original session was limited in time to two and a half hours, so it was not possible to include presentations on the latter two topics. Their importance has been acknowledged, however, by their inclusion in the present volume.

As a group, all eight essays focus on issues that have not been fully explored in John Bartlett's 1989 volume or in the set of essays dealing primarily with archaeological issues relating to the Iron I period in Edom and Moab by Piotr Bienkowski and so complement the latter two works nicely. My opening article traces the history of Edom and Seir as geographical terms, taking into consideration the changes that took place as political Edom grew beyond the original confines of geographical Edom and entered the ʿArabah and Cisjordanian territory of Seir. The two studies of Edom in the biblical texts by John Bartlett and Beth Glazier-MacDonald focus on possible changes in attitude toward Edom over time. These two scholars were assigned the difficult task of trying to place references to Edom in nonprophetical and prophetical texts, respectively, in a tentative chronological sequence to determine if there are any discernible changes in tone or attitude, however subtle or blatant, among various biblical writers.

As already mentioned, the article summarizing Edomite finds in Cisjordan by Itzhaq Beit Arieh is the first of its kind. Likewise, the summary of Edomite finds in Transjordan by Piotr Bienkowski, which includes a discussion of dating problems, a description of "Edomite" pottery, and then presents archaeological evidence relating to the Iron I, Iron II, and the end of the Edomite state, with full bibliography, is a unique resource for both the archaeologist and textual specialist. The historical reconstruction by E. Axel Knauf-Belleri, described above, offers an exciting new glimpse of the social and economic history of the Edomites.

The article on Edomite religion by J. Andrew Dearman explores the political, cultural, and territorial dimensions of the term, as well as issues associated with the identity of Qos as a main Edomite deity and evidence for the existence of an Edomite pantheon. The final article by David Vanderhooft reviews the current evidence from seals and inscriptions about the Edomite language and script and concludes that while a distinctive cursive script existed during the 7th and 6th centuries BCE, it is not clear that Edomite was an independent Canaanite dialect.

Diana Vikander Edelman
March 15, 1994

EDOM: A HISTORICAL GEOGRAPHY

Diana Vikander Edelman

Since the term Edom is used to describe both a territory and a state, any study of the history of the use of Edom as a geographical label must also include within its scope a study of its use as the name of a political state. Only a careful consideration of the development of both meanings can yield an adequate understanding of the complex history of the term. Edom means "red" and so would seem to have originated as a descriptive designation for a region characterized by red soil or rocks. However, it was then secondarily applied to the political organization that emerged within the territory it had first described. Once this occurred, the term was able to be used beyond its original geographical confines to designate additional territory that became part of the domain of political Edom outside the original territory of geographical Edom. Thus, tracing the history of Edom as a geographical term necessarily includes consideration of the history of the expansion of the "state" of Edom. The latter task is a difficult one due to the paucity of textual materials, the ideologies that influence the few available texts, and the use of additional terms as synonyms for Edom, particularly Seir and Teman, whose origins and histories also need to be traced before the history of the term Edom can be fully understood.

As Isa 34:6, 63:1, Jer 49:13, 22, 27; and Amos 1:11-12 attest, Bozrah became the central city of political Edom in the 8th and 7th centuries BCE. It was probably the seat of the Edomite kingdom that became a vassal to Adad Nirari III (810-783 BCE)[1] and the capital of Qos-malaku, vassal of Tiglath-Pileser III (745-727).[2] Bozrah almost certainly was the seat of the kingdom during Edom's vassalship to Sargon II (722-705 BCE)[3] as well as the capital of two subsequent Edomite kings: Aiarammu, the vassal of Sennacherib (704-681 BCE)[4] and Qos-gabr, the vassal of Esarhaddon (680-669 BCE)[5] and his successor Ashurbanipal (668-633 BCE).[6] Bozrah has been confidently identified with the modern site of el-

---

[1]For a convenient English translation of the text of the stone slab at Calah, see *ANET*, 281.

[2]*ANET*, 282, from a building inscription.

[3]*ANET*, 291, from broken Prism A.

[4]*ANET*, 287.

[5]*ANET*, 289, from Prism B.

[6]*ANET*, 294, from Cylinder C.

Buseirah, which sits on a natural land spur carved out of the surrounding plateau by the deep ravines of the Wadi el-Hamayida.[7]

As the center of the state that emerged within the geographical region of Edom, Bozrah's location provides a firm clue about the location of the original territory of Edom. It lay in the region east of the ʿArabah and south of the Dead Sea. More specific geographical boundaries must be deduced from textual information. While Egyptian texts provide the earliest known references to a land called Edom, they are too vague to allow the pinpointing of geographical boundaries. The earliest certain textual reference to Edom, found in the late 13th century Papyrus Anastasi (VI:54-56), states "we have just finished letting the *shasu* people of Edom pass the fortress of Merneptah-hotphima-'e (life, prosperity, health), which is in Tjeku, to the pools of Pi-tum."[8] This schoolboy's exercise, which is based on a document from a frontier official, uses the determinative for foreign land to describe Edom and refers to its inhabitants as *shasu*, "sand-dwellers," but is not explicit enough to indicate where the land of Edom lay.[9]

In the Bible, the northern boundary of geographical Edom is consistently called the Brook Zered, which is equated by consensus with the Wadi el-Ḥasa.[10] The southern geographical boundary is less clear. In early discussions, some scholars limited it to the region north of the Wadi al-Ghuweir (the region of el-Jibal),[11] but today most extend Edom

[7]The identification is based on name preservation. For the results of excavations at the site, see C. M. Bennett, "Excavations at Buseirah, Southern Jordan, 1972. Preliminary Report," *Levant* 5 (1973) 1-11; idem, "Excavations at Buseirah, Southern Jordan, 1972. Preliminary Report," *Levant* 6 (1974) 1-24; idem, "Excavations at Buseirah, Southern Jordan, 1973. Third Preliminary Report," *Levant* 7 (1975) 1-19; idem, "Excavations at Buseirah, Southern Jordan, 1974. Fourth Preliminary Report," *Levant* 9 (1977) 1-10.

[8]*ANET,* 259.

[9]W. Helck (*Die Beziehungen Agyptens zu Vorderasien im 3. und 2. Jahrtausend vor Chr.* [2d ed.; Weisbaden: O. Harrassowitz, 1971] 243) has suggested that Edom might be reflected in entries #98 and #128, *ʾi-d-ma,* in the campaign list of Tutmosis II from the 15th century BCE.

[10]So, e.g., F. Buhl, *Geschichte der Edomiter* (Leipzig: A. Edelmann, 1893) 21, 27; J. Lury, *Geschichte der Edomiter im biblischen Zeitalter* (Berlin: L. Wechselmann, 1896) 16; J. L. Porter, "Edom," *Smith's Dictionary of the Bible* (4 vols.; ed. H. B. Hackett; Boston: Houghton, Mifflin, & Co., 1896) 1.661; G. L. Robinson, *The Sarcophagus of an Ancient Civilization* (Chicago: MacMillan, 1930) 192; N. Glueck, "The Boundaries of Edom," *HUCA* 11 (1936) 143; J. Simons, *The Geographical and Topographical Texts of the Old Testament* (Netherlands Instituut voor het Nabije oosten; Studia Francisci Scholten Memoriae Dicata 2; Leiden: Brill, 1959) sec. 266; S. Cohen, "Edom," *IDB,* 2.24.

[11]This position was grounded on the erroneous assumption that the modern term "esh-Shera" preserves the ancient name of Seir, a region that originally was geographically distinct from Edom. The linguistic impossibility of this argument was recognized before the turn of the century, so that this position is found only in

as far south as Ras en-Naqb.[12] It should be noted that the region south of the Wadi al-Ghuweir includes Petra and its famous red Nubian sandstone, so that the characteristic red soil associated with the geographical region of Edom continues through this more mountainous southern region as well. The eastern and western borders of the original geographical Edom are fairly straightforward. The western border would have been the ʿArabah south of the Dead Sea; the eastern border would have been the desert edge.

Turning to Edom as a political designation, the Bible lists a number of sites, most of which are not identifiable, as lying within the borders of political Edom. According to 2 Kgs 14:7, the site of Selaʿ was stormed by Amaziah after he defeated the Edomite army in the Valley of Salt and was subsequently renamed Joktheel. The summary nature of the textual information need not require Selaʿ to be located in the Valley of Salt *per se*; the initial victory could have led to Judah's further advance to the strategic stronghold, which could have been located an unspecified distance north, south, east, or west of the valley being used for access. Since it is uncertain where the Valley of Salt was located, other than the general vicinity of the Dead Sea,[13] Selaʿ's proposed equations

---

very early discussion. So, e.g., J. L. Burckhardt *Travels in Syria and the Holy Land* (London: J. Murray, 1822) 410; E. Robinson and E. Smith, *Biblical researches in Palestine, Mount Sinai and Arabia Petraea: a journal of travels in the years 1838 and 1852* (3 vols.; London: J. Murray, 1841) 2. 552. It can be noted that while E. Robinson accepted the erroneous linguistic equation in a subsequent discussion (ed., *The Comprehensive Critical and Explanatory Bible Encyclopaedia* [Toledo: B. F. Rigg & Co., 1881] 415), he believed nevertheless that Seir originally included the western scarp of the plateau bordering both el-Jibal and esh-Shera.

[12]So, for example, B. Stade, *Geschichte des Volkes Israel* (2 vols.; Berlin: G. Grote, 1887) 1.122; Lury, *Geschichte der Edomiter,* 20; Robinson, *Sarcophagus,* 192; Glueck, "Boundaries of Edom," 144. Contrast Buhl (*Geschichte der Edomiter,* 22), who makes ʿAqaba the southern boundary.

[13]It is equated with the Wadi el-Milḥ in the Negeb by F. M. Abel, *Géographie de la Palestine* (2 vols.; 3d ed.; Paris: J. Gabalda, 1967) 1.407-8; Simons, *Geographical Texts,* sec. 221; C. H. S. Moon, "A Political History of Edom in the Light of Recent Literary and Archaeological Research" (Ph.D. dissertation, Emory University, 1971) 148-49; with es-Sebkah south of the Dead Sea by i.e. E. L. Curtis and A. A. Madsen, *A Critical and Exegetical Commentary on the Books of Chronicles* (ICC 11; New York: Charles Scribner's Sons, 1910) 235; D. Baly, *The Geography of the Bible* (New York: Harper, 1957) 115, 216; and with some place near the Wadi ʿArabah by i.e. M. Noth, *The History of Israel* (2d ed.; Philadelphia: Westminster, 1975) 182; Y. Aharoni, *The Land of the Bible* (revised and enlarged ed.; Philadelphia: Westminster, 1979) 296, 344. A location in northern Syria, on the other hand, is argued on the basis of 2 Sam 8:13 by L. Coleman (*An Historical Book and Atlas of Biblical Geography* [Philadelphia: Lippincott, Grambo and Co., 1854] 118). He places it 24 miles SE of Aleppo, some distance above Hamath, on whose SE margin lie the ruins of Zobah/Zebah.

with Kh. Silʿ[14] and Petra/Umm el-Biyara[15] must remain guesses only.

Two additional sites located within Edom according to the Bible are Ezion-geber and Elot/Elat,[16] mentioned in 1 Kgs 9:26 and 2 Chr 8:17. The latter is described to lay on the shore of the Red Sea in the land of Edom, while the former is a nearby site where Solomon was to have built a fleet. Both sites clearly lay within the ʿArabah valley and not the mountainous country of Edom proper. Thus, they testify to the widening of Edom as a geographical term to include new territories brought under control of the domain of the political entity Edom.

Genesis 36 and its parallel traditions in 1 Chr 1:43-50, 52-54 provide the additional Edomite place names Dinhabah, Avith, Masrekah, Rehoboth hannahar, and Pau/Pai (vv. 31-39); Elah, Pinon, Teman, Mibzar and Magdiel (vv. 40-41). Except for Elah or Elat/Elot[17] and Pinon or

[14]So, e.g., U. F. Seetzen, *Reisen durch Syrien, Palästina, Phonicien, Transjordan-Länder, Arabia Petraea und Unter-Aegypten, Herausgegben und commentiert von Prof. Dr. Fr. Kruse* (3 vols.; Berlin: G. Reimer, 1854-1859) 1.425; 3.19; R. Hartmann, "Die Namen von Petra," *ZAW* 30 (1910) 150; Aharoni, *Land of the Bible,* 40, 441.

[15]So, for example, Lury, *Geschichte der Edomiter,* 29; G. Horsfield and A. Conway, "Historical and Topographical Notes on Edom: With an Account of the First Excavation at Petra," *Geographical Journal* 76 (1930) 377; Abel, *Géographie,* 2.87; N. Glueck, *Explorations in Eastern Palestine II* (AASOR 15; New Haven: American Schools of Oriental Research, 1935) 49, 82; Simons, *Geographical Texts,* sec. 923; S. Cohen, "Sela," *IDB,* 4.262-3; S. Schulz, "Petra," *Biblisch-historisches Handwörterbuch* (4 vols.; ed. B. Reicke and L. Rost; Göttingen: Vandenhoeck and Ruprecht, 1962-1979) 3.1430.

[16]The identification of the site is disputed. F. Frank ("Aus der ʿAraba, I: Reiserberichte," *ZDPV* 57 [1934] 244) equated it with a ruined site 1 km N of mod ʿAqaba, while W. Ewing ("Elat," *The International Standard Bible Encyclopaedia* [5 vols.; ed. J. Orr; Chicago: Howard-Severance Co., 1955] 2.923) and Aharoni (*Land of the Bible,* 36, 434), for example, identified it with modern ʿAqaba. They almost certainly mean the section of ʿAqaba known as ʿAila, which is more specifically pinpointed by Buhl (*Geschichte der Edomiter,* 39) and Simons (*Geographical Texts,* secs. 832-3). A third popular option was proposed by N. Glueck (*The Other Side of Jordan* [New Haven: American Schools of Oriental Research, 1940] 89), who considered Elat to be the later name of Ezion-geber and equated both place names with the site of Tell el-Kheleifeh. He has been followed by S. Cohen, "Elat," *IDB,* 2.71 and K. Elliger, "Ezeon-Geber," *Biblisch-historisches Handwörterbuch* (4 vols; ed. B. Reiche and L. Rost; Göttingen: Vandenhoeck and Ruprecht, 1962-1979) 1.462. J. Bartlett (*Edom and the Edomites,* [JSOTSup 77; Sheffield: JSOT, 1989] 46) on the other hand, simply locates Elat at Tell el-Kheleifeh, without bringing Ezion-geber into the equation.

[17]Punon is widely equated with modern Feinan. So, e.g., Buhl, *Geschichte der Edomiter,* 38; Seetzen, *Reisen,* 3.17; Abel, *Géographie,* 2.42, 216, 410-411; Glueck, *Explorations,* 32; Simons, *Geographical Texts,* sec. 439; R. Knipperberg, "Pinon," *Biblisch-historisches Handwörterbuch* (4 vols.; ed. B. Reicke and L. Rost; Göttingen: Vandenhoeck & Ruprecht, 1962-1979) 3.1475; Aharoni, *Land of the Bible,* 440; Bartlett, *Edom and the Edomites,* 50.

Punon,[18] none can be identified with any confidence, regardless of the date assigned to the lists. Rassam Cylinder C names two additional sites, Azaril and Hirata-kasaia, which were places where Ashurbanipal routed fleeing Arabs.[19] Both lack identification. Unfortunately, these additional twelve names are of little help in elucidating the territory associated with political Edom or the growth of political Edom beyond geographical Edom.

A. Knauf's comparative study of the tribal names of Seir and Esau and the names of the *ʿallûpîm* of Edom in Genesis 36 (=1 Chr 1:38-42, 51-54) with modern south Jordanian toponyms that lack an Arabic etymology provides some promising localizations of thirteen Edomite groups.[20] They include Shobal, Magdiel, Manahath, Zibeon, Ebal, Uz, Mibzar, Thimna, Alwan, Dishon, Zerah, Hemam, and Ana. All are situated south of the Wadi el-Ḥasa, in the mountainous region that has been seen above to have been the original core of geographical Edom. If correct, they would tend to corroborate the centering of the early 7th century political state of Edom within geographical Edom.

The widening of political Edom to include the Negeb territory to the west of the ʿArabah eventually culminated in the transfer of the former geographical and political term to the southern Negeb as the provincial name Idumaea. When this provincial label became established is not clear from our present textual evidence, although it is firmly in place by the Hellenistic period. Nevertheless, its roots almost certainly are to be traced in part to Edomite presence in the western ʿArabah and eastern Negeb in the late monarchic period.[21]

Archaeological evidence for Edomite presence in the Negeb has been uncovered at a number of excavated sites: Tel Malḥatha, Tel Masos, Tel ʿIra, Tel ʿAroer, Tel Arad, Ḥorvat ʿUza, Ḥorvat Radum,

[18]This latter group was identified as a group of place names rather than personal names by J. Bartlett "The Edomite King List of Genesis 36:31-39 and I Chron. 1:43-50," *JTS* n.s. 16 (1965) 301-14.

[19]*ANET,* 298.

[20]"Edom: The Social and Economic History," in the present volume. Since I consider Mt. Seir to have originally been a label for the eastern Negeb highlands, I would question the proposed locations of Shobal, Dishon, Manahath, Ebal, Zibeon, Ana, and Hemam east of the ʿArabah, unless it can be demonstrated that by the era in which the author of Genesis 36 lived, political Edom had already gained control of the eastern Negeb highlands, allowing Seir and Edom to become interchangeable labels for the Edomite state. Even so, the author is making a distinction between the offspring of Seir, who are designated as "inhabitants of the land," and Esau's offspring in the land of Edom. This distinction suggests to me that Seir is being used as a geographical label to represent the territory west of the ʿArabah, in distinction to territory east of the ʿArabah, the land of Edom.

[21]For another important influential factor, see *ibid.*

Ḥorvat Qitmit, and Kadesh Barnea.[22] In all cases, the Edomite material is dated from the second half of the 7th century BCE to the beginning of the 6th century BCE. Neutron activation analysis of a number of the painted wares from Qitmit has indicated that they were locally produced, not imported through trade. The Edomite-style cooking pots, on the other hand, were not made locally. The reason for and nature of this Edomite presence west of the ʿArabah is not yet totally clear, but probably is to be linked to economic factors associated with the control of trade routes through the region.[23] Whether the Negeb was essentially unincorporated territory open to any group interested in it, part of the kingdom of Judah at this time, or territory monitored by the Assyrian and then Egyptian empires needs further investigation.[24]

A number of prophetical texts from the end of the monarchy condemn Edom for playing a role in Jerusalem's final demise in 587 BCE (Joel 4:19; Obad 10-16; Mal 1:4 cf Ps 137:7; and Lam 4:21-22), suggesting Edomite presence in Cisjordan. The exact nature of that role varies in the texts. While Jer 40:11 refers neutrally to the flight of Judahites to Edom, Joel 4:19 seems to allude to the killing of Judahite refugees in Edom, a theme that reappears in Obad 14. Obadiah similarly castigates Edom for its failure to help its brother Judah when the Neo-Babylonians took and looted Jerusalem in vv. 11-12; Ps 137:7 seems also to echo an onlooker's stance. The four latter statements condemn Edom for its failure to act on Judah's behalf, but do not suggest that Edom took an active part in the state's demise in 587 BCE.[25] On the other hand, in v. 13,

---

[22]For a discussion of all this material, see I. Beit Arieh, "The Edomites in Cisjordan," in the present volume.

[23]This explanation was suggested in a paper by R. Haak entitled "Zephaniah's Oracles Against the Nations" that was presented at the Chicago Society for Biblical Research on February 2, 1992. It has been taken up by B. Glazier-McDonald in her article, "Edom in the Prophetic Corpus," in the present volume. I. Finkelstein has independently raised the same possibility ("*Ḥorvat Qiṭmit* and the Southern Trade in the Late Iron Age II," *ZDPV* 108 [1992] 156-70).

[24]N. Naʾaman, for example, has raised the possibility that the fortress at Kadesh Barnea was built by the Assyrians and staffed by local Semites or mercenaries. He thinks that it was subsequently transferred to Egyptian control in the late 7th century BCE, citing the use of hieratic for record-keeping as evidence ("The Kingdom of Judah under Josiah," *Tel Aviv* 18 [1991] 48).

[25]So noted by Bartlett (*Edom and the Edomites,* 151-61), who concludes that the complaints raised against it in postexilic writings are based on prejudice without even circumstantial evidence to back them. He follows H. W. Wolff in rejecting Amos 1:11 and Joel 4:19 as late textual additions with no historical accuracy and traces the negativity against Edom back to David's conquest of Edom and Edom's later successful fight for independence, together with Edom's failure to fall to the Babylonians at the same time Judah did in 587. Because prophetical texts are often general rather than explicit in their accusations and threats, the lack of more *explicit*

Obadiah accuses Edom of also having entered the city and looted it, thereby assigning it an active role in Judah's destruction.[26] The entrance and looting could either have taken place during the Neo-Babylonian attack, with Edomite troops among those supplied by vassal states for the operation, or could have taken place in the wake of the neo-Babylonian attack and withdrawal from the area. The references to Edom in Lam 4:21-22 and Mal 1:4 are too vague to assign to either particular role, but reinforce the general hostility toward this country shortly after the fall of Jerusalem.

Further textual evidence for Edom's expansion into the region west of the ʿArabah may be provided by the equation of Edom with (Mt.) Seir. Seir itself generally is taken to mean "hairy," suggesting a forested region.[27] However, two other meanings would seem to be equally plausible, if not more so. One, probably derived from the same root sense of "hairy," would be "goaty." In this instance, Seir could either have been a dialectical form of the Judahite noun *sāʿîr*, "goat,"[28] or an adjectival form relating to the noun *sāʿîr*. The only drawback to the first option would be the lack of one of the standard endings like *-ôn* or *-ayîm* to indicate the geographical scope of the term "goat land."[29] Yet, linguists cannot be certain that such locative suffixes were an absolute prerequisite in geographical names. The frequent appearance of the term *har*, "mountain," before Seir might have eliminated the need for the standard geographical suffix, indicating that the region in question was "goat mountain." No geographical ending would have been needed were Seir an adjective.

---

statements of Edom's direct role in aiding the Neo-Babylonians in the destruction of Jerusalem in 587 does not rule out such a situation.

[26]Bartlett (*ibid.*, 154-55) does not believe that Obad 13 is an authentic chronicle of Edom's active role in Jerusalem's fall. He argues that the verse is the poet's projection of himself into the past and his vivid imagining of Jerusalem's fall, warning Judah's ancient enemy against stereotypical hostile behavior. He cites the references to Edom's gloating, rejoicing and boasting in vv. 12-14 as attitudes rather than active participation. Yet of the three verbs in verse 13 specifically, only one, "boasting," reflects an attitude; the other two, "enter" and "loot," describe physical activities. The reference to Edom's burning of the temple during the destruction in 587 in 1 Esd 5:5, on the other hand, may well be based on the claims in Obad 13 rather than reflecting an independent tradition or collective memory.

[27]This was first argued apparently by P. de Lagarde (*Uebersicht über die im aramäischen, arabischen und hebräischen übliche Bildung der Nomina* [Abhandlungen der königlichen Gesellschaft der Wissenschaften zu Göttingen 35; Göttingen: Dieterich, 1889] 92) and his conclusion is routinely quoted in discussions of the term.

[28]So, for instance, G. B. Gray, *Studies in Hebrew Proper Names* (London: A. and C. Black, 1896) 94, n. 2.

[29]This point was raised by E. A. Knauf in private correspondence.

The second option to be considered would derive Seir from *sʿr* II, "sweep or whirl away." Seir could be an adjective meaning "whirled away" or "made bare," needing no geographical ending. Mt. Seir would then be a mountainous region that was windswept and barren.

It is commonly concluded that Mt. Seir is to be located east of the ʿArabah, either as a synonym for the Edomite territory in general,[30] or more specifically, as the western scarp of the Edomite plateau[31] or the southern part of the Edomite plateau, the esh-Sherah region between the Wadi al-Ghuweir and Ras en-Naqb.[32] A few scholars have argued that Seir included the mountains and rough steppe on both sides of the ʿArabah.[33] However, the biblical testimony tends to indicate that it was originally a geographical term at home in the mountains bordering the western ʿArabah, i.e. the eastern Negeb highlands.[34]

---

[30]So, e.g., G. A. Smith, *The Historical Geography of the Holy Land* (26th ed.; London: Hodder & Stoughton, 1935) 557; Coleman, *Historical Book,* 34; Buhl, *Geschichte der Edomiter,* 30; Robinson, *Sarcophagus,* 176; Glueck, *Other Side of the Jordan,* 134, 149; Simons, *Geographical Texts,* secs. 68, 435; M. Seligsohn, "Edom, Idumea," *The Jewish Encyclopaedia* (12 vols; ed. I Singer; New York: Funk and Wagnalls, 1903) 5.40.

[31]So, e.g., J. P. Lawson and J. M. Wilson, *A Cyclopaedia of Biblical Geography, Biography, Natural History and General Knowledge* (2 vols.; London: A. Fullarton & Co., 1870) 1.722; Porter," Edom, Idumaea," 661-62; A. Musil, *The northern Hagaz* (New York: Czech Academy of Sciences and Arts and Charles J. Crane, 1926) 251-52; W. F. Albright, "The Oracles of Balaam," *JBL* 63 (1944) 207-209, 229 n. 120; Cohen, "Edom," 2.24; Aharoni, *Land of the Bible,* 40; E. A. Knauf, "Seir," *ABD,* 5.1072.

[32]See note #11. Buhl (*Geschichte der Edomiter,* 29), while opting for the more general equation with Edom, implies strongly that this more limited meaning was the original one, being found in early texts.

[33]So, e.g., Lury (*Geschichte der Edomiter,* 11), who includes the ʿArabah as well; A. H. Sayce, "Edom, Edomites," *A Dictionary of the Bible* (5 vols.; ed. J. Hastings; New York: Charles Scribner's Sons, 1911) 1.644; Smith, *Historical Geography,* 560; Simons, *Geographical Texts,* secs. 68, 435; apparently, Moon, "Political History of Edom," 7-11.

[34]This was argued early by Stade (*Geschichte des Volkes Israel,* 1:122) and W. Baudissin ("Edom," *Realencyclopadie für protestantische Theologie und Kirche* [24 vols; ed. J. J. Herzog; Leipzig: J. C. Hinrichs, 1896-1913] 5.163). It was subsequently taken up again by Abel (*Géographie,* 1.281-85; 389-91) and by H. P. Rüger ("Seir," *Biblisch-historisches Handwörterbuch* [4 vols.; ed. B. Reicke and L. Rost; Göttingen: Vandenhoeck & Ruprecht, 1962-1979] 3.1760). It was reasserted by J. R. Bartlett ("The Land of Seir and the Brotherhood of Edom," *JTS* n.s. 20 [1969] 5, 18) and then adopted by L. E. Axelsson (*The Lord Rose Up from Seir: Studies in the History and Traditions of the Negev and Southern Judah* [ConBOT 25; Lund: Almqvist & Wicksell, 18987] 70). In subsequent work, Bartlett has more specifically located Seir in "the wilder, scrubby land south of Judah and Mt. Halak and between Kadesh and the Gulf of ʿAqaba" (*Edom and the Edomites,* 44). Recently, N. Naʾaman also has recognized the association of the label Seir with the region west of the ʿArabah in certain Egyptian and biblical texts and seems to favor this area as the original location of the geographical term, even though he argues that the equation of Seir and Edom goes back to a very early time ("Israel, Edom and Egypt in the 10th Century B.C.E.," *Tel Aviv* 19 [1992] 74).

The genealogical lists in Genesis 36 state outright that the Edomites secondarily came into control of Seir, "displacing," absorbing, and intermarrying with the native inhabitants of the region. Timnaᶜ is named as a native female offspring of Seir. The site of Timnaᶜ is located in the southwestern mountains facing the ᶜArabah, not on the eastern Edomite side. Timnaᶜ reappears as the concubine of the main son of Edom, Eliphaz, whose union produces Amalek. The Amalekites are traditionally associated with the southern Negeb region, and Timnaᶜ's status as a concubine rather than full wife suggests some sort of secondary association between the Edomites and the region of Timnaᶜ.[35]

In the poem in Deuteronomy 33, Yahweh is associated with the geographical regions of Sinai, Seir and Paran. Sinai and Paran are commonly located somewhere west of the ᶜArabah, down into the Sinai peninsula. This suggests in turn that the remaining term Seir is to be located west of the ᶜArabah as well, probably in the Negeb highlands.

Seir's location west of the ᶜArabah also seems to be indicated by el-Amarna letter #288, in which Abdi-Ḫepa, king of Jerusalem, reports to pharaoh that there is war against him as far as the land of Seir and as far as Gath-Carmel.[36] While it is reasonable to believe that Abdi-Ḫepa had laid claim to the Negeb regions adjoining the southern hill country of Judah, it seems less likely that he would have controlled the mountainous scarp east of the ᶜArabah. It would not have been contiguous to his own holdings unless he had also controlled the eastern Negeb highlands. The two other references to Seir in Egyptian texts are too vague to allow one to favor a location on either the east or west side of the ᶜArabah. Both link the region with *shasu*. Ramses II (ca. 1279-1212 BCE) claims to have laid waste the land of the *shasu*, plundering Mt. Seir with his valiant arm.[37] Ramses III (ca. 1172-1141 BCE) claims to have destroyed the people of Seir among the *shasu*, razing their tents and carrying off their people, property and cattle into captivity.[38]

Additional textual evidence for Edom's expansion across the ᶜArabah into the former region of Mt. Seir and even further north, into the territory of Judah, is supplied by the book of Deuteronomy. The writer has systematically avoided the use of Edom in favor of Seir. This is particularly clear from a comparison of the account of the wilderness

---

[35]For further arguments about the location of other names in this genealogy west of the ᶜArabah, see E. Meyer (*Die Israeliten und ihre Nachbarstämme* [Halle: M. Neimeyer, 1906] 328-54) and Bartlett ("The Land of Seir," 2-5; idem, *Edom and the Edomites,* 87-8).

[36]*ANET,* 488.

[37]P. Montet, *Les nouvelles fouilles de Tanis, 1929-1932* (Publications de la Faculté des Lettres de Strasbourg, II.10; Paris: Les Belles Lettres, 1933) 70-72.

[38]*ANET,* 262, from Papyrus Harris I.

wandering in Deuteronomy 1-2 with the same account in Numbers 20. Numbers uses Edom consistently; Deuteronomy uses Seir and the sons of Esau instead.[39] Nevertheless, the writer of Deuteronomy betrays his deliberate policy of substitution because he uses the geographical term Seir to designate territory beyond the Negeb highlands proper as though it were the name of a political entity as well. In 1:44, for example, Seir refers to the hill country of Judah inhabited by the Amorites, who beat the Israelites back as far south as Hormah.

Since there is no evidence of a state of Seir that emerged from the territory of the same name, and it is clear that Seir has been systematically used in place of the term Edom, the use of Seir in the book of Deuteronomy to designate territory in southern Judah as well as the Negeb and Negeb highlands can be seen to provide indirect evidence that the state of Edom spread westward and claimed land west of the ʿArabah. Once political Edom controlled Mt. Seir, the two terms came to be used as synonyms, although in most cases "Seir" seems to be used to refer to Cisjordanian Edomite territory, maintaining its long-standing geographical associations. The expression *śᵉdēh ʾᵉdôm*, "flatland or field of Edom," in Gen 32:4 and Judg 5:4 apparently arose after Edom's occupation of the Negeb, as evidenced by its use beside "Seir" to describe Cisjordanian Edomite holdings.[40]

Finally, the term Teman needs comment. It is a *taw*-preformative noun from the root YMN meaning "south." As such, it could be a general description for any southern region, covering a wide amount of territory. However, Amos 1:12 speaks of the fire that Yahweh will hurl on Teman that will consume the palaces of Bozrah, Ezek 25:13 threatens the Edomites "from Teman to Dedan," and in Gen 36:11, Teman is the first-born of Edom's eldest or most prominent son Eliphaz. These three passages suggest that Teman originally was a designation for the northern portion of the Edomite plateau, the region surrounding Bozrah.[41]

---

[39]The sole use of Edom/Edomite in Deuteronomy is found in 23:8: "You shall not abhor an Edomite, for he is your brother." This prohibition presumes a history of hostility between Judahites and Edomites that is deep-rooted enough to be hard to reverse. In my opinion, the law presumes the social setting of the community in the Persian or Hellenistic period and may well date from the Hasmoneans' forced conversion of Idumaea to Judaism.

[40]So earlier, e.g., Buhl, *Geschichte der Edomiter,* 28, 29. Contrast Lury (*Geschichte der Edomiter,* 11 n 5), who suggests that the expression *śᵉdēh ʾᵉdôm* refers to the ʿArabah.

[41]So, for example, E. A. Knauf, "Teman," *ABD,* 6.347-48. Contrast R. de Vaux ("Téman, ville ou région d'Edom?" *RB* 76 [1969] 385), who argues that it originally designated the southern esh-Shera region of Edom but became a synonym for Edom in general. Bartlett (*Edom and the Edomites,* 40) suggests on the basis of Ezek 25:12-14 that it represents the Wadi Ḥisma region south of Ras en-Naqb, with Dedan being el-ʿUla in the Hejaz region of northern Arabia. Buhl (*Geschichte der Edomiter,* 30) had

After the state emerged at Bozrah, this local term came to be synonymous with the core territory of the state, so that Jer 49:7, 20 and Obad 9 could use Teman as a synonym for Edom.

To summarize, Edom originated as a geographical term designating the plateau and adjoining western scarp characterized by red soil and rocks between the Wadi el-Ḥasa and Ras en-Naqb on the eastern side of the ʿArabah. The northern portion of the plateau also came to be known as Teman. After the Edomite state emerged with its capital at Bozrah, the term "Edom" spread beyond its original confines as the state grew and added new territory to its domain. In the process, the ʿArabah came to be part of Edom, as did the eastern Negeb highlands, otherwise known as Mt. Seir, the Negeb and southernmost Judah. With the emergence of the province of Idumaea that was located completely west of the ʿArabah, a total territorial transfer of the original geographical term was accomplished.

---

long ago argued against this location as being too far south on the basis of the identical text.

EDOM IN THE NONPROPHETICAL CORPUS

John R. Bartlett

My primary responsibility is to discuss how "Edom" has been used by the biblical writers within the nonprophetical corpus. I have been asked to explore whether the texts reflect changes in attitude towards the nation of Edom and perhaps to suggest a relative chronology for uses of "Edom." My "nonprophetic" brief will include the Pentateuch, the Deuteronomistic History work, and the Psalms; genuinely prophetic works will be discussed by Beth Glazier-McDonald.

Poetic texts mentioning Edom will be examined first. Following Albright and Freedman, many scholars assume that these texts—in particular the Song of Moses, the final oracle of Balaam, and the Song of Deborah—are premonarchic and can therefore be taken to reflect a very early view of Edom.[1] Others, including myself, are not convinced that these texts were composed at such an early date. The Song of Moses, Exodus 15, after celebrating God's mighty actions on behalf of his people Israel, describes their effect on the surrounding peoples:

> The peoples have heard, they tremble;
> pangs have seized on the inhabitants of Philistia.
> Now are the chiefs of Edom dismayed;
> the leaders of Moab, trembling seizes them;
> all the inhabitants of Canaan have melted away. (Exod 15:14-15)

Here the terms Philistia, Edom, Moab and Canaan seem to have territorial reference, each region having its identifiable inhabitants, chiefs or leaders. Kings are not mentioned, so the poem might predate monarchy in Edom and Moab—but not necessarily. There are other indications in the poem that might suggest its origins in the Israelite monarchic period. In either case, the poet knows of distinguishable political territories and territories understood to be hostile to Israel. These places are Israel's enemies, and Yahweh's salvific activity for Israel naturally and rightly dismays Israel's enemies. The question needs to be asked, "When were

---

[1]See, e.g., W. F. Albright, "The Oracles of Balaam," *JBL* 63 (1944) 207-33; D. N. Freedman, "Early Israelite History in the Light of Early Israelite Poetry," *Unity and Diversity: Essays in the History, Literature and Religion of the Ancient Near East* (ed. H. Goedicke and J. J. M. Roberts; Baltimore: Johns Hopkins University, 1975) 3-35; idem, "'Who is Like Thee among the Gods?' The Religion of Early Israel," *Ancient Israelite Religion* (ed. P. D. Miller, P. D. Hanson and S. D. McBride; Philadelphia: Fortress, 1987) 315-36.

Philistia, Moab, Edom and Canaan seen as Israel's political enemies?," and, *pace* Freedman,[2] a *terminus post quem* in the time of Saul and David, the period of the beginning of Israel's national self-awareness, seems more plausible.

The next poetic reference to Edom comes in the last oracle of Balaam, Num 24:17-19.

> A star shall come forth out of Jacob,
>   and a scepter shall rise out of Israel;
> it shall crush the forehead of Moab,
>   and break down all the sons of Sheth.
> Edom shall be disposessed,
>   Seir also, his enemies, shall be dispossessed,
>   while Israel does valiantly.
> By Jacob shall dominion be exercised,
>   and the survivors of cities be destroyed!

Here, the reference seems to be less to territories than to peoples; territorial terms (Moab, Edom, Seir) are used but peoples are in mind. The peoples are clearly hostile, to be crushed and dispossessed by Jacob/Israel. There is even a reference to the survivors of cities, which suggests that the poet belongs to a period when Edom and Moab had cities. The poet certainly belongs to a time when Edom and Seir can be closely linked in poetic parallelism and perhaps even, for the author's purposes, virtually identified. For reasons explained elsewhere,[3] it is unlikely that this can predate the Davidic period, and the association of these oracles with the figure of Balaam, now known from a nonbiblical 8th or 7th century BC inscription from Tell Deir ʿAlla,[4] suggests the monarchic period, probably the later monarchic period. This is perhaps supported by the reference to Assyrian captivity for the Kenite in Num 24:22. For all

[2]"Early Israelite History," 6-8.

[3]See J. R. Bartlett, "The Land of Seir and the Brotherhood of Edom," *JTS* n.s. 20 (1969) 1-20.

[4]For the *editio princeps* of these texts, see J. Hoftijzer and G. van der Kooij, *Aramaic Texts from Deir ʿAlla* (Leiden: Brill, 1976). H. J. Franken suggested a Persian period dating for them ("Texts from the Persian Period from Tell Deir ʿAlla," *VT* 17 [1967] 480-81). J. A. Hackett (*The Balaam Text from Deir ʿAlla* [Chico, CA: Scholars Press, 1984]) proposed a 7th century date on the basis of comparisons with the letter forms used in 7th century Ammonite inscriptions, but most scholars prefer an 8th century dating on grounds of stratigraphy, carbon-14 dating, and epigraphic comparisons; see J. Naveh, "The Date of the Deir ʿAlla Inscription in Aramaic Script," *IEJ* 17 (1967) 256-58; A. Lemaire, "L'inscription de Balaam trouvée à Deir ʿAlla: épigraphie," *Biblical Archaeology Today: Proceedings of the International Congress on Biblical Archaeology, Jerusalem, April 1984* (ed. J. Amitai; Jerusalem: Israel Exploration Society, 1985) 313-25. See also A. Caquot and A. Lemaire, "Les textes araméens de Deir ʿAllā," *Syria* 54 (1977) 189-208; H. and M. Weippert, "Die "Bileam"-Inschrift von Tell Der ʿAlla," *ZDPV* 98 (1982) 77-103.

these reasons, this oracle would seem to reflect an attitude towards Edom and Moab that belongs to the monarchic period.

Judges 5 contains the famous passage:

> Lord, when you went forth from Seir,
> when you marched from the region of Edom,
> the earth trembled,
> and the heavens dropped,
> yea, the clouds dropped water.
> The mountains quaked before the Lord,
> yon Sinai before the Lord, the God of Israel. (Judg 5:4-5)

Here Edom and Seir are undeniably territories, and there is no hostile reference to their peoples. Edom and Seir, remarkably, are seen as the base camp of the Lord; it is from here that Yahweh comes to rescue Israel. This probably reflects an older conception of Yahweh that has been preserved to surface in a court epic from monarchic times in the kingdom of Israel. The bard is singing before kings and princes (Judg 5:3), probably at the court of the king of Israel, extolling the valor of the northern tribes and their leaders in the ancient battle against the kings of Canaan, long ago in the days of Shamgar and Jael.[5] The bard's lay indirectly reveals that there was a time when Edom and Seir were not seen as hostile places, the homes of Israel's enemies, but were reckoned with Sinai, Paran, Kadesh, and Teman (cf. Deut 33:1; Hab 3:3) as the home territory of Yahweh.

Edom appears again in the poetic oracle in Ps 60:6-8, 9 (cf. Ps 108:7-9, 10) (MT: Ps 60:8-10, 11; 108:8-10, 11):

> God has spoken in his sanctuary:
> "With exultation I will divide up Shechem
> and portion out the Vale of Succoth.
> Gilead is mine; Manasseh is mine;
> Ephraim is my helmet;
> Judah is my scepter.
> Moab is my washbasin;
> upon Edom I cast my shoe;
> over Philistia I shout in triumph."
> Who will bring me to the fortified city?
> Who will lead me into Edom?

Moab and Edom here are clearly territories, and the oracle given from the sanctuary, apparently in Jerusalem, seems to declare that Edom, with Moab and Philistia and other places, belongs under God's rule, exercised through Judah (God's scepter). The oracle is set in the context of the psalmist's complaint that God's people have suffered defeat and feel

---

[5]See J. R. Bartlett, *Edom and the Edomites* (JSOTSup 77; Palestine Exploration Fund Monograph Series 1; Sheffield: JSOT Press, 1989) 102.

rejected by God. The psalmist (the king?) prays for God's help, asking rhetorically,

> Who will bring me to the fortified city?
> Who will lead me to Edom?

The fortified city is perhaps Bozrah,[6] whose strongholds are referred to in Amos 1:12. Edom is clearly hostile, and the situation appears to be that the people, recently defeated by the Edomites, are seeking God's support for a successful counter-attack. All this sets the psalm firmly in the monarchic period, at a time when the people might hope for future success after an initial setback, possibly after Edom's successful rebellion in the mid-9th century BC, but probably later.

Having completed discussion of the poetic texts, narratives about Edom or involving Edom will now be examined, beginning with the story of Esau and Jacob in Genesis 25-33. This story of brotherly rivalry is given explicit political reference by the narrator; the Lord says in an oracle to the pregnant Rebekah,

> Two nations are in your womb,
> and two peoples, born of you, shall be divided;
> the one shall be stronger than the other,
> the elder shall serve the younger. (Gen 25:23)

The elder, Esau, is identified by a word play with Edom; he is tricked out of his dying father's blessing by the younger, to whom Isaac says,

> May God give you of the dew of heaven,
> and of the fatness of the earth,
> and plenty of grain and wine.
> Let peoples serve you,
> and nations bow down to you. (Gen 27:28-29)

The text recalls Gen 49:10-11, where Jacob promises in turn that Judah shall bear rule and win "the obedience of the peoples." To Esau/Edom, however, Isaac says,

---

[6]This is perhaps suggested by the parallelism of "fortified city" (*ʿîr māṣôr*) and "Edom," though elsewhere Edom is paralleled by "the land of Teman," just as Moab is paralleled by "the strongholds of Kerioth" (Amos 2:2). The parallel version in Ps 108:11 reads *ʿîr mibṣār* ("fortified city"); this might be connected with the Mibzar of Gen 36:42, which J. J. Simons (*The Geographical and Topographical Texts of the Old Testament* [Leiden: Brill, 1959]) following W. R. S. Smith ("Animal Worship and Animal Tribes among the Arabs and in the Old Testament," *JPhil* 9 [1880] 75-103, esp. 90) tentatively identified with Bozrah. The psalmist may have been thinking of Bozrah; certainly the modern Buseirah, on a spur of mountain surrounded on three sides by deep wadis, may be described as an *ʿîr māṣôr* or *ʿîr mibṣār*.

Behold, away from the fatness of the earth shall your dwelling be,
and away from the dew of heaven on high.
By your sword you shall live,
and you shall serve your brother;
but when you break loose
you shall break his yoke from your neck. (Gen 27:39-40)

This surely refers to Edom's servitude to the Davidic kingdom and to Edom's subsequent rebellion (2 Sam 8:14; 1 Kgs 8:20). Edom's readiness with the sword is emphasized also in Amos 1:11-12, where Edom's pursuit of his brother with the sword refers in my view[7] to the rebellion of Edom in Jehoram's day, and again in the narrative of Num 20:14-21. Edom's vindictiveness is underlined later in the Jacob-Esau story; Jacob fears his reunion with Esau, "lest he come and slay us all" (Gen 32:11). This whole narrative underlines from the start the enmity of Edom and Jacob, who here must be understood as standing for his son Judah; enmity began in the womb, where they struggled, continued in the subjugation of the older brother by the younger, and in the violence of the younger's rebellion and subsequent independence. This narrative thus clearly understands Edom politically as an independent, hostile people, and must date from the middle monarchic period, after the mid-9th century, at the earliest.

Much the same is true of the narrative in Num 20:14-21, where Moses sends messengers from Kadesh to ask for a transit visa for the Israelites. The narrator assumes Edom's hostility from the start and makes Moses' messengers plead hard for the required permission. The narrator also anachronistically assumes that Edom is a monarchic state, organized with a royal highway (or perhaps even an imperial Assyrian highway),[8] with fields, vineyards and wells, with territorial claims extending as far west as Kadesh, and an army ready to march out in defence of them; all of this again suggests that the narrative belongs to the middle or later monarchic period, when Judah has experienced Edom as a militaristic monarchy, capable of defeating Judah and denying her access to Edomite territory. A similar indication comes from the reference to Israel as Edom's brother; this identification cannot predate the Davidic interest in Edom, and probably belongs to the early monarchic period.[9] This narrative has close and complex links with the similar story about Israel's encounter with Sihon (Num 21:21-24), with the reference to the Egyptian bondage in Deut

---

[7]*Edom and the Edomites,* 85, 92, 180.

[8]See J. M. Miller, "Moab and the Moabites," *Studies in the Mesha Inscription and Moab* (ed. J. A. Dearman; Archaeological and Biblical Studies 2; Atlanta: Scholars Press, 1989) 12-13; B. Oded, "Observations on Methods of Assyrian Rule in Transjordania after the Palestinian Campaign of Tiglath-Pileser III," *JNES* 29 (1970) 177-86, esp. 182, n. 41.

[9]*Edom and the Edomites,* 175-80.

26:5-7, with the account in Judg 11:16-17, and with the rather different account in Deut 2:1-8. If, as van Seters and Miller have argued,[10] the Numbers narrative derives from a conflation of the accounts in Judges and Deuteronomy, then it is a very late narrative indeed, dating from well after the end of the Edomite kingdom. But whatever its pedigree, it cannot postdate the late monarchic period, when Edom was still a serious threat.

The Deuteronomistic version of this story in Deut 2:1-8, whatever its precise literary relationship with Numbers 20 and Judges 11, presents a notoriously different picture of Israel's relationship with Edom. Edom is not named; Israel deals with the children of Esau who live in Seir, territory given to Esau by God as a possession, and thus denied to Israel for *their* possession; the children of Esau are afraid of the Israelites and do not oppose them; and the Israelites can proceed through their land, purchasing what they need from its inhabitants. The Israelites must see the children of Esau as brethren and must not contend with them. Similarly, in Deut 23:8 the Deuteronomist commands that the Israelite must not abhor the Edomite, for he is his brother. Deut 2:1-8 is interesting in that it avoids referring to the sons of Esau as the hated Edomites, avoids reference to any hostile action on either side, and underlines the brotherly relationship. The Deuteronomistic author is clearly aware that Edom had been a threat to Israel; but Edom is no longer a threat and is to be treated with respect. This is in striking contrast with all other biblical writers and cries for explanation. Possibly the author writes from a late, postexilic situation when Edomites are no longer any threat. This later deuteronomistic theologian may be aware that Yahweh's roots were in Edom and the neighbouring regions of the south.

The Deuteronomistic historian, however, had no illusions about Edom's historical enmity with the Davidic dynasty. Simply to catalogue the references will be enough to demonstrate the point. Saul fights against Edom (1 Sam 14:47—if Edom, not Aram is the original reading here); David subdued Edom, slaying 18,000 Edomites, garrisoning Edom, and reducing Edom to the level of a subject state (2 Sam 8:12, 13-14; cf. 1 Kgs 11:15-16). Doeg the Edomite was a treacherous piece of work (1 Sam 21:7; 22:18-19,22). Edomite women were among Solomon's pagan wives (1 Kgs 11:1). Solomon's adversaries included Hadad the Edomite (1 Kgs 11:14-22). In the days of Jehoram king of Judah, Edom revolted from Judah and was still independent in the writer's day (2 Kgs 8:20-22), in spite of king

[10]See J. van Seters, "The Conquest of Sihon's Kingdom: A Literary Examination," *JBL* 91 (1972), 182-97. For a critique of this view, see J. R. Bartlett, "The Conquest of Sihon's Kingdom: A Literary Re-examination," *JBL* 97 (1978) 347-51 and van Seters' response, "Once Again: The Conquest of Sihon's Kingdom," *JBL* 99 (1980) 117-24. More recently, J. M. Miller has supported van Seters' proposal in "The Israelite Journey through (around) Moab and Moabite Toponymy," *JBL* 108 (1989) 577-95.

Amaziah's partially or temporarily successful attempt to recover Edom (2 Kgs 14:7, 10). Edom managed to evict the Judahites from their post in Elath at the head of the Gulf of ʿAqabah (2 Kgs 16:6). For this historian, Edom had been hostile from the days of David, or even of Saul, down to the time of the author. (I suspect that hostilities really began with David's conquests.) The Deuteronomistic Historian's understanding of Edom is precisely reflected in the narratives of Genesis 25-33 and Numbers 20 but not in the account of Deut 2:1-8, which is surely an important observation.

Lastly, references to Edom in archival material need to be examined. Care must be taken to detach genuinely archival material from its present context. Genesis 36, for example, as it stands, is part of the larger epic of Jacob and Esau and purports to show Esau/Edom's non-Israelite family. At the core of this chapter are three lists: the two primary lists of the descendants of Esau (vv. 10-14) and the sons of Seir (vv. 20-28), from which most of the other lists of the chapter are constructed, and the Edomite king-list of vv. 31-39, itself visibly a compilation from different materials.[11] This list is based on the assumption that Edom was a kingdom, though the information contained in it raises many questions about the nature of that kingdom. The introductory sentence—"These are the kings who reigned over the land of Edom, before any king reigned over the Israelites"—suggests that the editor is looking back over some period of time. If the second clause be translated "before any king reigned (over Edom) *for* the Israelites," as is possible,[12] then the editor is perhaps looking back to the time before David's conquest of Edom and reveals awareness of Edom's difficult relationship with Judah. However, apart from this introduction, the list itself gives no hint of Edom's hostility to Judah; its editor did his archival job with admirable neutrality. The editor reveals knowledge of Bozrah and Teman, known otherwise only from sources of the later monarchic or exilic period, and this list, with its use of the formula common in the Deuteronomistic History, "x died, and y reigned in his stead," is probably an Israelite compilation from various sources in the 8th-7th century BC, edited by a Deuteronomistic hand before incorporation into its present context. Axel Knauf-Belleri, on the other hand, argues for the Persian period.[13]

Other archival references to Edom are few. Topographic reference to Mount Hor, "on the edge of the land of Edom," appears in the itinerary in

[11]*Edom and the Edomites*, 94-102.

[12]Cf. F. Buhl, *Geschichte der Edomiter* (Leipzig: Edelmann, 1893), 47; J. Skinner, *Genesis* (ICC 1; Edinburgh: T. & T. Clark, 1910) 434; Simons, *Geographical and Topographical Texts*, 24, n. 9.

[13]E. A. Knauf, "Alter und Herkunft der edomitischen Königslisten Gen. 36:31-39," *ZAW* 97 (1985) 245-53.

Num 33:37, and reference is made to the common boundary of Judah and Edom in the boundary description of Josh 15:1-12. Josh 15:21-30 lists cities of Judah in the south "toward the boundary of Edom." Edom is known as a separate state, clearly marked off from Judah. The description of Solomon's shipbuilding in 1 Kgs 9:26-28, presumably deriving from some archival source, notes that Solomon built his ships at Ezion-geber, "which is near Eloth, in the land of Edom." The explanatory phrase was presumably not needed in the original archive and is the historian's own gloss. It can hardly predate Edom's capture of Eloth (2 Kgs 16:6) ca. 735 BC. Again, there are no overt suggestions of hostility in these references, which focus on topography rather than politics and people.

In summary, the Song of Deborah and the archival material betray no animus against Edom, but this does not necessarily mean that they are to be dated earlier than the Davidic conquest of Edom. The Song of Deborah is not at all concerned with relationships between Judah and Edom, and the archivists have been properly neutral in setting out their material. The remaining texts portray Edom as hostile. The poems—the Song of Moses, the last oracle of Balaam, and Psalm 60—all reflect the hostility of the Edomite nation, and the narratives of Genesis 25-36 and Num 20:14-21 go out of their way to stress the archetypal hostility of Edom. The Deuteronomistic history knows and accepts that from David's time Edom has been Judah's enemy; however, Deuteronomy 2 and 23 deliberately tone down this tradition. Apart from the DtrH material and Deuteronomy 2; 23:8, the poems and prose narratives probably derive from the middle to late monarchic period, when Edom is known to be a kingdom hostile to Judah. To be more precise, they date from the period after Edom's fierce rebellion in the days of Jehoram, when Judah seems to have conducted a running war with Edom, evidenced by Amaziah's campaign ca. 800 BC, Edom's capture of Elath ca. 735 BC, and the political situation reflected in the reference to "the evil that Edom has done" in the ostracon from Stratum VIII at Arad, perhaps from the time of Sennacherib's invasion in 701 BC.[14] It is not necessary to suppose that these passages have been influenced by the events of 587/6 BC because reliable evidence for Edom's physical and actual participation in the destruction of Judah is nonexistent.[15] It was the record of the hostility of the monarchic period that led later writers to attribute hostile behavior to Edom in 587/6 BC. The attitude of the account in Deut 2:1-8 and Deut 23:8, however, belongs to the postmonarchic situation or to a totally different theological

---

[14]For this ostracon, see Y. Aharoni, "Three Hebrew Ostraca from Arad," *BASOR* 197 (1970) 16-42; idem, *Arad Inscriptions* (Jerusalem: Israel Exploration Society and Massada Press, 1981) 70-74, n. 40.

[15]J. R. Bartlett, "Edom and the Fall of Jerusalem, 587 B.C.," *PEQ* 114 (1982) 13-24.

appreciation of the relationship between Edom and Judah, or to both. Nevertheless, it still reveals a conscious attempt to undo the hostile attitude and underlines how deep that went.

EDOM IN THE PROPHETICAL CORPUS

Beth Glazier-McDonald

One of the very few things that can be stated with absolute certainty is that Edom's press agent in Jerusalem was totally ineffective, overwhelmed by Israelite/Judahite propaganda. After all, how can one respond to rhetoric like that of Amos in the mid-700s BCE?

> For three transgressions of Edom,
> and for four, I will not revoke the punishment;
> because he pursued his brother with the sword,
> and utterly destroyed his allies . . .
> So I will send a fire on Teman,
> and it shall devour the strongholds of Bozrah. (1:11)

And then there is Obadiah in the 500s BCE.

> The house of Jacob shall be a fire,
> and the house of Joseph a flame,
> and the house of Edom stubble;
> they shall burn them and consume them,
> and there shall be no survivor of the house of Edom. (v. 18)

Finally, note the hostility of Isaiah 34, postexilic perhaps.

> When my sword has drunk its fill in the heavens,
> lo, it will descend upon Edom,
> upon the people I have doomed to judgment.
> For Yahweh has a day of vengeance . . . .
> And the streams of Edom shall be turned into pitch,
> and her soil into sulfur;
> From generation to generation it shall lie waste;
> no one shall pass through it forever and ever. (vv. 5, 8, 9, 10)

When this Edom-baiting began and what caused it are matters of conjecture. I do not believe, however, that the anti-Edom bias, so frequently and vehemently attested in the prophetic corpus, began with the prophets, "for their message depends on previous messages; the prophet is not the first to find, nor does he make the morality he expounds."[1]

---

[1]M. Walzer, *Interpretation and Social Criticism* (Cambridge, MA: Harvard University Press, 1987) 71. Walzer remarks that "we can detect a certain theological revisionism in some of the later prophets, but none of them presents an entirely new doctrine," 71.

Bruce Cresson points to the late development of what he graphically describes as "Damn Edom" theology.[2] Edom's participation "with a fury" in the destruction of Judah and Jerusalem in 587 BCE, and its grasping of traditionally Judahite territory in the south were both causes for the emergence of virulent anti-Edom feeling and thus, for the prominence of "Damn Edom" theology in early postexilic Judaism. Indeed, Cresson maintains that all the relevant prophetic texts exhibit the same hard-line, anti-Edom sentiment and all are to be dated to the exilic or postexilic period.[3]

John Bartlett remarks, however, that Edom has been falsely accused in the prophetic texts and cannot be held in any way responsible for the destruction of Judah and Jerusalem in 587 BCE.[4] Instead, Bartlett points to Jer 40:11 as the only firm evidence that some Judahites found refuge from the Babylonian onslaught in Edom. He writes that "the historic experience which influenced prophetic complaints against Edom's behavior, derived from earlier history, rather than anything done by Edom in 587."[5] While Bartlett's view admits of historical development in the Edom—Israel relationship (as viewed through the textual material and archaeology), his repeated references to poor, maligned Edom are not convincing precisely because nothing he adduces in his numerous reviews of the generations-long struggle between Edom and Israel seems sufficient to account for the thoroughgoing anti-Edom bias in the prophetic corpus. Edom was not just an enemy like Tyre, the Philistine city states, or even Assyria; Edom became the enemy *par excellence*, the epitome of wildness and lust for power, the symbol of Yahweh's foes throughout the world who oppose the deity in the eschaton.

The pivot on which the see-saw struggle between Israel and Edom hinged seems to have been control of the trade route north from the Gulf of ʿAqaba. The recognition of this Edomite asset likely followed David's early 10th century (ca. 990 BCE) occupation of Edom and Judah's subsequent ability to explore Edomite territory. Significantly, two periods of Israelite prosperity—during Davidic/Solomonic times and during the Omride era—coincide with Israelite control of this land west of the ʿArabah. As might be suspected, anti-Edom rhetoric escalates when Edom recovers its territory. It is interesting, however, that such

[2]B. C. Cresson, "The Condemnation of Edom in Postexilic Judaism," *The Use of the Old Testament in the New and Other Essays* (ed. J. M. Efird; Durham: Duke University Press, 1972) 125.

[3]Cresson, "The Condemnation of Edom," 134-140.

[4]J. R. Bartlett, *Edom and the Edomites* (JSOTSup 77; Sheffield: JSOT Press, 1989) 157.

[5]J. R. Bartlett, "Edom and the Fall of Jerusalem, 587 B.C.," *PEQ* 114 (1982) 23.

propaganda continues when Israel regains control, perhaps because of Edom's retaliatory strikes in attempts to inflict damage on its overlord.

Having said all that, were it asked whether there really is one hard-line anti-Edom sentiment pervading the prophetic texts, the answer would have to be—no. It may be an answer inferred from silence, yet sometimes silence yields important possibilities for historical reconstruction.

By Amos' time (in the mid-8th century BCE) the battle lines are clearly drawn. Although scholars continue to argue that Amos' oracles against Tyre (1:9-10), Edom (1:11-12) and Judah (2:4-5) are late additions to contemporize the book of Amos for use in Judah during the exilic and postexilic periods,[6] John Priest and others have convincingly demonstrated that the Tyre and Edom oracles at least, are authentic words of Amos.[7] Along with the oracle against Gaza in 1:7-8, they derive from that period beginning in the mid-9th century when Edom rebelled against King Jehoram of Judah and regained its independence. In fact, it is possible that the Tyre and Gaza oracles that involve Edom as slave trading middleman (1:7-8, 9-10) and the Edom oracle (1:11-12) reflect two different situations within this period.

A key factor in the economic prosperity of the Omride era was the wide treaty network in which Israel, Judah, Phoenicia and Philistia participated. The alliance of Phoenicia, Israel and Judah implied by the marriages of Ahab and Jezebel and later Jehoram and Athaliah may have been conceived in order to revive and expand the sort of beneficial commercial arrangements that had existed in Solomon's day. Then, as during the Omride era, Edom was subject to Israel, and its Red Sea port was connected by overland routes through Judah and Israel to Phoenician seaports on the Mediterranean and probably to Philistine seaports as well. The identical charge delivered by Amos against both Tyre and Gaza (1:7-8, 9-10) suggests that not only were Tyre and Israel linked by a בְּרִית אַחִים, a covenant of brothers, but that Israel and the Philistines had a similar treaty relationship.[8] Indeed, as many have

---

[6]J. L. Mayes, *Amos* (OTL; Philadelphia; Westminster, 1969) 13.

[7]J. Priest, "The Covenant of Brothers," *JBL* 84 (1965) 400-406; K. Schoville, "A note on the oracles of Amos against Gaza, Tyre and Edom," *Studies on Prophecy. A Collection of Twelve Papers* (ed. G. W. Anderson *et al.*; VTSup 26; Leiden: Brill, 1974) 55-63; M. Haran, "Observations on the Historical Background of Amos 1.2-2.6," *IEJ* 18 (1968) 201-212.

[8]Schoville notes the possibility that "such a brotherly covenant had existed between Israel and the Philistines, thus providing a similarity of situation that is reflected in the identical charge of delivering over a galut shelemah which was levelled at Gaza as well as at Tyre" ("Amos Against Gaza, Tyre and Edom," 58).

pointed out, "brotherhood was an integral element in treaties between groups and nations which had no real kinship ties."[9]

It was Jehu's coup (ca. 841 BCE), the deaths of Ahaziah, Joram and Jezebel and the *herem* carried out on the worshippers of the Tyrian Baal that shattered all those favorable relationships and set the stage for the oracles against Tyre and Gaza involving Edom. Phoenicians and Philistines are accused of manstealing, of handing over a גָּלוּת שְׁלֵמָה, "a whole captivity," to Edom. Both Gaza and Tyre were centers of slave traffic. They are referred to together again in Joel 4:4-8 and accused this time of selling the children of Judah and Jerusalem into slavery. Further evidence of the ties between Tyre and the Philistine city states can be found in Zech 9:3-6 and Jer 47:4. In the case of the Amos oracles, it may be that the Philistines invaded Judah (now vulnerable from the loss of Omride protection) and the Phoenicians invaded Israel (depleted and similarly vulnerable, thanks to Jehu). The expression גָּלוּת שְׁלֵמָה, "a whole captivity," suggests relatively large numbers of captives. Certainly, more slaves meant more money for the trading partners, but in this case, handing over a גָּלוּת שְׁלֵמָה was also likely the violent retaliatory action of Philistines and Phoenicians to Jehu's purge. That Edom, by this time independent and in control of the trade passing through its borders, should act as middleman for slave buyers in Africa and south Arabia was surely a fitting way to get back at its former overlord.

Then, around 800 BCE, Amaziah achieved victory over Edom at Gey Melah, the Valley of Salt. Although Edom was not newly subjugated by Judah, Amaziah apparently regained Edomite territory between Judah and the gulf of ʿAqaba. He thus achieved free access along the ʿArabah route to Elath, which King Uzziah later rebuilt.[10] It is to this incident that Amos' oracle against Edom in 1:11-12 points. Surely Judah's takeover of that strategic bit of land after one-half century of Edomite control would have incited bitter acts of vengeance by Edomites against Judah and would have provoked the sort of animosity that would not die down quickly, but that asserted itself over and over again in acts of רָדְפוֹ בַחֶרֶב, "pursuit with the sword."

---

[9]Priest, "The Covenant of Brothers," 406.

[10]Haran contends that the only concrete result of Amaziah's victory was the capture of Selaʿ (2 Kgs 14:17), which he identifies as el-Salʿ in the northern part of Edom. "This strategic place, controlling the mountain passes, the valley of Bozrah and part of the 'King's Highway,' is situated in the vicinity of the road leading to Elath and guarantees its security from the east. The location of el-Salʿ on the outskirts of Edom coincides with the fact that its capture by Amaziah was not concomitant with the subjugation of all Edom" ("Observations on the Historical Background of Amos 1.2–2.6," 212).

During the reign of King Ahaz, when Judah was hard pressed on all sides by Rezin and his supporters in the anti-Assyrian coalition, Edom recovered control of the trade routes and occupied the seaport city of Elath, presumably with Rezin's help (2 Kgs 16:6; 2 Chron 28:16). It is interesting to note that at this time, while the Philistines made slave raids on the Shephelah and the Negeb, Edom was raiding Judah. Further, Edomites began to extend their influence into the southern regions of Judah. As has been noted, they probably had enough in common with the tribes of the border country to make movement and intermarriage relatively easy.[11] This friendly intermingling of Edomites with Judahites (in the Judahite south) was politically a wise move on Edom's part for it seems to have mitigated the hostility that Judahites must have felt upon losing Elath and trade (notice the lack of hostile prophetic literature here). Such a move may also have initiated a period of amiable relations between Judah and Edom. In fact, Zephaniah, who spewed forth oracles against just about everyone, makes no mention at all of Edom. Clearly, Zephaniah's oracles are all against areas that had long been dominated by Assyria and remained in Assyria's camp during a period when its power in the west was on the decline, ca. 640-633 BCE.[12] If these oracles against the nations are reflective of political reality, then Zephaniah's failure to denounce Edom suggests that Edom and Judah may have supported a move away from Assyrian domination during this period of Assyrian weakness. It may be that by working together, they hoped to exploit for themselves the trade routes and trade connections that had been developed during the period of Assyrian control.[13]

We seem to have taken our cue about Judahite/Edomite relations from the conflict and vehement rhetoric that characterize the Babylonian period, especially post-587 BCE. It is very interesting to note, however, that in the course of the 7th century there is increasing interaction between the two peoples as both participate in the trade that crossed the Negeb on its way to the coast. There is also growing evidence of Edomite presence in traditionally Judahite areas.[14] In fact, there does not seem to be archaeological evidence for Judahite/Edomite conflict

---

[11]Bartlett, *Edom and the Edomites*, 143.

[12]R. Haak, "Prophets and History: Zephaniah." Unpublished paper given in Jerusalem (5/91) as an NEH Fellow-AIAR, 23-24.

[13]Haak, "Prophets and History: Zephaniah," 25.

[14]I. Beit Arieh, "New Data on the Relationship between Judah and Edom Toward the End of the Iron Age," *Recent Excavations in Israel: Studies in Iron Age Archaeology* (ed. S. Gitin and W. G. Dever; Winona Lake, IN: ASOR by Eisenbrauns, 1989) 125-31. (See now also the article below on 33-40. Ed.)

until the end of the 7th century.[15] Therefore, what seems to have made Edom's participation, or perhaps the lack of it, in the Babylonian destruction of 587 BCE so heinous was the fact that relations between Judah and Edom had improved significantly in the previous century. Even as late as 594/93 BCE, Edomites and Judahites were found together, prepared to join with Ammonites, Moabites and others to plan strategy or perhaps plot rebellion against the Babylonians. No longer cutthroat enemies, Edom and Judah had reached a *rapprochement.*

John Bartlett remarks that hard evidence for Edom's behavior when the Babylonians attacked Jerusalem in 587 BCE is less easy to find than is often supposed.[16] Although I agree that sifting truth out of the morass of prophetic accusations is difficult, it seems unrealistic to conclude that only Jer 40:11, which states that Edom offered a haven to Judahite refugees, provides reliable information. Unless the Edomites were extremely myopic, they saw the Babylonians coming and recognized that their survival meant dissociation from Jerusalem. In fact, that Edom survives the Babylonian onslaught argues for some accommodation to/cooperation with Babylon. Further, there were likely perceived benefits to an association with Babylon, especially territorial gain. Jeremiah's oracle against the Ammonites (49:1-5) suggests that they had taken advantage of Judah's weakness to settle in areas formerly regarded as belonging to the tribe of Gad. It should not be surprising that neighboring lands were only too ready to prey upon a weakened Judah. In Edom's case, penetrating and occupying the Judahite south (with Babylon's approval) might have enabled it to control trade to Philistia and the Mediterranean port of Gaza and might have safeguarded Edom's handle on trade with south Arabia by ensuring that should Judah recover from the devastation, it would now be too far removed geographically to reclaim control.[17] Traditionally, Edom was a poor country; it is not inconceivable, therefore, that Edomites would have joined in the looting of Jerusalem (Obad 13). Nor should it be surprising that some Edomites, responding to their government's change of alignment, would have cut off Judahite fugitives and handed them over to the Babylonians (Obad 14; Ezek 35:5).

---

[15]Note the Arad ostraca, especially the "Ramoth-negeb" ostracon, a military dispatch concerning an impending Edomite attack. John Lindsay contends that it "best fits the period of guerilla warfare around about 600 BC" ("The Babylonian Kings and Edom, 605-550 B.C.," *PEQ* 108 [1976] 25).

[16]Bartlett, *Edom and the Edomites,* 151.

[17]Beit Arieh notes that "the Edomite shrine at Qitmit, c. 10 km south of Arad, served an Edomite population located in Judean territory around the time that Judah was already weakened by the Babylonian conflict, or a few years after Judah's destruction" ("New Data on the Relationship between Judah and Edom," 111).

Obadiah 11 clearly mirrors the disbelief of the Judahites at Edom's about-face—"You, Edom, who shared such a close relationship with us, upon whose support we thought we could depend, you acted like one of them!" It was the fact of Edomite association with the Babylonians, not the extent of its participation, that returned Edom to its former status as an "enemy" who, as in times past, took undue advantage of Judah during a period of weakness. Consequently, Judah's early hope (as mirrored in Obad 15, 19; Amos 9:11-12) was that Edom's deeds would recoil on its own head, that it would experience what Judah had experienced and, that just as Edom was dominating part of Judah, so Israel/Judah would once again dominate Edom. Indeed, so Israel's early hope went, all the territory that originally had belonged to David's kingdom would be recovered, especially Edom: "In that day I will raise up the booth of David that is fallen and I will build it as in days of old that they may possess the remnant of Edom and all the nations" (Amos 9:11-12). Notice that the reincorporation of Edom is clearly associated with the restoration of Israel (Obad 19). Further, the wording of the Amos passage, שְׁאֵרִית אֱדוֹם, "the remnant of Edom," suggests that when this addition was composed, likely in the exilic or early postexilic period, Edom was tottering, still a recognized political entity but no longer as intact as it had been during its heyday in the Assyrian period.

When Edom's destruction is viewed through prophetic lenses, it is similarly allied with Israel's restoration. Joel warns that Edom will be a desolate wilderness for the violence against the Judahites, whereas Judah will be inhabited forever (4:19-20). Jeremiah announces that Edom "shall become an object of horror and ridicule, a waste and an object of cursing; and all her towns shall be perpetual wastes" (49:13). In Ezek 25:13, Yahweh announces: "I will stretch out my hand against Edom, and cut off from it humans and animals and I will make it desolate." It is interesting to note that Edom, whose destruction is coming, does not stand alone. In these prophecies, Edom is one of many neighboring nations that will experience the wrath of Yahweh. With Malachi 1:2-5, the scene has shifted somewhat, for this prophet treats Edom as already having fallen. Edom's destruction, an event within his hearers' memory, is used by Malachi to "prove" Yahweh's love and concern for Israel. "How have you loved us?" Israel queries. "Well," responds Yahweh, "remember Edom? . . ." Thus, prophecies like Jeremiah 49, Joel 4 and Ezekiel 25 seem to represent an early phase in the drama of Edom's downfall, the culmination of which is viewed through Malachi's eyes. Unfortunately, the dating of Edom's demise is complicated both because of the lack of sufficient information from which to reconstruct Edom's history and because archaeological investigation has not resolved some of the major questions regarding Edom's fate. Further, the dating of the relevant prophecies is not universally agreed upon. Nevertheless, these prophecies reveal that Edom's downfall was a clearly visible process—one could see it coming. It was a process that likely started as the 7th century ended and the 6th century began. Perhaps Assyria's demise and the resulting unsettled political situation were responsible. Perhaps a retaliatory strike by Nebuchadnezzar in 582 BCE or Nabonidus' attempt to gain control of the trade routes ca. 552 BCE set the wheels in motion. It seems logical to assert that the breakdown of centralized political organization led to Edom's loss of ability to control and profit from the trade between Arabia and the Mediterranean. Further, as political authority decayed, there was increasing belligerent activity from nomadic desert tribes, among whom were likely the Nabateans. As they began pushing into Edom, some Edomites left, finding refuge in the Judahite south, while others were gradually absorbed by the Nabateans. John Bartlett has argued for direct continuity between Edomites and Nabateans.[18] While this may hold true for some areas (Tell el-Kheleifah, Petra, Buseirah, perhaps), direct continuity cannot be advocated across the board. As J. M. Myers notes and as the excavations of Crystal Bennett show, a large number of sites were abandoned in the 6th century BCE.[19] Further, on the Edomite plateau (the Jebel esh-Shera) evidence indicates that civilization collapsed sometime in the 5th century BCE (when I date Malachi) and did not reemerge until the Nabatean period.[20]

To emphasize again, the prophetic texts seem to witness to the process of Edom's loss of control. Although Malachi's assertion that Edom has fallen, never to rise again, may not be correct strictly speaking, it seems to reflect a knowledge, gained perhaps from resettling Edomites, that in some areas at least, Edomite civilization was wiped out. With nomadic groups wandering around at will, any desire to rebuild one's former way of life would not be easily realized (note Malachi 1:4—"Although Edom says, 'We are beaten down, but we will return and rebuild the ruins,' thus says Yahweh, 'They may rebuild but I will tear down'").

---

[18]J. Bartlett, "From Edomites to Nabataeans," *PEQ* (1979) 66.

[19]J. M. Myers, "Edom and Judah in the 6th-5th c. B.C.," *Near Eastern Studies in Honor of William Foxwell Albright* (ed. H. Goedicke; Baltimore: Johns Hopkins Press, 1971) 389; C. Bennett, "Excavations at Buseirah (Biblical Bozrah)," *Midian, Moab and Edom: The History and Archaeology of the Late Bronze Age and Iron Age Jordan and Northwest Arabia* (ed. J. Sawyer and D. Clines; JSOTSup 24; Sheffield: JSOT Press, 1983) 17.

[20]S. Hart, "The Edom Survey Project 1984-85: The Iron Age," *Studies in the History and Archaeology of Jordan III* (ed. A. Hadidi; Amman: Dept. of Antiquities, 1987) 287-90; B. Glazier-McDonald, *Malachi the Divine Messenger* (SBLDS 98; Atlanta: Scholars Press, 1987) 14-18.

The tension between Ezekiel 25 and 35 reveals movement toward Edom's final transformation. In Ezekiel 25, Edom's judgment is seen as part of a series of judgments that it will share with other hostile nations. In chapter 35, all this has changed and Edom has become the enemy, the quintessential symbol of hostility toward Judah and its deity. Edom's destruction is viewed as the indispensable prelude to Israel's restoration, a view shared by Obadiah (16-17) and Isaiah (34; 63). Further, this transformation of Edom from "an" enemy to "the" enemy is clearly attributed to Edom's movement from its own land to southern Judah, which is Yahweh's land. Perhaps this transformation was the bitter reaction of exiles to a pattern of settlement they were powerless to stop. Perhaps it points to a time after the temple was rebuilt when Yahweh was believed to dwell in Judah again among his people. Indeed, as Ezekiel laments, Edom claimed ownership of the land "although Yahweh was there" (35:10). Most likely, Edom came to symbolize the hostile, encroaching world when the hope of an actual restoration of Israel was being vitiated by the recognition of human powerlessness in the face of cold political reality—as Babylonian hegemony gave way to Persian. Restoration hopes did not cease; they took on new forms. There is a movement toward apocalyptic complete with cosmic catastrophes where Edom is put forward as a symbolic example of the wider process of universal destruction. In Isa 34:5-7, the Edomites, the eschatological foe, are exterminated in the course of Yahweh's bloody sacrificial feast, the marks of which are stamped on the earth forever. In Isaiah 63, Yahweh's bloody vengeance is pictured as taking place in Edom. Only when Yahweh's judgment on Edom has been carried out will wilderness be transformed into paradise; only then will the redeemed return home on a processional way to Zion.

Edom and Israel were neighbors and neighbors squabble. Tensions erupt, animosities flare and property is disputed. In essence, the prophets' diatribes against Edom are not very different from their diatribes against other neighbors and sometime allies like Ammon, Tyre and Gaza. It is only when their oracles against the nations give way to oracles against a nation, when Edom, an enemy, becomes Edom, the enemy, that there is a need to search for deeper explanations.

The silence of Zephaniah on the subject of Edom points to a time, perhaps as long as a half-century, of friendly accommodation between the two countries.[21] Edom and Judah cooperated in the trade arena and intermingled peacefully in southern Judah. That Judah would expect support from such a friend during a time of dire need should not be surprising. Nor should it be surprising that Judah reacted to Edom's

[21]Haak, "Prophets and History," 18, 24-25.

defection around 587 BCE with disbelief and with anger. When Edomites began to claim land in Judah and settle there as their own country foundered, and by so doing failed to recognize the indissoluble unity of Yahweh, Yahweh's people and Yahweh's land, Judah's anger burned white hot. All grievances against the nations were subsumed under the major grievance of territorial usurpation by Edom, and upon its shoulders were heaped all the nations' sins that Yahweh, the cosmic warrior, must surely avenge. Indeed, Edom's transformation is complete when it is depicted as the eschatological foe whose bloody destruction is the precondition for cosmic restoration and for Israel's triumphant return to Zion.

THE EDOMITES IN CISJORDAN

Itzhaq Beit Arieh

In order to recognize traces of an Edomite presence outside the territory of Edom itself, it is necessary first to establish the identifying characteristics of Edomite culture. In my opinion, the findings from sites excavated by Crystal Bennett and others in Edomite territory[1] provide only two salient criteria by which the Edomite culture may be identified. These are the pottery and the script.

Edomite sites have been dated by their excavators and other researchers to the time span between the 8th and 6th centuries BCE.[2] This has been done mainly on the evidence of the pottery, but also by reference to the written material that has been found, for which parallels exist in the Assyrian documents. It may be noted that several types of the ceramic ware found at the sites are known from the Judean Negeb, and this helps to establish the dates of the Edomite sites. Nevertheless, the dates of the sites in the land of Edom itself, which are being queried even at this time by some scholars, would seem in need of further consolidation. To resolve this problem it appears to be necessary to rely on the well-established dates of the Judahite sites in the strata of which Edomite material has been uncovered.

Edomite material has been exposed in Judah either at one-stratum sites or else in occupation strata dating from the second half of the 7th century BCE to the beginning of the 6th century BCE, as at Tel Malḥata, Tel Masos, Tel ʿIra, Tel ʿAroer, Tel Arad, Ḥorvat ʿUza, Ḥorvat Radum, and Kadesh Barnea.[3] It may be noted that the chronologically relevant

---

[1]For Umm el-Biyara, see C. M. Bennett, "Fouilles d'Umm el Biyara. Rapport préliminaire," *RB* 73 (1966) 372-493. For Buseirah, see C. M. Bennett, "Excavations at Buseirah, Southern Jordan, 1971. Preliminary Report," *Levant* 5 (1973) 1-11; idem, "Excavations at Buseirah, Southern Jordan, 1972. Preliminary Report," *Levant* 6 (1974) 1-24; idem, "Excavations at Buseirah, Southern Jordan, 1973. Third Preliminary Report," *Levant* 7 (1975) 1-19; idem, "Excavations at Buseirah, Southern Jordan, 1974. Fourth Preliminary Report," *Levant* 9 (1977) 1-10. For Tawilan, see C. M. Bennett, "Excavations at Tawilan in Southern Jordan," Levant 16 (1984) 1-23.

[2]So, e.g. Bennett, "Excavations at Buseirah, 1974," 9-10.

[3]See M. Kochavi, "Malḥata, Tel," *EAEHL* 3.771-75; A. Kempinski *et al.*, "Excavations at Tel Masos: 1972, 1974, 1975," *EI* 15 (1981) 154-80 (Hebrew); I. Beit Arieh, "Tel ʿIra—A Fortified City of the Kingdom of Judah," *Qadmoniot* 18 (1969/70) 17-25 (Hebrew); A. Biran and R. Cohen, "Notes and News: Aroer," *IEJ* 26 (1976) 138-40; Y. Aharoni, *Arad Inscriptions* (Jerusalem: Israel Exploration Society and Masada Press, 1981); I. Beit Arieh and B. Cresson, "Ḥorvat ʿUza: A Fortified Outpost on the Eastern

vessels that are dated to the above period are known as imitations of Assyrian palace ware. These types are found along with the Edomite material in the same strata, which accounts for their importance.

Three main types of pottery can be identified as Edomite:

(1) Vessels painted with black stripes in a variety of combinations (Fig. 1:3-5; 16);

(2) Perforated incense cups and/or fenestrated incense vessels, sometimes with triangular decoration around the vessel (Fig. 1:9, 10, 12, 13);

(3) Cooking pots with stepped rims, produced from clay containing Nubian sandstone from the region of Petra (Fig. 1:7, 8, 11).

In addition to these main types, others, which occur less frequently, are clay lamps with low compartments or with high sockets, holemouth jars with broadstepped rims, sometimes painted red, and cylindrical holemouth jars (Fig. 1:15, 4).

The Script

It should be noted at the outset that the characteristics of Edomite script are at present based only on a small corpus of inscriptions, most of which are fragmentary, that have been discovered in the territory of Edom and Judah.[4] This small corpus includes ink-written ostraca, inscriptions incised on pottery vessels, and seal impressions. Despite the limitations necessarily imposed on paleographic analysis by the small number of inscriptions, it is still possible to conclude that the Edomite script, both in the cursive and lapidary forms, differs in certain respects from the northwest Semitic script used in the countries adjoining Edom, namely, Judah, Moab, and Ammon. Several Edomite letters show the influence of the Aramaic script that entered the region in the wake of the Assyrian conquest.[5] Some characteristics of Edomite script include the following: the *he* resembles a mirror-image "R" (Я), the *waw* is shaped like an inverted "h," the *mem* has a large head, the *sammekh* has a zigzag line on the top, the *qof* has a looped top, and the *tav* resembles a flag on a staff.

The theophoric personal names incorporating the word Qos, the name of the principal Edomite deity, also belong within the scope of a discussion of Edomite inscriptions. Undoubtedly, these names furnish an

---

Negev Border," *BA* (1991) 126-35; I. Beit Arieh, "A Small Frontier Citadel at Ḥorvat Radum in the Judean Negev," *Qadmoniot* 24 (1991) 86-89 (Hebrew); and R. Cohen, "Excavations at Kadesh-Barnea 1976-1978," *BA* 54 (1981) 100.

[4]For a convenient description and discussion of the various inscriptions, see J. R. Bartlett, *Edom and the Edomites* (JSOTSup 77; Sheffield: JSOT Press, 1989) 209-27. (See now also the article by D. Vanderhooft below, 137-87. Ed.)

[5]So J. Naveh, *Early History of the Alphabet* (Jerusalem: Magnes Press, 1982) 104-105.

important and reliable index to ethnic identification. Granted that these criteria for Edomite identification are adequate, it is possible to investigate the extent of Edomite culture outside the territory of Edom itself, or, in other words, the presence of the Edomites in Cisjordan, which is the subject of this paper.

Aside from some casual small finds, significant Edomite remains have been discovered outside Transjordan only in the eastern Negeb, the biblical Judean Negeb. This region began to be investigated systematically by archaeologists in 1962 when the late Professor Aharoni excavated at Tel Arad. From the content of Arad ostracon No. 24,[6] Aharoni conjectured that stratum VI of the site was destroyed following the penetration of Edomites into the region. The text of the ostracon is concerned with the military deployment of the kingdom of Judah against an anticipated attack by the Edomites. Its closing sentence, "lest Edom come there," led Aharoni to assume that the Edomites were responsible for the destruction of the Arad fortress in 596/5 BCE.[7]

Since the excavation of Arad, most of the large sites in the eastern Negeb have been excavated with results that point to unprecedented fortification activity in this region during the 7th century BCE, greater than at any other time in its history.[8] This is indicated on the accompanying map in Fig. 2. Fortified settlements dating from this period include Kh. Tov, Arad, Kh. ʿUza, Kh. Radum, Kh. ʿAnim, Tel ʿIra, Tel Malḥata, and Tel ʿAroer. This fortification effort is consonant with the content of Arad ostracon No. 24 that warns of a coming Edomite attack on the Judahite frontier settlements in the eastern Negeb. This apprehension is evidently confirmed by the findings from some of these sites, which indicate that the Edomites indeed penetrated into the region at the end of the 7th or the beginning of the 6th century BCE.

Significant Edomite finds have not been uncovered in any other part of Israel. However, before reviewing the material evidence from the individual sites, I want to bring to your attention the Edomite cultic site at Ḥorvat Qitmit that was excavated by my expedition a few years ago in the eastern Negeb.[9] The Edomite identity of this shrine was predicated primarily on the basis of numerous Edomite sherds found at this site (Fig. 1:4, 6-10). However, the resemblance of several of the figurines found there (see Fig. 3) to those discovered in Edom itself and

---

[6]For a description and translation, see Aharoni, *Arad Inscriptions*, 46.

[7]*Ibid.*

[8]I. Beit Arieh, *Ḥorvat Qitmit, an Edomite Shrine in the Judean Desert*, forthcoming.

[9]I. Beit Arieh, "The Edomite Shrine at Ḥorvat Qitmit in the Judean Negev. Preliminary Excavation Report," *Tel Aviv* 18 (1991) 93-116.

the presence of inscriptions incorporating the name Qos give added weight to the Edomite identity of the site.

Aside from its location within a region of Judahite settlement—a matter which in itself is of considerable historical importance—there are the unique finds from this site. These are of no less historical importance, testifying as they do to the integration of Edomite culture into the general cultural scheme of the Mediterranean basin. Neutron activation analysis of the Qitmit pottery[10] indicates that the cooking pots, most of which were Edomite types, were produced most likely in a "foreign land perhaps from certain areas in Edom."[11] In my opinion, they originated in the region of Nubian sandstone in Transjordan, the region that historically is considered the land of Edom. On the other hand, examination of the Qitmit painted wares indicates that they were produced in the eastern Negeb, as were most of the cultic vessels and the sculpted material. It may therefore be concluded that Qitmit represents the permanent settlement of an Edomite population at this location and that the Edomite material found within its limits did not originate from trade relations with outside factors. At most, it can be concluded that it served as an Edomite station for Edomite caravans on their way to the port of Gaza.

Significant Edomite finds that can be interpreted as evidence for Edomite presence in the eastern Negeb were also discovered at other sites besides Qitmit. The most important of these are: Kh. ʿUza, Tel ʿAroer, and Tel Malḥata. At Kh. ʿUza, a Judahite tower fortress that dominated the "Way of Edom,"[12] an ostracon in Edomite script was discovered. It was sent by an Edomite functionary to another Edomite functionary who was resident at Kh. ʿUza or at one of the other settlements in the eastern Negeb.[13] The ostracon reads:

Transcription

1. ʾmr. lmlk. ʾmr. lblbl.
2. hslm. ʾt. whbrktk
3. lqws. wʾt. tn. ʾt. hʾkl.
4. ʾsr. ʾmd. ʾhʾmh [ ]
5. whrm ʾ[z]ʾl. ʾl mz[bh(?) . . .]
6. [ ] hmr. hʾkl.

Translation

---

[10]J. Gunneweg and H. Mommsen, "Instrumental neutron activation analysis and the origin of some cultic objects and Edomite vessels from the Ḥorvat Qitmit Shrine," *Archaeometry* 32 (1990) 7-18.

[11]*Ibid.*, 13.

[12]Beit Arieh and Cresson, "Ḥorvat ʿUza," 126-35.

[13]I. Beit Arieh and B. Cresson, "An Edomite Ostracon from Ḥorvat ʿUza," *Tel Aviv* 12 (1985) 96-101.

1. (Thus) said Lumalak (or <E> limelek): Say to Blbl!
2. Are you well? I bless you
3. by Qos. And now give the food (grain)
4. that Ahiʾma/o . . .
5. And may U[z]iel lift [it] upon (the altar?) . . .
6. [lest] the food become leavened(?)

The Edomite finds from Tel ʿAroer include a seal inscribed "Leqosa," a small ostracon fragment, and a collection of pottery including cooking pots, geometrically decorated vessels and bowls with denticulated decoration.[14] The pottery uncovered during two seasons (1968 and 1971) at Tel Malḥata, probably a central city in the eastern Negeb during the 7th century, included ca. 25% ware of Edomite origin.[15]

Recently, excavations have been renewed at Malḥata and have yielded significant results. Two humanoid figurines and other small clay models were uncovered in 1993. Their style and characteristics indicate that they were produced in the same workshop, maybe even by the same artisan, as the figurines found at Qitmit. One of the figurines depicts a man playing a reed flute. It shares identical artistic and technical features with the head of the three-horned goddess found at Qitmit. It is likely that the workshop that produced the figurines at both sites was located at Malḥata, where the water necessary for a ceramic industry and a permanent settlement was located, unlike at Qitmit. A high percentage of the pottery from the 7th century strata was Edomite, and although the exact amounts have not yet been quantified, they may exceed the 25% found in the earlier excavations.[16]

As indicated previously, the largest distribution of Edomite finds is mainly in the eastern Negeb, though other finds have surfaced elsewhere in southern Israel. Especially noteworthy are two sites that are located at some distance from the frontiers of the eastern Negeb. One of these is Kadesh Barnea, a fortress site in the Negeb highlands along the road to northern Sinai. Geometrically decorated Edomite pottery has been found within the fortress.[17] The second site, located in the center of the ʿArabah near the present-day settlement of Ḥatzeva, is currently under excavation.[18] Here, two forts dating from the third phase of the Iron Age have been uncovered. The forts are built one on top of the

---

[14] Biran and Cohen, "Notes and News: Aroer," 138-40.

[15] Kochavi, "Malḥata, Tel," 774.

[16] For preliminary details, see I. Beit Arieh, "Tel Malḥata," *Had Arkh* 101-102 (1994) 111 (Hebrew).

[17] R. Cohen, *Kadesh Barnea. A Fortress from the Time of the Judean Kingdom* (Israel Museum Catalogue 233; Jerusalem: Israel Museum, 1983) xx.

[18] R. Cohen, "ʿEin Ḥazebah 1988-1989," *Had Arkh* 96 (1991) 38-39 (Hebrew).

other. The dimensions of the lower, earlier casemate fort with towers and a four-chamber gate are 100 m x 100 m, while the upper, later fort measures 36 m x 36 m. Dr. Cohen, director of the excavations, has identified the site as biblical Tamar. Within the limits of the later fort, which has tentatively been dated to the second half of the 7th century BCE, a cultic structure of uncertain nature (chamber? open air platform? favissa?) has been exposed. It contained ceremonial vessels and figurines that closely resemble the ensemble from Qitmit. Edomite vessels were found in association with this later fort, but what percentage of the entire assemblage they constituted remains to be determined.[19] Since the excavations are still in progress, it is too early to reach definitive conclusions regarding the site's connections to the nearby land of Edom. Nevertheless, it is possible to claim that we now possess sufficient clues to suggest a westward expansion of Edom in the 7th century BCE (see Fig. 2).

In conclusion, complete answers are still lacking to many questions concerning the complex relationship between Edom and Judah during the monarchic period. Important issues needing further exploration are the nature and significance of their relationship, the authenticity of the biblical depiction of their interactions, and the interpretation of Edomite remains outside the territory of Edom. For the current status of these topics, the reader should refer to Professor Bartlett's book, *Edom and the Edomites.* It seems that the description of wars and the manifestations of enmity between Judah and Edom as related in the historiographical and prophetic literature of the Bible reflect to a greater or lesser degree the historical reality of the situation prevailing toward the end of the monarchic period. However, if scholarly differences exist concerning the historical interpretation, there can be no dispute concerning the material evidence of the Edomite culture. The Edomite presence in the eastern Negeb is an objective fact, though the interpretation of this Edomite presence is likely to evoke further controversy.

---

[19]For preliminary details, see *ibid.* I wish to thank Dr. R. Cohen for kindly showing me the site, the ceramics and the cultic materials.

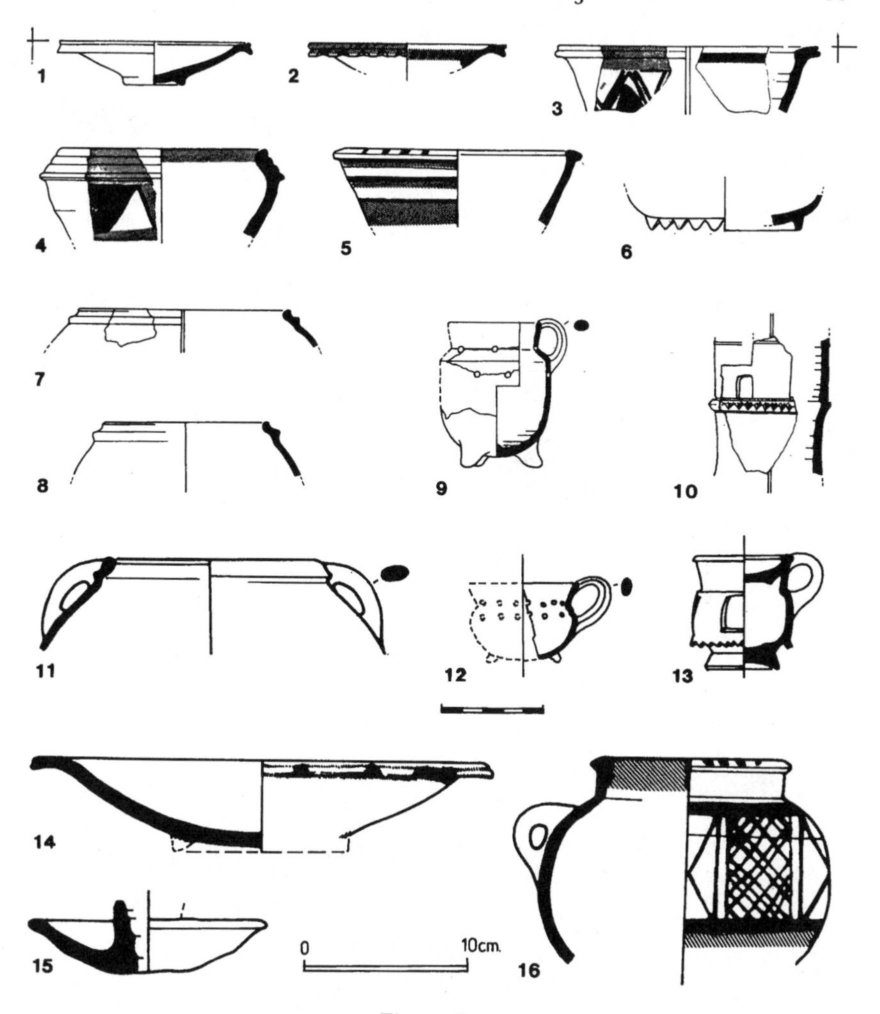

Figure 1

1–10	Vessels from Qitmit
12–13	Vessels from Tell el-Kheleifeh (After N. Glueck, "Some Edomite Pottery from Tell el-Kheleifeh," *BASOR* 188 [1967] 32, fig. 3:8; p. 37, fig. 5:1)
11, 14–16	Vessels from Buseirah (After M. F. Oakeshott, "A Study of the Iron Age II Pottery of East Jordan with Special Reference to Unpublished Material from Edom" [Ph.D. Thesis, University of London] pls. 2:17, 18:13, 26:11, 41:13)

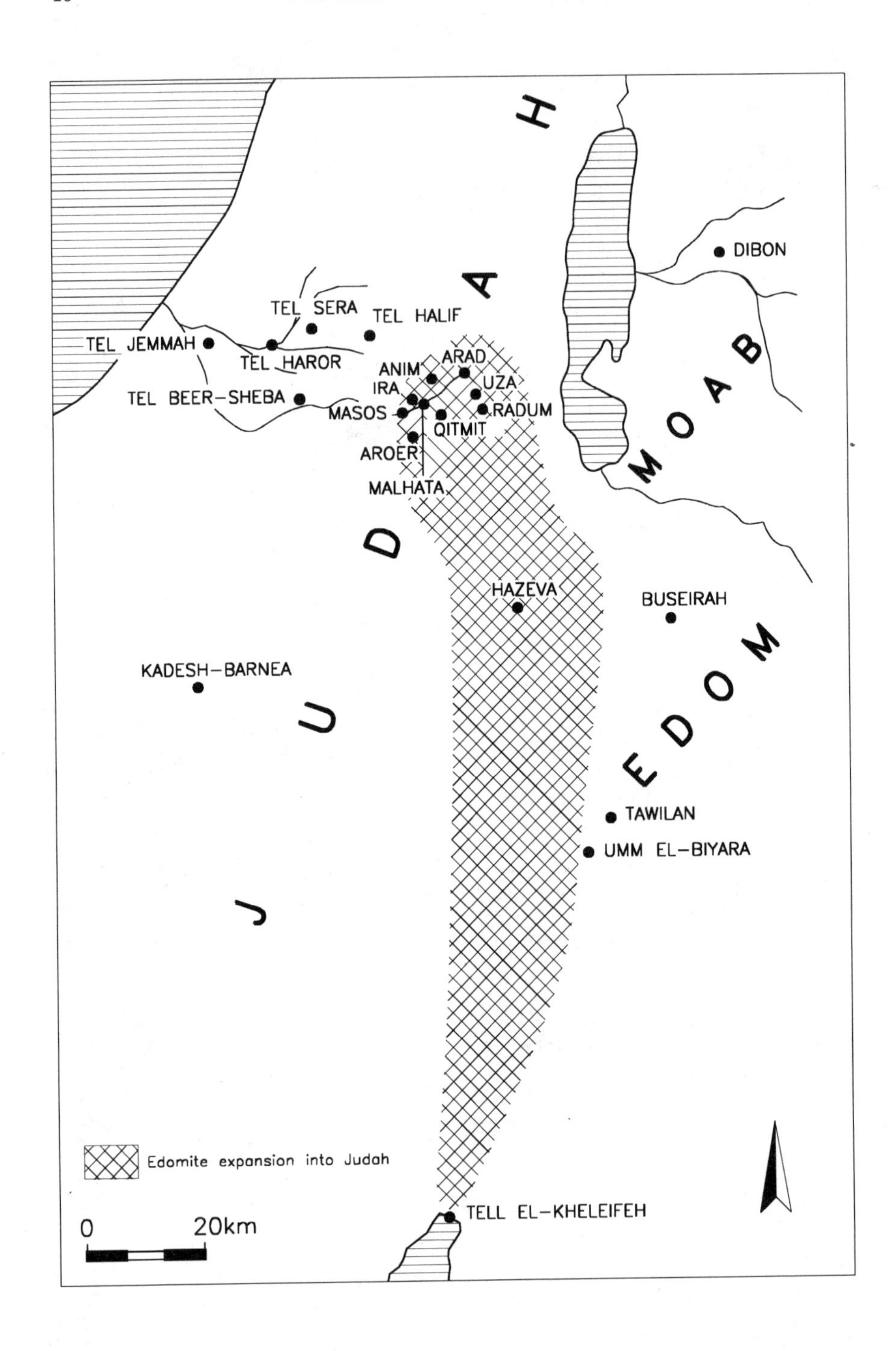

JUDAH
MOAB
EDOM
DIBON
TEL SERA
TEL HALIF
TEL JEMMAH
TEL HAROR
ANIM
ARAD
UZA
IRA
TEL BEER-SHEBA
MASOS
RADUM
QITMIT
AROER
MALHATA
HAZEVA
BUSEIRAH
KADESH-BARNEA
TAWILAN
UMM EL-BIYARA
Edomite expansion into Judah
0 20km
TELL EL-KHELEIFEH

Figure 2

The Edomites: The Archaeological Evidence from Transjordan

Piotr Bienkowski

Introduction

Until 1960, the generally accepted synthesis of Edomite archaeology was that of Nelson Glueck. Following his exhaustive survey of Transjordan from 1932-34, he postulated a thriving Edomite kingdom from the 13th century BC on and an occupational gap from the end of Iron II to the Hellenistic and Nabataean periods (i.e. 6th-4th centuries BC).[1]

Crystal Bennett's excavations at Umm el-Biyara from 1960 to 1965 clearly dated Edomite pottery to the 7th century BC. Her work at Tawilan and Buseirah revealed some evidence for continued occupation into the Persian period.[2] These excavations were responsible for creating the current framework for Edomite archaeology, which stresses the lack of stratified Iron Age deposits in southern Jordan prior to the end of the 8th century BC.

Nevertheless, no final report has yet been published on any Edomite site, and evidence for a good chronological sequence is still largely lacking. None of the Edomite sites so far excavated appears to have a continuous Iron Age sequence, nor do they have any pre-Iron Age remains. In addition to Glueck's original survey, the corpus of material now at our disposal consists of the following (see Fig. 1):

Excavated sites: Glueck's excavations at Tell el-Kheleifeh;[3] Crystal Bennett's excavations at Umm el-Biyara, Tawilan and Buseirah;[4]

---

[1]See conveniently J. A. Sauer, "Transjordan in the Bronze and Iron Ages: A Critique of Glueck's Synthesis," *BASOR* 263 (1986) 1-26.

[2]Cf. P. Bienkowski, "Umm el-Biyara, Tawilan and Buseirah in Retrospect," *Levant* 22 (1990) 91-109.

[3]Cf. G. D. Pratico, "Nelson Glueck's 1938-1940 Excavations at Tell el-Kheleifeh: A Reappraisal," *BASOR* 259 (1985) 1-32; idem, *Nelson Glueck's 1938-1940 Excavations at Tell el-Kheleifeh: A Reappraisal* (ASOR Archaeological Reports 3; Atlanta: Scholars Press, 1993), with full bibliography of earlier reports.

[4]Bienkowski, "Umm el-Biyara, Tawilan and Buseirah in Retrospect," with full bibliography of earlier reports.

Stephen Hart's excavations at Ghrareh;[5] and the archaeometallurgical investigations in Feinan by Andreas Hauptmann and Gerd Weisgerber.[6]

Surveys: those conducted by Burton MacDonald in the Wadi el-Ḥasa, the southern ghor and northeast ʿArabah;[7] Stephen Hart's Edom Survey Project between Ṭafila and Ras en-Naqb, including limited soundings;[8] William Jobling's ʿAqaba-Maʿan survey (a primarily epigraphic survey searching for Thamudic rock inscriptions);[9] Manfred Lindner's surveys and soundings at Baʿja III, es-Sadeh and Jebel al-Kser in the Petra area and at Selaʿ near Buseirah;[10] surveys at Khirbet Abu Banna and Khirbet Mashmil by Manfred Weippert;[11] three sites—es-Safi, Feifeh and Khanazir—from the Southeastern Dead Sea Plain survey by Walter Rast

---

[5]S. Hart, "Excavations at Ghrareh, 1986: Preliminary Report," *Levant* 20 (1988) 89-99; idem, "The Archaeology of the Land of Edom" (doctoral dissertation, Macquarie University, 1989) 9-20 and pls. 1-28 for pottery.

[6]A. Hauptmann, "Die Gewinnung von Kupfer: Ein uralter Industriezweig auf der Ostseite des Wadi Arabah," *Petra: Neue Ausgrabungen und Entdeckungen* (ed. M. Lindner; Munich/Bad Windsheim: Delp, 1986) 31-43; for the latest overview, see A. Hauptmann and G. Weisgerber, "Periods of Ore Exploitation and Metal Production in the Area of Feinan, Wadi ʿArabah, Jordan," *Studies in the History and Archaeology of Jordan IV* (ed. M. Zaghloul, *et al.*; Amman: Department of Antiquities, 1992) 61-66.

[7]B. MacDonald, *The Wadi al Hasa Archaeological Survey 1979-1983, West-Central Jordan* (Waterloo, Ontario: Wilfrid Laurier University Press, 1988); idem, *The Southern Ghors and Northeast ʿArabah Archaeological Survey* (Sheffield: J. R. Collis, 1992). For area covered by these two surveys, see Figs. 19-21 here.

[8]S. Hart, "Some Preliminary Thoughts on Settlement in Southern Edom," *Levant* 18 (1986) 51-58; idem, "Five Soundings in Southern Jordan," *Levant* 19 (1987) 33-47; idem, "The Edom Survey Project 1984-85: The Iron Age," *Studies in the History and Archaeology of Jordan III* (ed. A. Hadidi; Amman: Department of Antiquities, 1987) 287-90; idem, "The Archaeology of the Land of Edom," 83-111 for site list, pls. 59-66 for pottery.

[9]In particular, W. J. Jobling, "Preliminary Report on the Archaeological Survey between Maʿan and ʿAqaba, January to February 1980," *ADAJ* 25 (1981) 110 for five Iron Age sites; idem, "The 1982 Archaeological and Epigraphic Survey of the ʿAqaba-Maʿan Area of Southern Jordan," *ADAJ* 27 (1983) 189 for Iron Age surface sherds from Tell el-Kharaza.

[10]Conveniently, M. Lindner, "Edom outside the Famous Excavations: Evidence from Surveys in the Greater Petra Area," *Early Edom and Moab: The Beginning of the Iron Age in Southern Jordan* (ed. P. Bienkowski; SAM 7; Sheffield: J. R. Collis, 1992), with full bibliography of earlier reports; J. P. Zeitler, "'Edomite' Pottery from the Petra Region," *Early Edom and Moab* (ed. P. Bienkowski; Sheffield: J. R. Collis, 1992) for pottery from Ba'ja III and es-Sadeh. Cf. also S. Hart, "Selaʿ: The Rock of Edom?" *PEQ* (1986) 91-95. Lindner's survey at Jebel al-Kser, another "mountain-top" site in the Petra region, is still unpublished.

[11]M. Weippert, "Remarks on the History of Settlement in Southern Jordan during the Early Iron Age," *Studies in the History and Archaeology of Jordan I* (ed. A. Hadidi; Amman: Department of Antiquities, 1982) 153-62.

and Thomas Schaub;[12] and an unpublished survey by Alistair Killick in the Udhruh region, east of Petra.[13]

This chapter is divided into six sections:

1. The Problem of Dating
2. "Edomite" Pottery
3. Archaeological Evidence for the Beginning of the Iron Age in Edom
4. Edom in the Iron II
5. Archaeological Evidence for the End of the Edomite Kingdom
6. Conclusion

1. The Problem of Dating

1.1. Terminology

The standard terminology for dating the Iron Age in Transjordan is based on the system used for the Palestinian Iron Age:[14]

Iron IA (ca. 1220–1000 BC) — from the end of the Late Bronze Age to the United Monarchy in Jerusalem
Iron IB (ca. 1175–1000 BC) — in the north Jordan valley
Iron IC (ca. 1000–918 BC) — corresponding to the United Monarchy
Iron IIA (ca. 918–721 BC) — the period of the two kingdoms of Israel and Judah until the fall of Samaria to the Assyrians
Iron IIB (ca. 721–605 BC) — from the fall of Samaria to the end of the Assyrian empire
Iron IIC (ca. 605–539 BC) — the Neo-Babylonian period until the fall of Babylon to the Achaemenid Persians
Persian (ca. 539–330 BC) — until the fall of Persepolis to Alexander the Great.

At present, this detailed scheme cannot be applied to Edom as there is no site with a complete Iron Age sequence; nor, of course, does the historical framework for Palestine bear any relation to the material cultural framework of Transjordan. If there is Iron I in Edom, there is no real evidence for its dates. Iron II in Edom cannot at present be dated prior to the 7th century BC, although an earlier date cannot be discounted. Iron II pottery may well have been used into the Persian

---

[12] W. E. Rast and R. T. Schaub, "Survey of the Southeastern Plain of the Dead Sea, 1973," *ADAJ* 19 (1974) 5-53, esp. 16-18 for dates.

[13] Killick reports that the Iron Age occupation is extensive; cf. Hart, "The Archaeology of the Land of Edom," 127. Near the Roman site of Udhruh is an Edomite "hill fort," Tell Udhruh; cf. A. Killick, "Udruh—1980, 1981, 1982 Seasons: A Preliminary Report," *ADAJ* 27 (1983) 236 and fig. 7a.

[14] See for example Sauer, "Transjordan in the Bronze and Iron Ages."

period, with no independently diagnostic Persian-period pottery identified so far (see below for detailed arguments).

It would seem more appropriate at this stage of knowledge to use the following less specific terminology for Edom (indeed, present evidence leaves no choice but to use it):

Iron I (ca. 1220–1000 BC)
Iron II (ca. 1000–?539 BC)
Persian (ca. 539–330 BC)

The following review of dating criteria for Edom begins with the Iron II period, leaving the Iron I and Persian periods for secondary consideration, as they are still shadowy in terms of solid dating evidence.

1.2. Iron II (ca. 1000–?539 BC)

The only clear evidence from any Edomite site for absolute dating is the clay seal impression of Qos-Gabr from Umm el-Biyara (Fig. 2). The impression shows a winged sphinx moving to the right, between two lines of text. The text is slightly damaged, but has been restored convincingly as *qws g*[*br*] /*mlk* ʾ[*dm*], "Qos-Gabr King of Edom."[15] This is the only example of a king's seal from Iron Age Jordan. Qos-Gabr (or "Qaus-gabri") is probably the king who is mentioned twice in Assyrian inscriptions: on Prism B of Esarhaddon, which is dated 673–672 BC,[16] and in a description of the first campaign of Ashurbanipal, dated 667 BC.[17] The two references to Qos-Gabr thus date between 673 and 667 BC, indicating a 7th-century BC date for the associated pottery and small finds.[18]

The dating of all the Edomite sites and their associated material is ultimately dependent entirely on the seal impression of Qos-Gabr, although there are a few other pieces of dating evidence. The epigraphic evidence from Buseirah—inscriptions on ostraca, seals, weights, and seal impressions on pottery—can be dated either side of 700 BC with a margin of about 30 years or so. Inscriptions from other

[15]Cf. J. R. Bartlett, *Edom and the Edomites* (JSOTSup 77; Sheffield: JSOT Press, 1989) 213.

[16]Cf. *ANET,* 291; R. Borger, *Die Inschriften Asarhaddons, Königs von Assyrien* (Beiheft AfO 9; Osnabrück: Biblio Verlag, 1956) Nin. A v. 56.

[17]Cf. *ANET,* 294; M. Streck, *Assurbanipal und die letzten assyrischen Könige bis zum Untergang Niniveh's* (3 vols; Vorderasiatische Bibliotek 7; Leipzig: J. C. Hinrichs, 1916) l.ccclx, 2.139.

[18]Cf. M. Oakeshott, "A Study of the Iron Age II Pottery of East Jordan with Special Reference to Unpublished Material from Edom" (Ph.D. dissertation, University of London, 1978) 96-99, 158-83 for comparisons and dating of the Umm el-Biyara pottery.

sites in Edom have been dated to the 7th-6th centuries BC (discounting later ostraca from Tell el-Kheleifeh, which may come from a post-Edomite occupation, see section 1.4).[19] There are considerable ceramic parallels with Dhiban, the Mount Nebo tombs, Hesban, and tombs in the Amman area, which date between the late 8th century and ca. 600 BC.[20] Pottery from Umm el-Biyara, Tawilan, Buseirah and Kheleifeh has parallels in the tomb of Adoni-Nur in Amman, whose seal dates the tomb to about 650 BC.[21] Definite Assyrian forms (in fact, copies of Assyrian forms) are present at all four sites, suggesting a date from the late 8th century BC on.[22]

At present, therefore, the evidence indicates a 7th-century BC date for the Edomite sites and their associated pottery, i.e. within the Iron II period. Of course, the seal impression of Qos-Gabr may give only a midpoint date—there is no real evidence to suggest how much earlier or later the pottery might date. It is generally assumed that the pottery stretches into the 6th century BC, but this is not based on any real evidence, other than the assumption that if Iron II finished in 539 BC then this Iron II pottery should also date at least as late as 539 (but see section 1.4). Similarly, the possibility cannot be discounted that the pottery also goes back earlier than the 7th century BC, to the 8th, 9th or even 10th centuries BC. Recent but still unpublished evidence from the Feinan region south of the Dead Sea may give an indication of an earlier (and later) date. Charcoal samples from Khirbet el-Jariye, Khirbet en-Nahas, Feinan 5 and Barqa el-Hetiye, apparently associated with standard "Edomite" pottery, have been C14-dated to between 900 and 400 BC (calibrated), although detailed publication is needed, especially of the context of the charcoal samples, before the true significance of these dates can be assessed.[23]

1.3. Iron I (ca. 1220–1000 BC)

In the last few years, surveys in northern Edom have reported sites of Iron I date, based on the dating of pottery sherds (Fig. 3).[24] The

[19]For a list of inscriptions from Edom, see Bartlett, *Edom and the Edomites*, 209-28.

[20]M. Oakeshott, "A Study of Iron Age II Pottery of East Jordan," 183; idem, "The Edomite Pottery," *Midian, Moab and Edom: The History and Archaeology of Late Bronze and Iron Age Jordan and North-West Arabia* (ed. J. F. A. Sawyer and D. J. A. Clines; Sheffield: JSOT Press, 1983) 61.

[21]Oakeshott, "A Study of the Iron Age II Pottery of East Jordan," 170-71; idem, "The Edomite Pottery," 62.

[22]Oakeshott, "A Study of the Iron Age II Pottery of East Jordan," 167-68.

[23]I thank Drs. A. Hauptmann, M. Najjar and M. Flander for sharing this information with me.

[24]Weippert, "Remarks on the History of Settlement in Southern Jordan," 156-61;

dating to Iron I was largely on the basis of pottery parallels from Palestinian and Syrian sites. In fact, much of the material that has been dated to Iron I is ambiguous and not diagnostic and could range from the Late Bronze Age to Iron II. Much of it can be paralleled with Iron II pottery from excavated Edomite sites, although some cannot and may well be earlier in date.[25] The problem at present is that all of the "Iron I" material comes from surveys. None of it has yet been found in a stratified sequence, so its relative date cannot be settled conclusively. Some support for an Iron I date may come from unpublished charcoal samples from Khirbet en-Nahas in the Feinan region, which have been C14-dated to between 1200 and 950 BC (calibrated) and are associated with a "Midianite" (or Qurayya painted ware) sherd, which would normally be dated to the end of the Late Bronze Age/Iron I.[26]

Clearly, there is not yet sufficient hard evidence to come to firm conclusions regarding the existence, dates and characteristics of Iron I in Edom. A group of sites on the banks of the Wadi el-Ḥasa in northern Edom has recently been identified as possibly containing a sequence from Late Bronze-Iron I-Iron II, and proposed fieldwork at these may provide the needed chronological evidence.[27]

Israel Finkelstein has argued that Iron I pottery has been published from between 27 and 30 sites throughout Edom, including Umm el-Biyara, Tawilan and Buseirah but was simply not identified as such.[28] His argument is essentially that certain storage jars from Edom have parallels to the well-known collared-rim jars from well-dated, rich Iron I assemblages in Palestine and Transjordan. The present writer has disputed Finkelstein's conclusions and upheld the Iron II dating. The stratigraphic evidence from the excavated Edomite sites shows clearly

---

MacDonald, *The Wadi al Hasa Archaeological Survey*, 171-81; idem, *The Southern Ghors and Northeast ʿArabah Archaeological Survey*; idem, "Evidence from the Wadi el-Hasa and Southern Ghors and North-east Arabah Archaeological Surveys," *Early Edom and Moab: The Beginning of the Iron Age in Southern Jordan* (ed. P. Bienkowski; SAM 7; Sheffield: J. R. Collis, 1992), 113-42.

[25]S. Hart, "Iron Age Settlement in the Land of Edom," *Early Edom and Moab: The Beginning of the Iron Age in Southern Jordan* (ed. P. Bienkowski; SAM 7; Sheffield: J. R. Collis, 1992) 93-98.

[26]Cf. n. 23. Jobling has reported Iron I material from the Wadi Rumman, between Ras en-Naqb and ʿAqaba, but without further details ("Preliminary Report on the Archaeological Survey between Maʿan and ʿAqaba, January to February 1980," *ADAJ* 25 [1981] 110 and pl. XXXI:1, 2 for Um Guweʿah, Rakbat Um Edgeyer and Jebel Utud).

[27]P. Bienkowski, "The Beginning of the Iron Age in Southern Jordan: A Framework," *Early Edom and Moab: The Beginning of the Iron Age in Southern Jordan* (ed. P. Bienkowski; SAM 7; Sheffield: J. R. Collis, 1992) 1-12, esp. 6.

[28]I. Finkelstein, "Edom in the Iron I," *Levant* 24 (1992) 159-66; idem, "Stratigraphy, Pottery and Parallels: A Reply to Bienkowski," *Levant* 24 (1992) 171-72.

that there were no Iron I strata below the Iron II occupations. The wide distribution throughout Jordan of collared-rim jars of varying sizes dating to the late Iron II period has now been firmly established, with well stratified evidence from Baluᶜa in Moab.[29] It has become quite clear that pottery development in Jordan is different from that in Palestine, and the Jordanian sequences must be determined on their own merits through rigorous and defensible local series based on stratigraphy, not by undue reliance on neighbouring parallels.

1.4. Persian Period (ca. 539–330 BC)

Evidence for dating anything in Edom to the Persian period is still ambiguous.[30] A cooking pot (Fig. 4) from the later phase of the Area C building at Buseirah has been dated to the Persian period, and Building A in Buseirah Area A was thought possibly to extend into the Persian period because of its similarity in plan to the Area C building (see section 4 and Figs. 28 and 30).[31] However, the Area C cooking pot is so far the only evidence cited for a date in the Persian period. Although it has the globular sack-shaped body, short neck, and handles from rim to shoulder of characteristic Persian-period cooking pots from Palestine,[32] a whole period cannot be dated on the evidence of just one pot. Particular caution must be used in Edom as there is no stratified Persian-period material and it cannot necessarily be assumed that Persian-period pottery here will be like Persian-period pottery in Palestine. Phoenician and Aramaic ostraca dated to the 5th and early 4th centuries and some 5th-century BC Greek sherds have come from the fragmentary Period V settlement at Tell el-Kheleifeh. However, this settlement was on a different alignment from the earlier fortified (possibly Edomite) settlement and might not even have been an Edomite site at this period (see section 4).[33] None of the major surveys in Edom has identified any

---

[29]P. Bienkowski, "The Beginning of the Iron Age in Edom: A Reply to Finkelstein," *Levant* 24 (1992) 167-169; idem, "The Date of Sedentary Occupation in Edom: Evidence from Umm el-Biyara, Tawilan and Buseirah," *Early Edom and Moab: The Beginning of the Iron Age in Southern Jordan* (ed. P. Bienkowski; SAM 7; Sheffield: J. R. Collis, 1992) 99-102, esp. 108; U. Worschech, "*Collared-Rim Jars* aus Moab: Anmerkungen zur Entwicklung und Verbreitung der Krüge mit 'Halswulst'," *ZDPV* 108 (1992) 149-55, with a list of other Iron II collared-rim jars from Jordan.

[30]P. Bienkowski, "The Chronology of Tawilan and the 'Dark Age' of Edom," *Aram* 2:1&2 (1990) 35-44.

[31]C.-M. Bennett, "Excavations at Buseirah, Southern Jordan, 1974: Fourth Preliminary Report," *Levant* 9 (1977) 8 and fig. 5:1201.

[32]Cf. E. Stern, *Material Culture of the Land of the Bible in the Persian Period 538-332 B.C.* (Warminster: Aris and Phillips, 1982) 100-102.

[33]Pratico, "Nelson Glueck's 1938-1940 Excavations at Tell el-Kheleifeh," 14.

Persian-period pottery.[34] The recent unpublished C14 date of 400 BC for the end of copper production at Feinan implies a Persian-period date, but publication of the associated data is awaited (see section 1.2 and n. 23).

Potentially the best evidence for the Persian period in Edom is the cuneiform tablet from Tawilan (Fig. 5).[35] This was a legal document drawn up in Harran in Syria concerning testimony to the disputed sale of two rams. The names of the buyer and of the seller are both Aramaic, but the name and patronymic of the man responsible for the testimony are both compounded with the name of the Edomite god Qos, probably indicating that he and his father were Edomites and perhaps explaining why this tablet went to Tawilan. The tablet is dated to the accession year of one of the Achaemenid kings named Darius: i.e. Darius I (521 BC), Darius II (423 BC) or Darius III (335 BC). Unfortunately, a certain attribution is impossible for this isolated text. Darius III may be unlikely, given the extreme rarity of cuneiform documents at the end of the Achaemenid era, even in Babylonia. Attribution to Darius I or II could be seen in the context of military movements in the Harran region in the accession years of both kings, which would explain the presence of a Babylonian scribe.[36] However, Darius I has been discounted on the basis of the king's title (i.e. "King of the Lands"), since he is not known to have taken it so early in his reign.[37] This would leave Darius II and a date of 423 BC for the tablet, but really none of the three can be definitely excluded.

The context in which the tablet was found is similarly unhelpful. Area II at Tawilan (see Fig. 22) was completely abandoned following a fire, with many of the walls collapsing. This was the end of Edomite settlement at the site. Following the abandonment, the surviving network of walls acted as a catchment for the accumulating silts and soils. The tablet was found next to a pillar within these fill-accumulation deposits. Thus, the tablet was found not in an occupation or even destruction context, but in an accumulation deposit following the end of Edomite occupation. Not only are its precise attribution and date uncertain, but its association with occupation at Tawilan cannot be

---

[34]Bienkowski, "The Chronology of Tawilan," 36 for references.

[35]S. Dalley, "The Cuneiform Tablet from Tell Tawilan," *Levant* 16 (1984) 19-22; idem, "The Cuneiform Tablet," *Excavations at Tawilan in Southern Jordan* (ed. C.-M. Bennett and P. Bienkowski; forthcoming); M. W. Stolper, "The Neo-Babylonian Text from the Persepolis Fortification," *JNES* 43 (1984) 309 n. 36.

[36]F. Joannès, "A propos de la tablette cunéiforme de Tell Tawilan," *Revue d'Assyriologie* 81 (1987) 165-66.

[37]I. Ephʿal, "Syria-Palestine under Achaemenid Rule," *Cambridge Ancient History IV* (2d ed.; ed. J. Boardman *et al.*; New York: Cambridge University, 1988) 151 n. 30.

conclusively demonstrated. All that can be concluded from the tablet, therefore, is that it was written in the Persian period far to the north in Harran, it involved an Edomite, and at some point it found its way to Tawilan, but it was not necessarily associated with the Edomite settlement at Tawilan.

The Persian period in Edom therefore appears to be very difficult to pin down in terms of hard archaeological evidence. No diagnostic Persian-period pottery has been identified as a separate corpus. It may be that Persian-period pottery in Edom is indistinguishable from the pottery of Iron II, i.e. that Iron II pottery simply continued unchanged through the Persian period. There is growing evidence that this was the case elsewhere in Transjordan. At Tell el-Umeiri south of Amman, typical Persian forms were missing, but 5th-century BC Attic sherds were found associated with standard Iron II pottery, suggesting that the Iron II pottery corpus lasted through the Persian period.[38] Continuity of pottery assemblages between Iron II and the Persian period, perhaps down to ca. 400 BC, has also been suggested for the Amman Citadel, Hesban and Tell el-Kheleifeh.[39] The possibility cannot be discounted that the same continuity of pottery assemblages occurred in Edom.[40]

2. "Edomite" Pottery

2.1. The Classification of "Edomite" Pottery

The first detailed classification of pottery from Edom was by Marion Oakeshott, based on her study of the pottery from Crystal Bennett's excavations at Buseirah.[41] Although Oakeshott's doctoral thesis embraced other sites inside and outside Edom, her detailed typology is essentially the Buseirah type series.[42] This type series is generally applicable to other Edomite sites, especially Tawilan, which with some

---

[38]L. G. Herr, "The Late Iron II-Persian Ceramic Horizon at Tell el-ʿUmeiri," *Studies in the History and Archaeology of Jordan V* (forthcoming); idem, "What Ever Happened to the Ammonites?" *BAR* 19/6 (1993) 35.

[39]Personal communications from M. Najjar (Amman Citadel) and J. A. Sauer (Hesban); Pratico, *Tell el-Kheleifeh* (cf. n. 3) 50.

[40]A few characteristic Persian-period forms have been identified elsewhere in Transjordan. For Moab, see R. Brown, "Ceramics from the Kerak Plateau," *Archaeological Survey of the Kerak Plateau* (ed. J. M. Miller; ASOR Archaeological Reports 1; Atlanta: Scholars Press, 1991) 203-205. Brown carefully acknowledges the difficulty of distinguishing Iron II from Persian.

[41]Oakeshott, "A Study of the Iron Age II Pottery of East Jordan"; cf. also idem, "The Edomite Pottery."

[42]Oakeshott, "A Study of the Iron Age II Pottery of East Jordan," 28-58.

exceptions has much the same range of forms as Buseirah, but less so for Umm el-Biyara (see section 2.2).[43]

Oakeshott's classification was based on a typological study and not on stratigraphy, since properly analyzed stratigraphical evidence was not available at the time of her study. More recently, Stephen Hart has attempted to determine a relative and absolute chronology for Edomite pottery and has generally followed Oakeshott's classification.[44] His dating hypothesis is considered below (see section 2.2).

No Edomite site has yet been fully published, so no complete assemblage of vessels is available. The classification of characteristic pottery from Edom that follows is that for the site of Tawilan, since final publication of this site by the present writer is imminent. Tawilan has stratigraphic evidence for eight architectural stages, five of them within Iron II.[45] The Tawilan pottery has been prepared for publication by Stephen Hart, and the classification used here is based on his work.[46]

The most common vessel types at Buseirah and Tawilan are platters and flat dishes (Fig. 6). The inside is usually decorated with black bands, often with groups of slash or dribble marks on the rim. Carinated bowls with the rim folded outwards horizontally (Fig. 7:1-12) are quite common, but are normally undecorated. Occasionally they are decorated with simple black bands. Straight-rimmed carinated bowls (Fig. 7:13) are not common at Tawilan. Bowls with triangular-section rims (Fig. 8) sometimes have a bar handle or a ridge below the rim and are occasionally decorated with simple black bands.

Fine-ware bowls (Fig. 9:1-17) are defined by the thinness of their walls and are usually decorated with bands of black paint, with some burnishing and slash or dribble marks over the rim. A characteristic at Tawilan is the use of thumb impressions (Fig. 9:9, 10), some outlined with incisions (Fig. 9:16). "Assyrian" bowls (Fig. 9:18-22) were probably influenced by Assyrian prototypes but manufactured locally. Mugs or bowls with a single handle (Fig. 10) may have been a variant of the "Assyrian" bowl, although the fabric is coarser, there is no decoration, and a single loop handle is attached.

Necked bowls (deep bowls with a short neck) (Fig. 11) show the standard black-banded decoration on some examples, although occasionally there is more complex decoration. Kraters (deep bowls with handles) (Fig. 12) are undecorated but vary quite a lot in shape.

---

[43]*Ibid.*, 18-19.

[44]Hart, "The Archaeology of the Land of Edom," 77-82.

[45]Bienkowski, "Umm el-Biyara, Tawilan and Buseirah in Retrospect," *Levant* 22 (1990) 96-97.

[46]Hart, "The Archaeology of the Land of Edom," 3-5, 47-49.

There is a wide range of large storage jar or pithos types (Fig. 13:1-11), e.g. the common "triple-ridged" form (Fig. 13:1-3), and jars with an external ridge below the rim (Fig. 13:7, 9). Fig. 13:12 is a very large bowl, perhaps best described as a hybrid krater/storage jar.

Large jugs with a ridged rim (Fig. 14) have one handle from shoulder to rim, with the rim shaped by an inward fold followed by a single outward fold. Only occasionally are they decorated.

Cooking pots (Fig. 15:1-12) at Tawilan normally have a ridged rim continuing the line of the shoulder, but occasionally they have a short neck (e.g. Fig. 15:6, 7), sometimes an unridged rim (Fig. 15:8), or are miniature variants (Fig. 15:9-12). Lamps (Fig. 15:13-16) show little distinction from standard Iron Age forms and ware. Negeb ware (Fig. 16) is a coarse, handmade pottery that occurs throughout Edom and the Negeb. It seems to date throughout the whole Iron Age, and probably earlier and later.[47]

The striking and characteristic painted pottery from Edom is generally termed "Edomite" pottery. This is an unfortunate term that has caused confusion, as it begs a lot of chronological and cultural questions. Just because this pottery is called "Edomite" does not mean that wherever it is found it must be Edomite. There is insufficient evidence to indicate that this pottery was confined to a specific ethnic group, rather than being the standard Iron II (and later?, see section 1.4) painted pottery of an area extending beyond Edom proper. The new term that has been proposed is "Buseirah painted ware," which has no ethnic presuppositions, just as elsewhere in the Near East reference is made to "Jemdat Nasr pottery."[48]

2.2. The Dating of the Pottery from Edom

Stephen Hart has attempted a relative and absolute dating of the main Edomite sites based on comparison of their pottery.[49] He suggests that the sites can be dated relatively as Umm el-Biyara (earliest), Buseirah Area D (whose three phases provide a rare example of stratified pottery), Ghrareh and Tawilan (latest). He proposes that Area D is one of the earliest areas of occupation at Buseirah, where occupation might extend into the Persian period in Area C (but see section 1.4).

Hart suggests the following sequence for the pottery:

---

[47]Pratico, "Nelson Glueck's 1938-1940 Excavations at Tell el-Kheleifeh," 23; idem, *Tell el-Kheleifeh,* 35-36.

[48]Bienkowski, "The Beginning of the Iron Age in Southern Jordan."

[49]Hart, "The Archaeology of the Land of Edom," 81-82.

1. Painted decoration on pottery in Edom did not become common until at least later than ca. 670 BC (i.e. the Umm el-Biyara settlement).
2. Two possible early forms are elongated bottles and rounded jugs, found at Umm el-Biyara (Figs. 17:93, 212; 18 left).
3. Later forms might be fine-ware bowls (Fig. 9:1-17) and "Assyrian" bowls (Fig. 9:18-22), and storage jars with a rounded rim and a ridge below externally (Fig. 13:7, 9).
4. Examples with elaborate painted decoration, plastic decoration, denticulation or complicated shapes (e.g. Fig. 9) are more likely to be of a late date. The majority of these examples occur at Tawilan. Hart finds it significant that many of the painted examples of Buseirah painted ware found in the Negeb, an area of what he calls later Edomite expansion, exhibit quite complicated geometric decoration, sometimes with incised or applied denticulation.

The evidence for this proposed sequence is sparse, and caution must be used when employing it. Hart's attempt at a relative and absolute date for this pottery makes several stated assumptions.[50] The most critical of these are:

1. The seal impression from Umm el-Biyara (see section 1.2 and Fig. 2) refers to the Qos-Gabr known from Assyrian annals and so dates to ca. 670 BC. This assumption is probably correct. Almost without exception, the Umm el-Biyara pottery is undecorated (cf. Figs. 17-18).[51] Since the Umm el-Biyara settlement can be dated to ca. 670 BC, Hart assumes that painted decoration only became common after that date—and therefore that the Edomite sites that contain painted pottery date later than ca. 670 BC. This assumption appears to receive support from the low incidence of painted pottery in the earliest phases at Buseirah Area D, but Hart himself concedes that this may be related to the low sample size.[52] However, variations in pottery typology between sites are not necessarily a function of chronology. As well as Umm el-Biyara, the other "mountain-top" sites in the Petra region—es-Sadeh and Baʿja III—also have little painted pottery.[53] While a chronological difference from Edomite sites with painted pottery remains a possibility, there are other factors to be considered. A regional difference is discounted, since nearby Tawilan has a high percentage of painted pottery. A difference based on site location is a possibility, since all three are on high, almost inaccessible mountains (see section 4).

---

[50]*Ibid.*, 58-60.

[51]Cf. *ibid.*, 51-52.

[52]*Ibid.*, 25-42.

[53]Cf. Zeitler, "'Edomite' Pottery from the Petra Region."

2. The cuneiform tablet from Tawilan (Fig. 5) dates to the accession year of Darius I (521 BC). An unstated assumption by Hart is that the Tawilan tablet is associated with the Edomite settlement at Tawilan, and thus, that the tablet can contribute to the dating of the settlement and associated pottery. Hart further assumes that Tawilan was unlikely to have been occupied for more than a century,[54] and he concludes that the tablet indicates a 6th-century BC date for the occupation. However, a certain attribution and date for this tablet is not possible, and even its association with occupation at Tawilan cannot be demonstrated conclusively (see section 1.4). If the Tawilan tablet was not associated with the Edomite occupation, a 7th or 6th-century BC-occupation terminating prior to the date of the tablet cannot be excluded; but if an association is assumed, a 6th, 5th or 4th-century BC date cannot be discounted for the occupation because of the uncertainty as to which Darius is meant.

While it is possible that Hart's proposed sequence is correct, the evidence on which it is based is far from clear, and even Hart agrees that at the very least there was considerable overlap in pottery types. It must therefore be concluded that while we probably have a workable classification of "Edomite" pottery, there is not yet sufficient evidence for a proper, defensible sequence.

3. Archaeological Evidence for the Beginning of the Iron Age in Edom

3.1. Pre-Iron Age Settlement Patterns

Nelson Glueck's synthesis of the archaeology of Transjordan in the Bronze and Iron Ages concluded that there was a major phase of occupation during the latter part of the Early Bronze Age, a gap during most of the Middle and Late Bronze Ages, and a rise in occupation in Iron I-II.[55] The Middle to Late Bronze Age gap has now disappeared in northern and central Transjordan, where major tell sites are well attested.

South of the Wadi el-Ḥasa, in what later became Edom, while there are Palaeolithic, Neolithic, Chalcolithic and Early Bronze Age sites, there is still a gap in the Middle and Late Bronze Ages. This was followed by a virtual explosion of settlement in the Iron Age.

The only sites south of the Wadi el-Ḥasa where Middle Bronze Age material has allegedly been found are Tell el-Kharaza, a rock shelter cave in the Wadi Hisma area,[56] and Selaʿ near Buseirah.[57] However,

---

[54]Hart, "The Archaeology of the Land of Edom," 44-47.

[55]See conveniently Sauer, "Transjordan in the Bronze and Iron Ages."

[56]W. J. Jobling, "The 1982 Archaeological and Epigraphic Survey of the ʿAqaba-Maʿan Area of Southern Jordan," *ADAJ* 27 (1983) 189-92.

none of the pottery has been published and a Middle Bronze Age date cannot be confirmed.

Only six Late Bronze Age sites have been identified south of the Wadi el-Ḥasa, by the Wadi el-Ḥasa Survey in northern Edom (Fig. 19).[58] These were in the best agricultural land in the western area of the survey, but no structures have been definitely dated to the Late Bronze Age. Furthermore, there is no proof for metal production in the Feinan region, the major copper production area of the southern Levant, during the 2nd millennium BC, after heavy exploitation in the Chalcolithic through to Early Bronze IV.[59]

3.2. Iron I Settlement?

Several sites in northern Edom have been dated to Iron I (Figs. 20-21).[60] The inadequacies of the evidence for dating Iron I in Edom have been dealt with above (see section 1.3). The sites dated to Iron I in the Wadi el-Ḥasa Survey were, like Late Bronze Age sites, mostly in the west of the survey area, in the best agricultural land (Fig. 20). In the Southern Ghors and Northeast ʿArabah Survey, the heaviest concentration of sites dated to Iron I was found in the Wadi Ghuweib in the south of the survey area (Fig. 21). These sites appear to be cemeteries, camps, sherd scatters and smelting sites. However, no site dated to Iron I has yet been excavated, so no structures can be assigned to this period.

4. Edom in the Iron II

The evidence of surveys carried out in Edom indicates a considerable rise in settlement in Iron II: there is a huge increase in the number of sites, perhaps reflecting a growth in population (cf. Figs. 20-21).[61] Of course, until more is known about Iron I, it is impossible to be certain how sudden this dense Iron II settlement really was. At present, though, the pattern appears to show light Iron I settlement in northern Edom, with heavy settlement appearing in Iron II across the whole

---

[57]M. Lindner, "Es-Selaʿ: Eine antike Fliehburg 50 km nördlich von Petra," *Petra und das Königreich der Nabatäer* (5th ed.; ed. M. Lindner; Munich/Bad Windsheim: Delp, 1989) 271-285; idem, "Edom outside the Famous Excavations."

[58]MacDonald, *The Wadi al Hasa Archaeological Survey,* 166-170; idem, "Evidence from the Wadi el-Hasa and Southern Ghors and North-east Arabah Archaeological Surveys."

[59]Hauptmann, "Die Gewinnung von Kupfer"; Hauptmann and Weisgerber, "Periods of Ore Exploitation," 63.

[60]Cf. n. 24.

[61]S. Hart, "Some Preliminary Thoughts on Settlement in Southern Edom," *Levant* 18 (1986) fig. 2; Bartlett, *Edom and the Edomites,* Maps 1 and 2 on 230-31.

Edomite plateau. Present evidence indicates a 7th-6th-century BC date for this Iron II expansion, but an earlier date cannot be discounted (see section 1.2).

The nature of many of these surveyed but unexcavated Iron II sites is uncertain, because later remains, often Nabataean, have concealed the earlier deposits and so Iron II sherds could not be associated with any structures.[62] During his pioneering survey in 1932-34, Nelson Glueck identified many Iron Age sites in Edom (and indeed elsewhere in Transjordan) as military forts, concluding that the boundaries of Edom were protected by a system of border fortresses.[63] This has long been an influential theory, and it is admittedly easy to get the subjective impression that many unexcavated sites with Iron II pottery were essentially defensive.[64] Nevertheless, the evidence for a string of border forts is not decisive and has been questioned.[65] A purely military function for these "forts" has not been adequately demonstrated, and there is evidence to suggest that they had a variety of functions, for example as agricultural facilities and settlements, which perhaps might have included defence.[66] A number that Glueck specifically identified as Iron Age forts show predominantly Nabataean or Roman surface pottery, sometimes to the exclusion of Iron Age forms.[67] No doubt some of the sites were Iron Age, but whether they were forts is a matter of interpretation. What little evidence there was, Glueck filled in with sites that may or may not have been Iron Age forts, to create a "string" of forts to fit his preconceived notion of a "Greater Edom" (and, in Moab, of a "Greater Moab") monarchy.[68] The question of the "border forts" has yet to be fully resolved, since it cannot be confirmed without

---

[62]Hart, "Some Preliminary Thoughts," 51.

[63]N. Glueck, *Explorations in Eastern Palestine II* (AASOR 15; New Haven: American Schools of Oriental Research, 1935) 138-39.

[64]E.g., Hart, "Some Preliminary Thoughts," 51; Bartlett, *Edom and the Edomites,* 137.

[65]R. H. Dornemann, *The Archaeology of the Transjordan in the Bronze and Iron Ages* (Milwaukee: Milwaukee Public Museum, 1983) 123-24; B. MacDonald, "The Wadi el Hasa Archaeological Survey," *The Answers Lie Below* (ed. H. O. Thompson; Lanham, MD: University Press of America, 1984) 113-28; idem, *The Wadi al Hasa Archaeological Survey,* 291; J. M. Miller, "Early Monarchy in Moab?" *Early Edom and Moab: The Beginning of the Iron Age in Southern Jordan* (ed. P. Bienkowski; SAM 7; Sheffield: J. R. Collis, 1992) 77-92, esp. 79.

[66]Cf. R. Kletter, "The Rujm el-Malfuf Buildings and the Assyrian Vassal State of Ammon," *BASOR* 284 (1991) 139-41 for the Ammonite "forts."

[67]MacDonald, *The Wadi al Hasa Archaeological Survey,* 291; Hart, "The Archaeology of the Land of Edom," 85-87; Dornemann, *Archaeology of Transjordan.*

[68]Miller, "Early Monarchy in Moab?," 77-92.

excavation that the sites were fortified during the Iron Age, and so far not one of these "forts" in Edom has been excavated.[69]

Most of the settlements in Edom in fact appear to be open villages and farms, sometimes located on almost inaccessible mountain tops.[70] There are exceptions, such as Buseirah (see below), or Ghrareh, which was on a spur surrounded by an enclosure wall.[71] Building plans are generally rectangular, with dry-stone walls, sometimes with long corridor-like rooms with smaller rooms adjoining, although within this there was considerable variation.[72] Pillars were occasionally used, for example at Tawilan and Ghrareh (Figs. 22-23), the main building at the latter having a central pillared courtyard. The pillars would probably have been roof supports, but they are not very stable and are unlikely to have carried either a very heavy or a large roof. All these sites seem to have been agricultural and domestic, judging from the presence of querns, grinding stones, loom weights, spindle whorls and cisterns.

Umm el-Biyara (Fig. 24), Baʿja III and es-Sadeh are linked in that they are all "mountain-top" sites in or near Petra, and their Iron II pottery was overwhelmingly plain, while at other Edomite sites painted pottery was plentiful (see section 2.2). It might be possible to explain this difference by site location: all three are on high mountains; at es-Sadeh and Umm el-Biyara there are large rectangular buildings with long corridor rooms, perhaps reflecting the paucity of timber for roofing, while at Baʿja III and es-Sadeh other habitations were rock shelters.[73] The remote location and difficult access may suggest deliberate inaccessibility and seclusion from the sites on the Edomite plateau and from any centralized control from the capital, Buseirah. In any case, it is not known how centralized a state Edom ever became, and there is much to suggest that statehood—and by implication central control—was fairly superficial.[74]

Tell el-Kheleifeh, about 500 m from the north shore of the Gulf of ʿAqaba, remains an enigma. Pratico's reappraisal of Glueck's 1938-40 excavations proposes two major occupational phases: a casemate for-

---

[69]Cf. Bienkowski, "The Beginning of the Iron Age in Southern Jordan."

[70]See P. Bienkowski, "The Architecture of Edom," *Studies in the History and Archaeology of Jordan V* (forthcoming).

[71]For Ghrareh, cf. n. 5.

[72]For details of individual sites, with full bibliographies of excavations, see n. 2 and 5, and Bartlett, *Edom and the Edomites*, 132-37.

[73]Zeitler, "'Edomite' Pottery from the Petra Region"; M. Lindner, "Edom outside the Famous Excavations."

[74]E. A. Knauf, "The Cultural Impact of Secondary State Formation: The Cases of the Edomites and Moabites," *Early Edom and Moab: The Beginning of the Iron Age in Southern Jordan* (ed. P. Bienkowski; SAM 7; Sheffield: J. R. Collis, 1992) 47-54.

tress with a six-roomed building in the center (Fig. 25), and a fortified settlement in an insets/offsets design with a four-chambered gate (Fig. 26).[75] All the construction is in mudbrick. The dating is still fairly flexible, but appears to be between the 8th and 6th centuries BC, although the end-date may even go down as far as ca. 400 BC (see section 1.4 and n. 39). Whether or not Kheleifeh was an Edomite foundation is debatable: if Edom proper is restricted to the area north of the Wadi Ḥisma,[76] then Kheleifeh was not technically in Edom, although in an age of ever-changing boundaries that did not mean very much. Pratico has compared the casemate fortress to the Negeb fortresses but has called the groundplan "chronologically, functionally, and typologically irrelevant."[77] Bartlett suggests that the fortified settlement represents an Edomite rebuilding,[78] but again there are similarities with Arad, Tell el-Qudeirat and Ḥorvat 'Uza in the Negeb.[79] The function and origins of Kheleifeh remain uncertain. Bartlett has called it a fortified caravanserai.[80] It may have been connected with the Arabian trade: although the route of the Arabian trade through Transjordan in the Iron Age is speculative, in later periods Elath was one of the links on the route between Maʿan and Egypt and Gaza.[81]

The major buildings at Buseirah remain unique in Edom. Excavations revealed what might be an administrative center dominated by two or three large buildings and fortified by a town wall (Figs. 27-30).[82] The area excavated probably embraced only the central part of the ancient city, the rest being hidden under the present-day village to the south. There is evidence for a division of the city into Upper and Lower Towns. The Upper Town consisted of the "acropolis" or "citadel" (Area A) with buildings that have been described as palaces or temples, built on a deep fill or mound. The Lower Town consisted of what might have been ordinary domestic buildings on the terraces surrounding the citadel (Areas B and D). The Upper Town was cut off from the Lower Town by a battered enclosure wall, which has been

[75]Cf. n. 3.

[76]Bartlett, *Edom and the Edomites*, 34.

[77]Pratico, "Nelson Glueck's 1930-1940 Excavations at Tell el-Kheleifeh," 15.

[78]Bartlett, *Edom and the Edomites*, 133-34.

[79]Pratico, "Nelson Glueck's 1930-1940 Excavations at Tell el-Kheleifeh," 15-17.

[80]Bartlett, *Edom and the Edomites*, 36.

[81]I. Ephʿal, *The Ancient Arabs: Nomads on the Borders of the Fertile Crescent, 9th-5th Centuries B.C.* (Jerusalem: Magnes Press/Leiden: Brill, 1982) 14-17.

[82]C.-M. Bennett, "Excavations at Buseirah (Biblical Bozrah)," *Midian, Moab and Edom: The History and Archaeology of Late Bronze and Iron Age Jordan and North-West Arabia* (ed. J. F. A. Sawyer and D. J. A. Clines; JSOTSup 24; Sheffield: JSOT Press, 1983); Bienkowski, "Umm el-Biyara, Tawilan and Buseirah in Retrospect," 101-103.

traced between Areas B and A (Fig. 27). Area C also probably contained a public building (Fig. 28). There appear to be five architectural phases.[83]

The major building on the citadel (Area A), built on a deep fill, appears to have two main phases, called Building B and Building A (Figs. 29-30). Building B, the earlier, had overall dimensions of 77m x 38m, with two entrances on the northeast side, both off-center, approached by a ramp (Fig. 29). In the main central courtyard was a cistern into which water flowed through one or two drains, one emerging from another room. At the end of the courtyard was a flight of shallow steps flanked by plinths, possibly forming the bases of two columns. These steps led into a long narrow room. All the floors and walls were plastered. There was some evidence for a mudbrick superstructure.

Building A was built on top of Building B and was smaller (48 x 36 m) (Fig. 30). There was a large central space, with surrounding rooms or corridors. The corners of the walls seem to curve outwards, hence its colloquial title, the "Winged Building." The main entrance was now on the opposite, southwest, side.

Buildings B and A have a generic similarity to the so-called Assyrian "open-court" buildings in Palestine and to Neo-Assyrian palaces and residencies in Mesopotamia and the north Syrian provinces, both in plan and in their situation on a raised artificial citadel.[84] These resemblances strongly suggest that the Buseirah buildings should be considered as palaces. Although they are quite unique for Edom, it cannot necessarily be concluded that they were influenced by Assyria, since similar arrangements are attested in north Syria at Tell Halaf, Zinjirli and Til Barsip, and in Palestine at Lachish, Megiddo and elsewhere.[85] They are an example of selective borrowing, comparable to the engraved *Tridacna squamosa* shell from Buseirah, the ivory lion from Tawilan, and "Assyrian"-type pottery,[86] all of which may have

---

[83]P. Bienkowski, "Umm el-Biyara, Tawilan and Buseirah in Retrospect"; idem, "The Date of Sedentary Occupation in Edom."

[84]For full discussion of these similarities, see P. Bienkowski, "The Architecture of Edom"; cf. also C.-M. Bennett, "Neo-Assyrian Influence in Transjordan," *Studies in the History and Archaeology of Jordan I* (ed. A. Hadidi; Amman: Department of Antiquities, 1982) 187; R. B. K. Amiran and I. Dunayevsky, "The Assyrian Open-Court Building and its Palestinian Derivatives," *BASOR* 149 (1958) 25-32; R. Reich, "Palaces and Residencies in the Iron Age," *The Architecture of Ancient Israel from the Prehistoric to the Persian Periods* (ed. A. Kempinski and R. Reich; Jerusalem: Israel Exploration Society, 1992) 219-20.

[85]Bienkowski, "The Architecture of Edom."

[86]Bennett, "Neo-Assyrian Influence in Transjordan"; idem, "Some Reflections on Neo-Assyrian Influence in Transjordan," *Archaeology in the Levant* (ed. P. R. S.

parallels in Assyria or north Syria, but reflect not so much direct influence as imitation.

The material culture of Edomite sites appears to be overwhelmingly agricultural and domestic.[87] About half of the nonceramic objects excavated at Tawilan were connected with food preparation, consumption and storage. Almost a quarter were connected with textile manufacture, and nearly a fifth were items of personal adornment or connected with the preparation of cosmetics. The remainder were tools, religious or cult items, toys, attachments or inlay for furniture, and a very small proportion could be identified as military equipment. Iron slag found at Tawilan and Tell el-Kheleifeh suggests that smelting was carried out there.[88] The evidence of seeds and animal bones from Tawilan suggests that the subsistence of the majority of the population depended on a combination of animal herding with crop cultivation; that is, agropastoralism. Over 80% of the animal bones identified were of sheep or goat.

It is difficult and probably premature to compare the material culture of Edomite sites with that of neighboring areas, since so little from Iron Age Jordan has been published in final form. It may well be that the painted pottery from Edom is the most characteristic product. The assemblage of other objects seems to be characterized less by what is present than by what is absent. Much of the material is fairly crude and utilitarian, with a narrower typological range than that found at sites in Cisjordan and even northern Jordan, for instance, Tell es-Saʿidiyeh.

An apparent exception is the hoard of gold jewellery from Tawilan (Fig. 31). This consisted of 18 gold rings and earrings with 334 carnelian beads inside a badly encrusted bronze bowl placed on a thick coarse-ware sherd. It was found in an accumulation level following the end of Edomite occupation.[89] Although the preliminary dating was between the 9th and 5th centuries BC,[90] the group is now regarded as homogeneous and is dated to the 10th–9th centuries BC.[91] As with the cuneiform tablet, the hoard cannot be associated conclusively with any occupation

---

Moorey and P. J. Parr; Warminster: Aris and Phillips, 1978) 165-71.

[87]C.-M. Bennett and P. Bienkowski, *Excavations at Tawilan in Southern Jordan* (forthcoming).

[88]F. L. Koucky and N. R. Miller, "The Metal Objects from Tell el-Kheleifeh," in Pratico, *Tell el-Kheleifeh*, 65; cf. n. 87.

[89]Cf. D. Petocz in C.-M. Bennett, "Excavations at Tawilan in Southern Jordan, 1982," *Levant* 16 (1984) 13.

[90]R. Maxwell-Hyslop, "The Gold Jewellery," *Levant* 16 (1984) 22-23.

[91]J. Ogden, "The Gold Jewellery," *Excavations at Tawilan in Southern Jordan* (ed. C.-M. Bennett and P. Bienkowski, forthcoming).

at Tawilan; if it was associated, it is likely that it was an heirloom, since there is no other indication of such an early date at Tawilan.

5. Archaeological Evidence for the End of the Edomite Kingdom

Archaeological evidence for dating the end of Edomite settlement in Transjordan is still ambiguous. Bartlett has argued for considerable continuity of population, though not necessarily settlement, through the Neo-Babylonian and Persian periods into the Nabataean period.[92] None of the excavated sites provides a firm archaeological anchor: although there is circumstantial evidence for continuity into the Persian period, none of it is beyond dispute (see section 1.4).

Despite the potential of the Tawilan cuneiform tablet, which dates to the Persian period (and at least proves some human activity if not necessarily settlement), it cannot be conclusively proven that Edomite occupation at the site extended that late. This negative picture is true also for the whole of Edom. There is evidence for destruction or fire in the latest Iron Age levels at Umm el-Biyara, Tawilan and Buseirah. Nevertheless, it cannot be demonstrated that these were deliberate destructions, or that they were contemporary. Even if it could be demonstrated, they cannot be dated and so no cause can be proposed. At present, no precise date for the end of Edomite settlement is possible on archaeological evidence.

If the way is now open for speculation, there are three main possibilities for the date (and perhaps the cause) of the end of Edomite settlement (and all sorts of uncertainties within those possibilities):

1. Edomite settlement continued into the 6th century BC but not beyond. The destructions at the main sites may therefore be a result of the campaigns of Nabonidus in southern Transjordan and northern Arabia in 552 BC.[93] There is some indication in the historical sources that Edom ceased to exist as an independent state sometime in the 6th century BC.[94]

2. Assuming that the Tawilan tablet was associated with the settlement, it can be concluded that settlement in Edom continued into the Persian period. How long into the Persian period is a separate matter: depending on which Darius is meant in the tablet, Edomite settlement at Tawilan at least may have continued into the late 6th, late 5th or late 4th centuries BC. This may fit with recent suggestions that

---

[92]Bartlett, *Edom and the Edomites*, 163-74; idem, "From Edomites to Nabataeans: The Problem of Continuity," *Aram* 2:1&2 (1990) 25-34.

[93]Bartlett, *Edom and the Edomites*, 157-61.

[94]*Ibid.*; idem, "From Edomites to Nabataeans."

"Iron II" pottery continued into the Persian period, perhaps as late as ca. 400 BC (see section 1.4).

3. The possibility also must be left open that settlements in Edom were destroyed, deliberately or accidentally, or abandoned at different times and that settlement may have continued beyond the demise of the Edomite state. Present evidence is so uncertain that none of these scenarios can be excluded.

6. Conclusion

A radically minimalist view of present evidence would conclude the following:

1. The only conclusive proof for dating Iron Age sites in Edom indicates a 7th-century BC date, within Iron II.

2. There is no decisive proof for the existence of Iron I in Edom.

3. There is no decisive proof for continuity of settlement into the Persian period in Edom.

Thus, it is not known when Edomite settlement began. The relative dating of the main sites and how much earlier than the 7th century BC the Iron II pottery might date are unknown. The period when Edomite occupation ended is also unknown. Any reconstruction beyond this series of negatives is of necessity hypothetical and open to change and challenge from new evidence. Despite this, historians must attempt to reconstruct and perhaps explain the emergence and development of Edom, accepting that evidence that falls short of absolute proof may nevertheless be admissable.[95]

Although there is a virtual settlement gap south of the Wadi el-Ḥasa during the Middle and Late Bronze Ages, Egyptian evidence proves that tent-dwelling pastoralists inhabited this region.[96] Settlement began again slowly in the Late Bronze Age and probably in Iron I, in the best agricultural land in northern Edom.[97] Edom remained largely nomadic perhaps until the 7th century BC. The great expansion of settlement in Iron II was due to improved economic circumstances: the resumption of mining activities at Feinan, the Arabian overland trade in luxury goods, particularly frankincense, and the political stability established by Assyrian control. Edom became a tributary of Assyria following Tiglath-pileser III's campaign of 734 BC but retained its independence and

---

[95]For a more detailed hypothesis on the emergence of Edom (and Moab), see Bienkowski, "The Beginning of the Iron Age in Southern Jordan: A Framework."

[96]K. A. Kitchen, "The Egyptian Evidence on Ancient Jordan," *Early Edom and Moab: The Beginning of the Iron Age in Southern Jordan* (ed. P. Bienkowski; SAM 7; Sheffield: J. R. Collis, 1992) 21-34, esp. 23-26.

[97]For possible causes, cf. n. 95.

autonomy. There is little evidence of direct Assyrian involvement in Edomite affairs and no evidence of Assyrian forts and garrisons throughout Edom, or indeed any of the other Transjordanian states. However, overall Assyrian control within a framework of tributary states probably produced a degree of political and economic stability that contributed to national development in Edom.[98]

Edom's statehood was relatively short-lived. It may have ceased to exist as an independent state sometime in the 6th century BC, perhaps as a result of the campaign of Nabonidus, although it is possible that state and settlement continued into the Persian period. There is no doubt, however, that even when the settlements were destroyed or abandoned, Edom was not depopulated but continued to be occupied, probably through to the Nabataean period. There is no evidence at all, however, of overlap between Edomite and Nabataean settlements.[99] The mountainous region of Edom had never been fully urban, and it is probable that a proportion of its population was always pastoralist and non-settled. Following the end of the Edomite state and the abandonment of the settlements, just as in the Middle and Late Bronze Ages, this nonsettled pastoralist lifestyle would have continued, leaving little or no identifiable archaeological remains. Edom is a marginal region and once the external stimulus of the *pax assyriaca* and its successors faded, perhaps there was no longer the incentive for a state or settlements to exist independently in a vacuum, at least until the favourable circumstances of the Nabataean era.

Acknowledgments

I thank Professor Burton MacDonald for permission to reproduce illustrations from his two published surveys (Figs. 3, 19-21) and Wilfrid Laurier University Press for permission for the Wadi el-Ḥasa Survey illustrations; Dr. G. D. Pratico for permission to reproduce two plans of Tell el-Kheleifeh (Figs. 25, 26); and Dr. Stephen Hart for permission to reproduce the plan of Ghrareh (Fig. 23). I am also grateful to Dr. Diana Edelman for her helpful editorial comments, and especially to Basia Chlebik and Amy de Joia for reading the manuscript.

---

[98]For Iron II expansion and Assyrian involvement, see Bienkowski, "The Beginning of the Iron Age in Southern Jordan: A Framework"; and A. R. Millard, "Assyrian Involvement in Edom," *Early Edom and Moab: The Beginning of the Iron Age in Southern Jordan* (ed. P. Bienkowski; SAM 7; Sheffield: J. R. Collis, 1992) 35-40.

[99]Bartlett, "From Edomites to Nabataeans"; Bienkowski, "The Chronology of Tawilan."

Illustrations

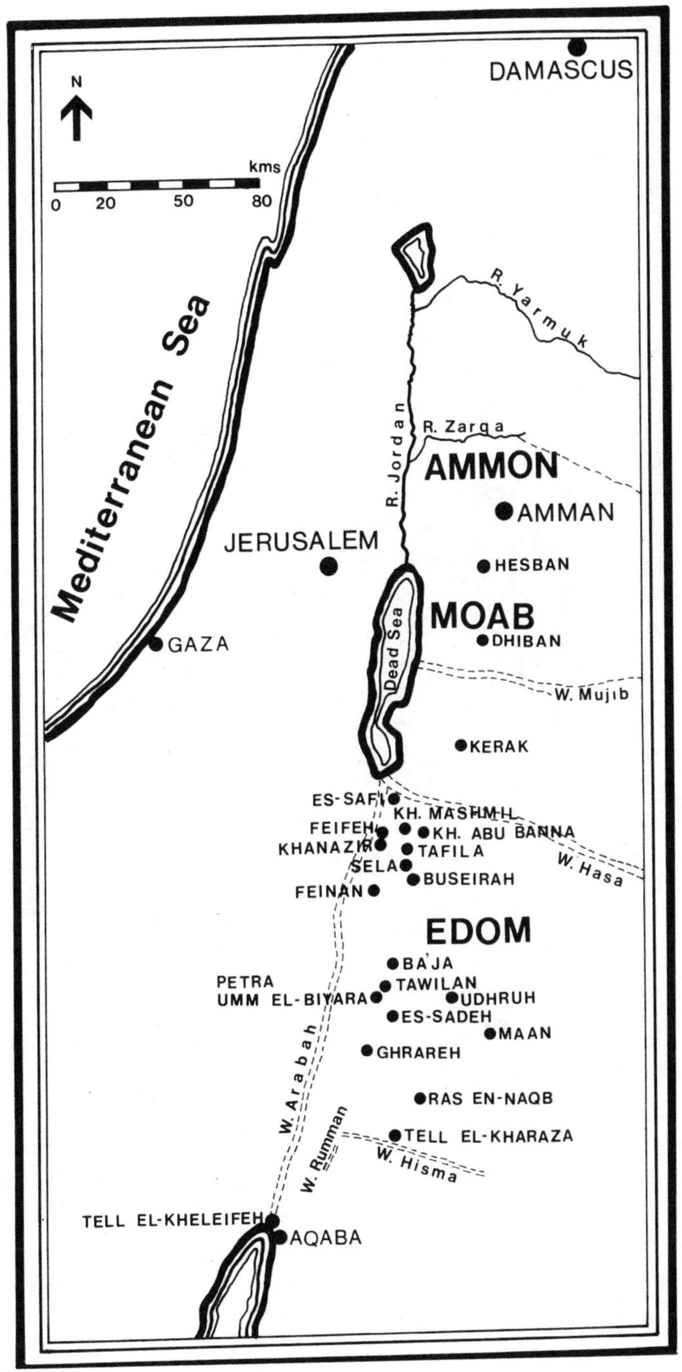

1. Map of Edom and surrounding areas, with sites mentioned in the text.

2. The seal impression of "Qos-Gabr King of Edom" from Umm el-Biyara.

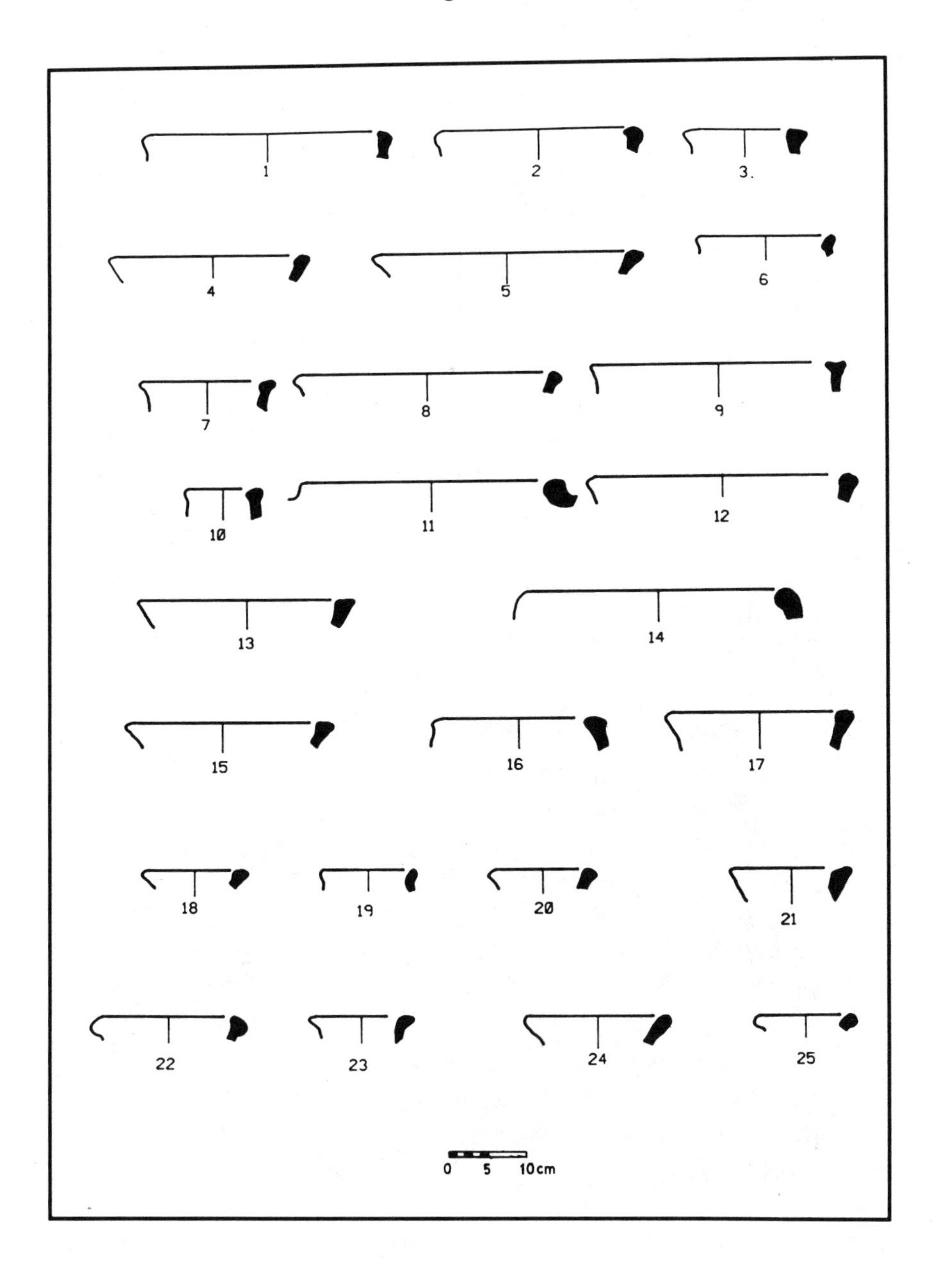

3. Iron I sherds from the Wadi el-Ḥasa Survey (from B. MacDonald, *The Wadi al Hasa Archaeological Survey 1979-1983* [Waterloo: Wilfrid Laurier University Press, 1988], pl. 7).

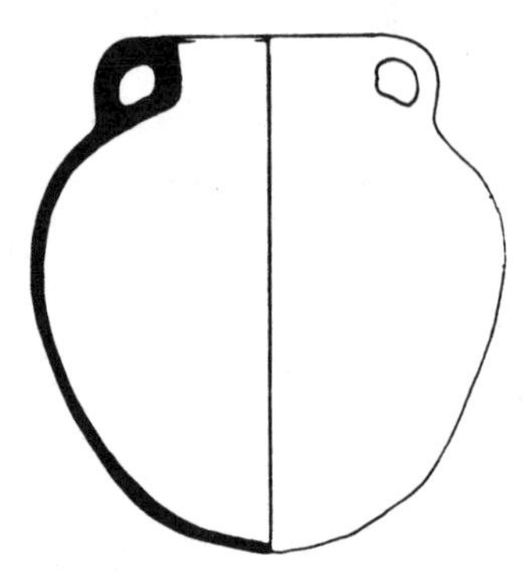

4. Cooking pot from Area C at Buseirah, tentatively dated to the Persian period.

5. The cuneiform tablet from Tawilan, dated to the accession year of one of the Achaemenid kings named Darius. Obverse.

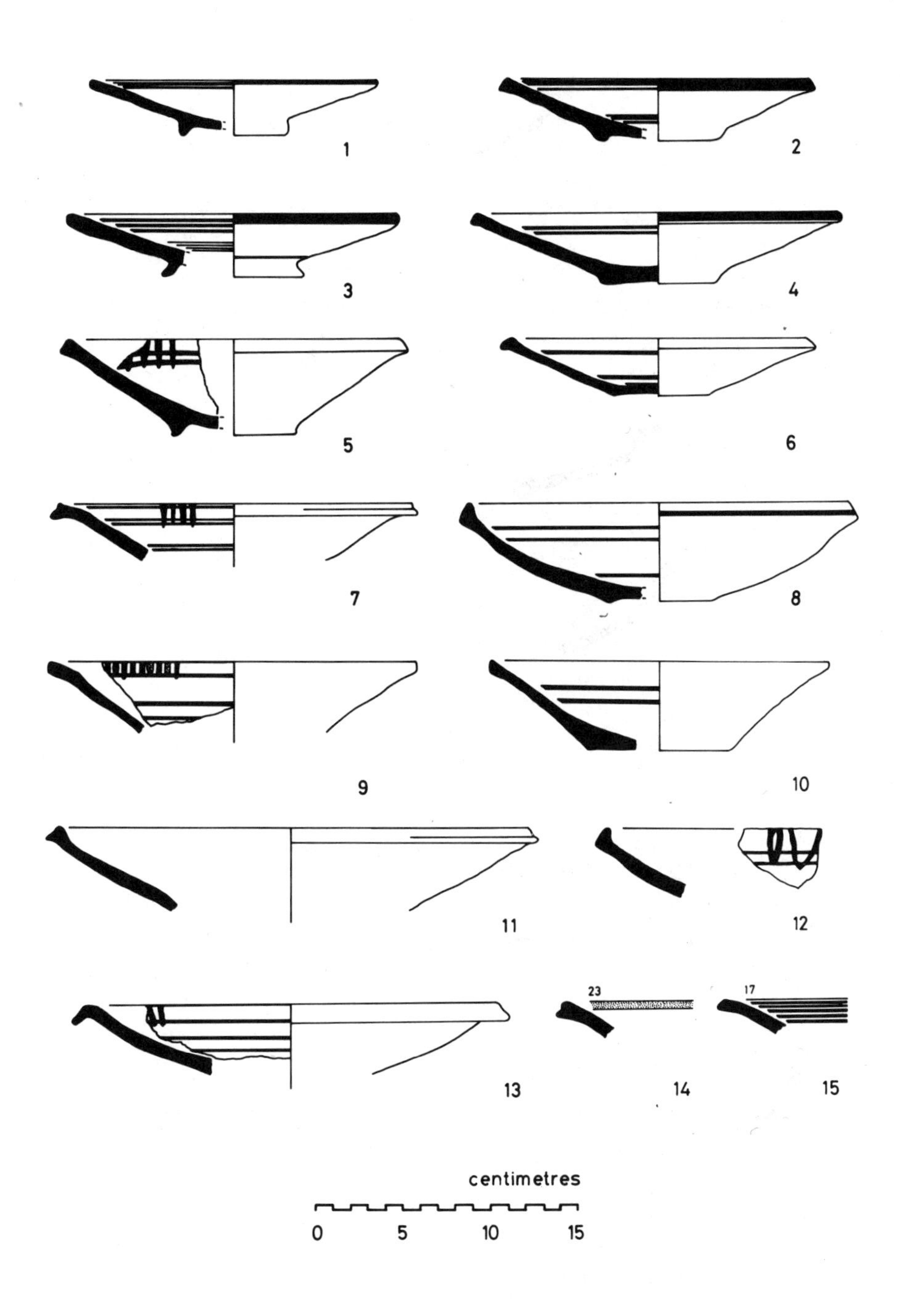

6. Platters and flat dishes from Tawilan.

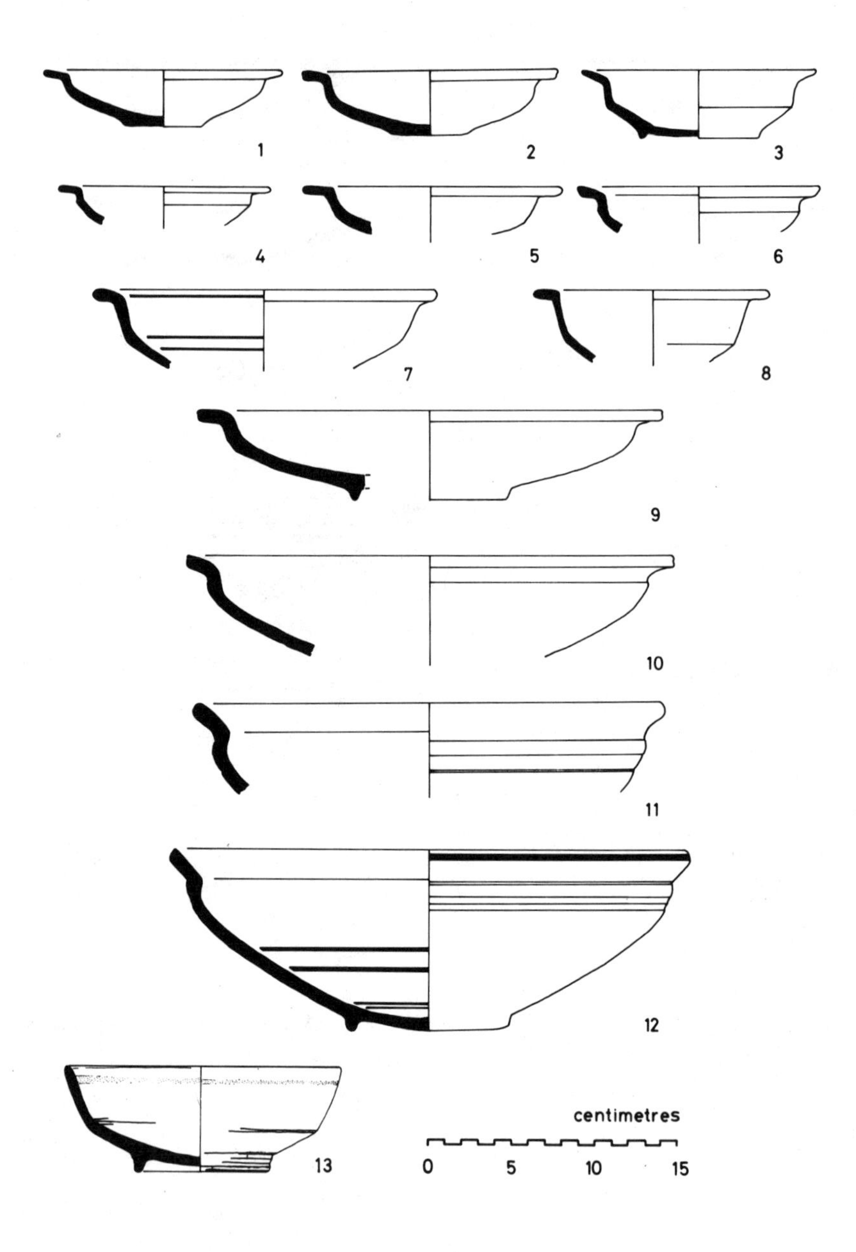

7. Carinated bowls from Tawilan.

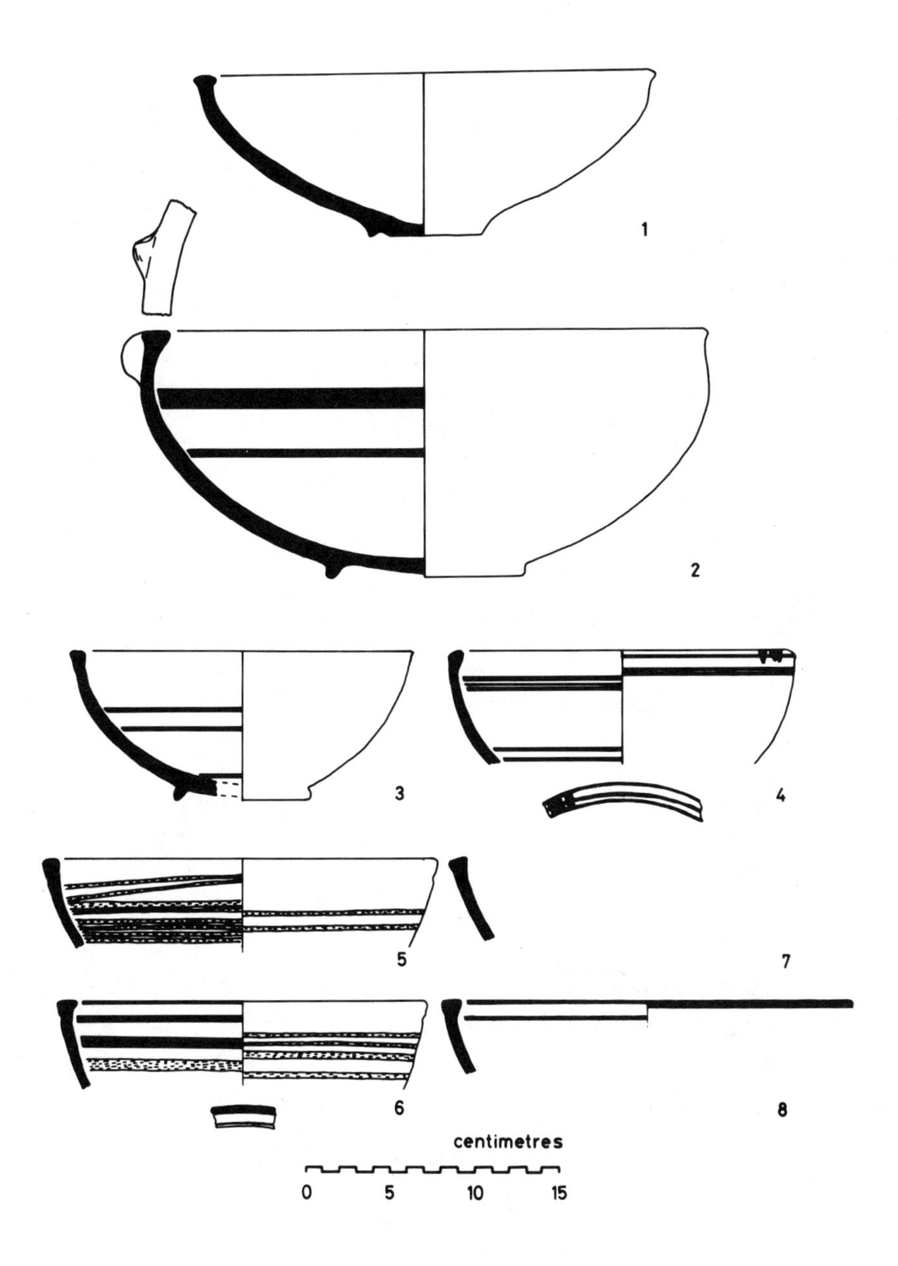

8. Bowls with triangular-section rims from Tawilan.

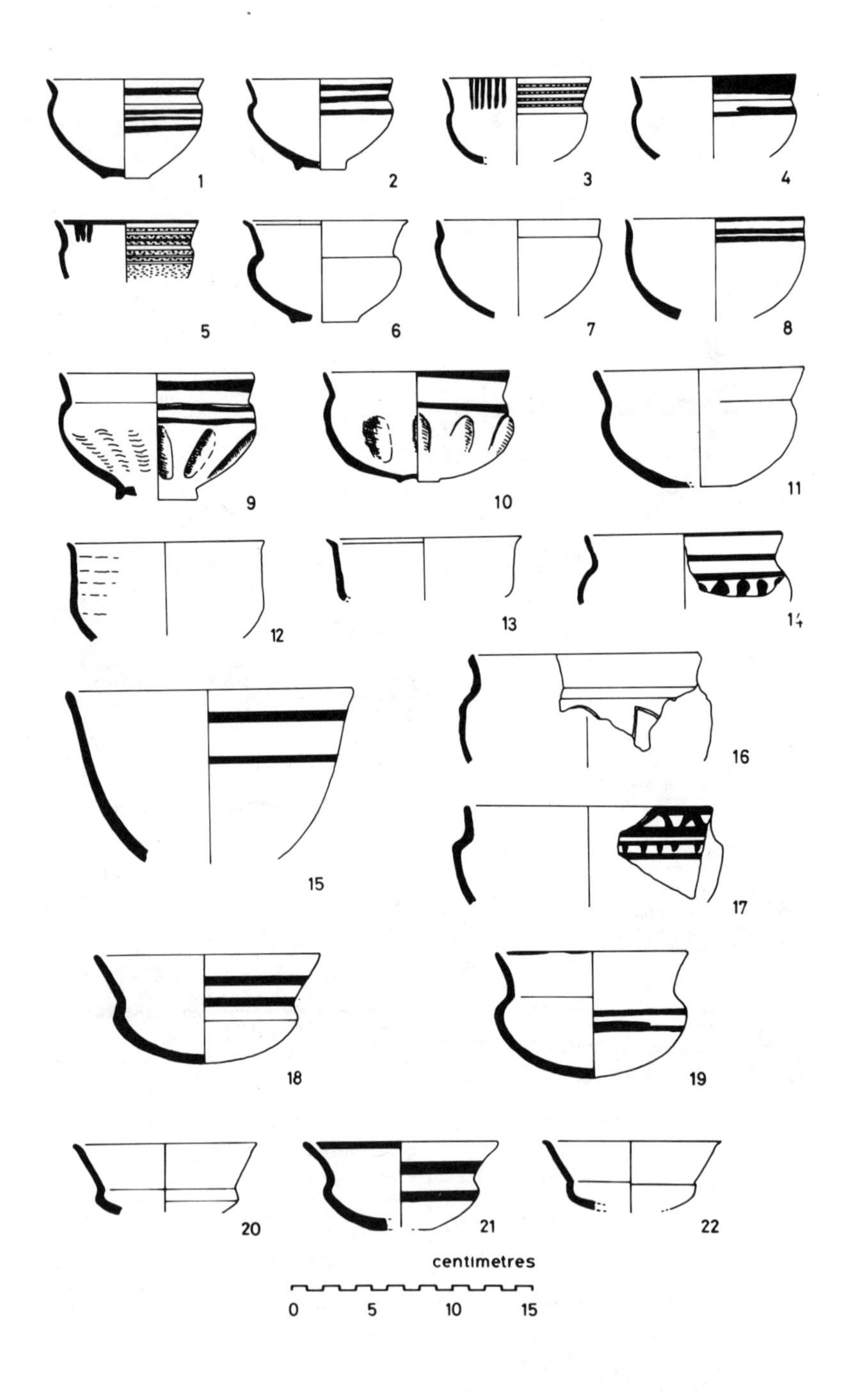

9. Fine ware bowls (1-17) and "Assyrian" bowls (18-22) from Tawilan.

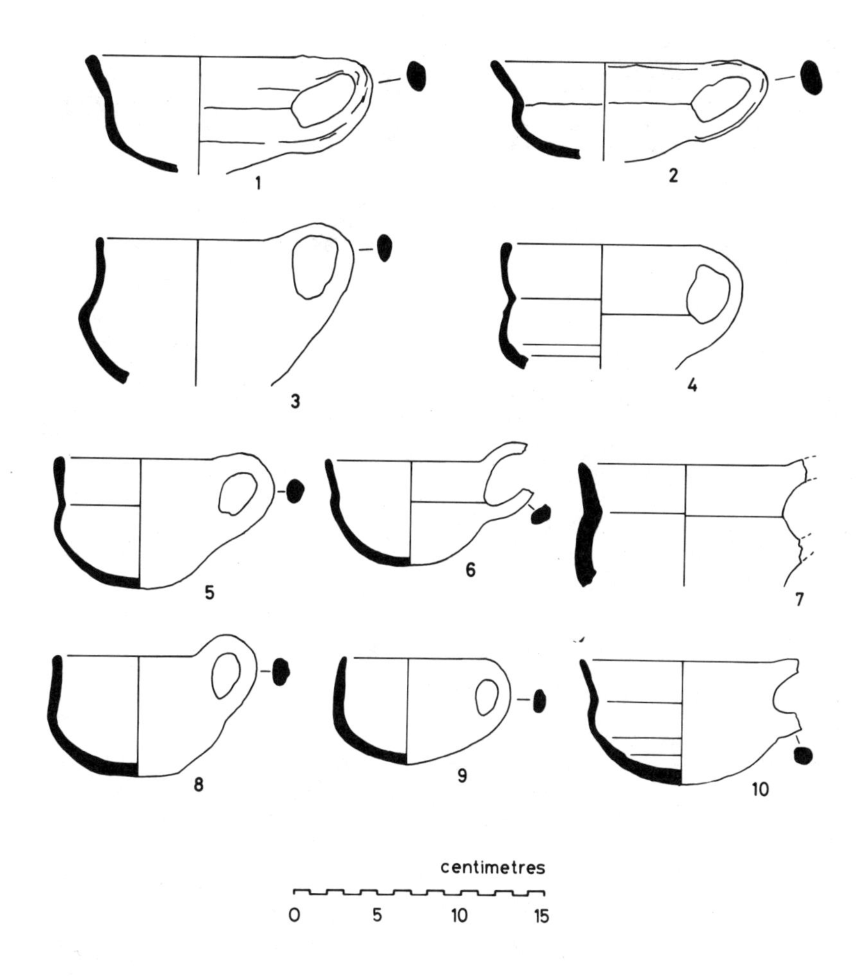

10. Mugs or bowls with a single handle from Tawilan.

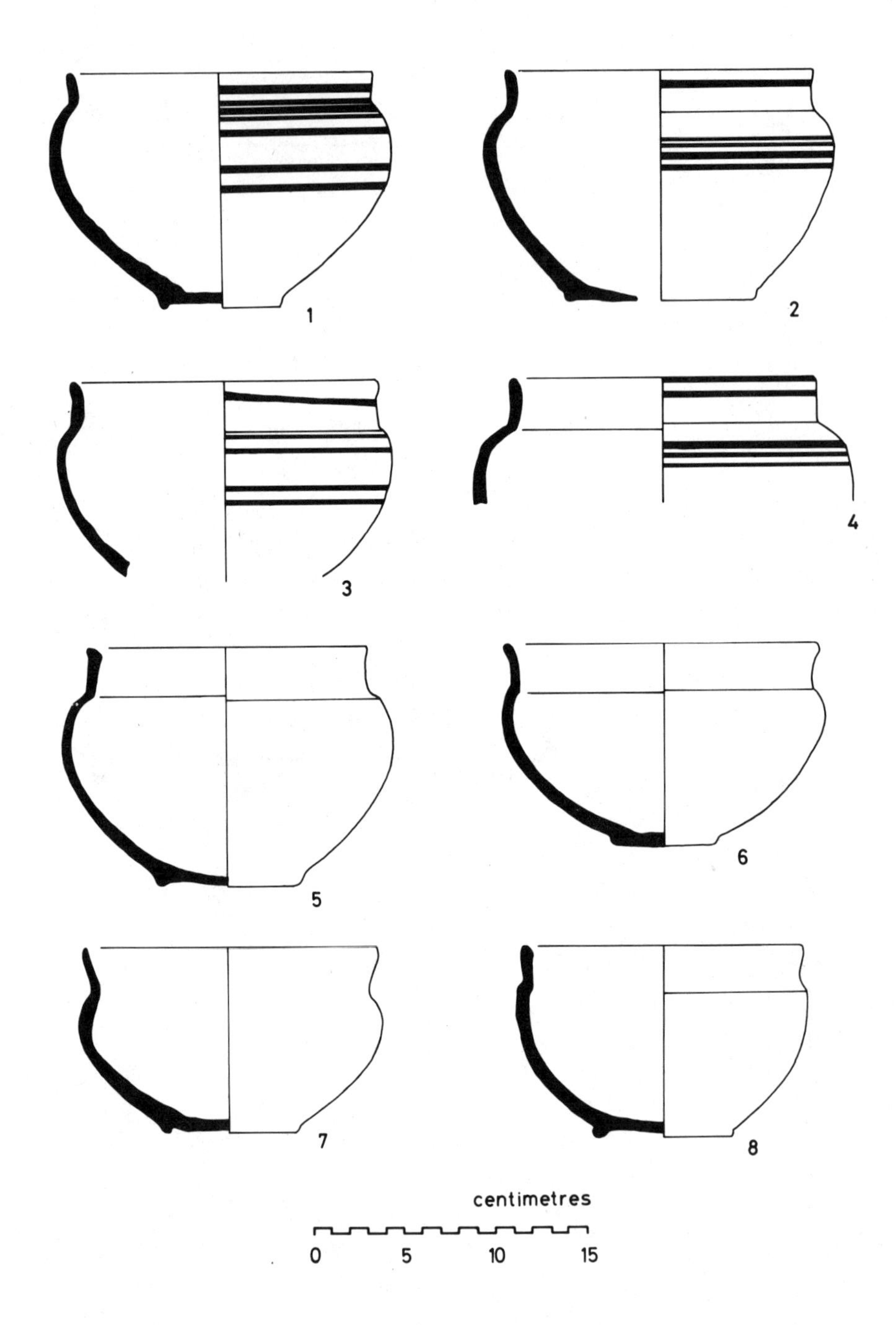

11. Necked bowls from Tawilan.

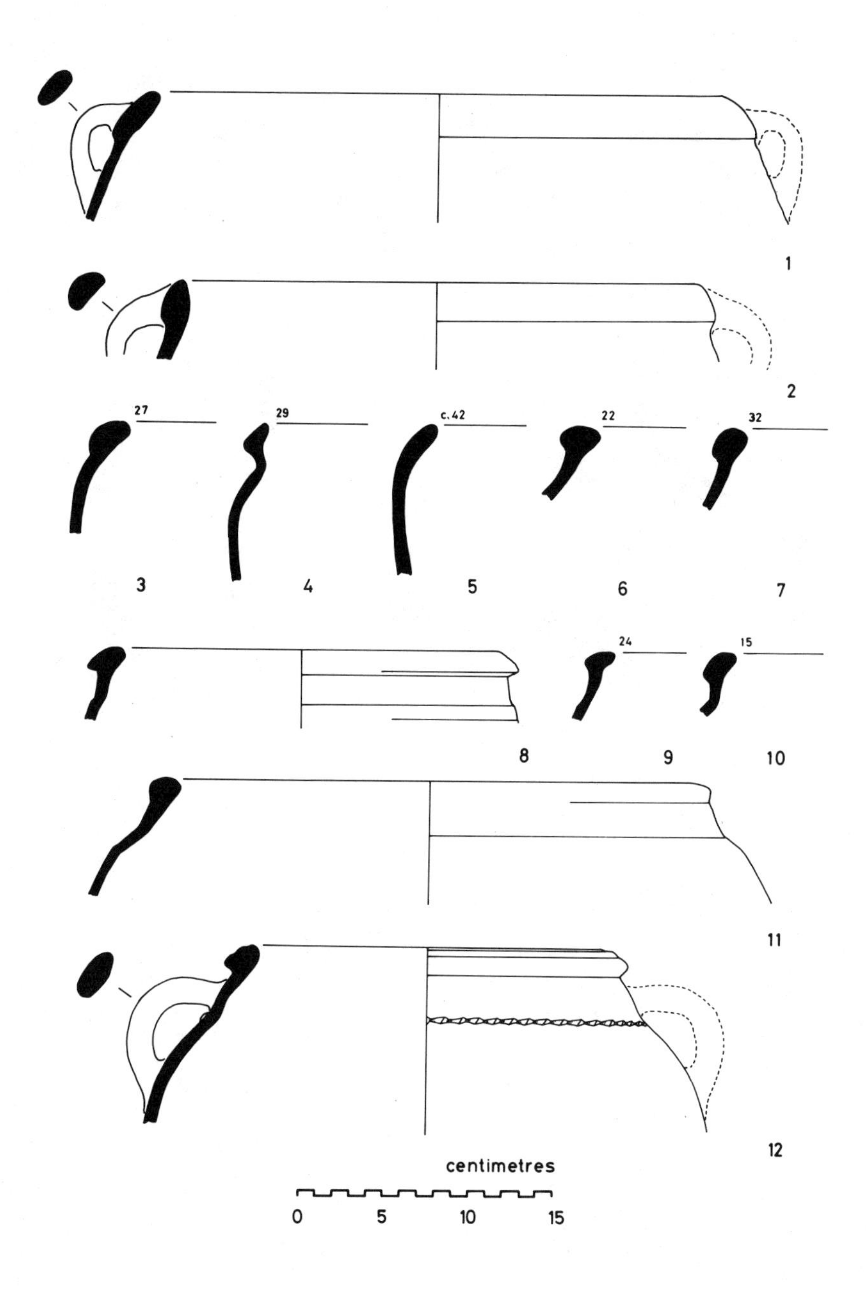

12. Kraters from Tawilan.

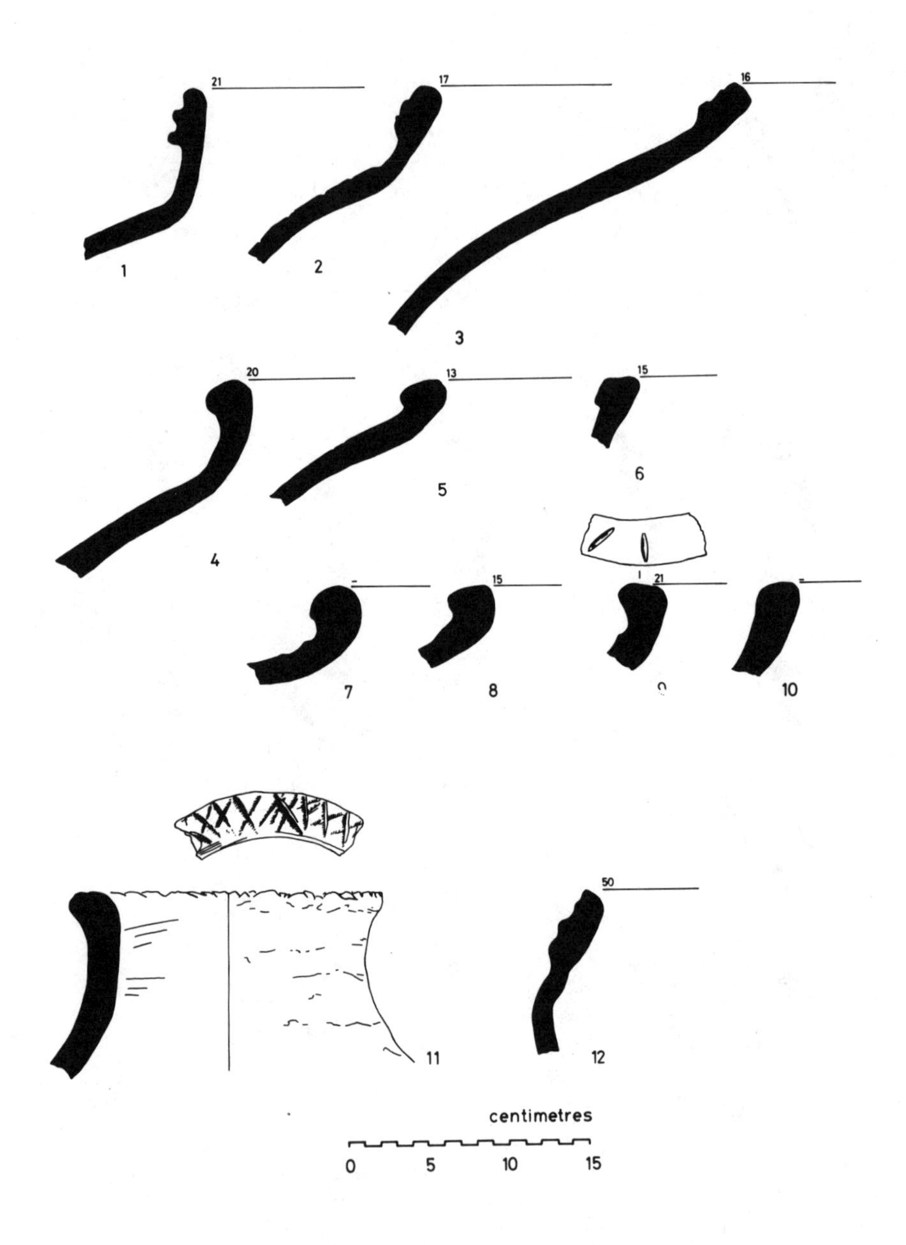

13. Storage jars (1-11) and very large bowl (12) from Tawilan.

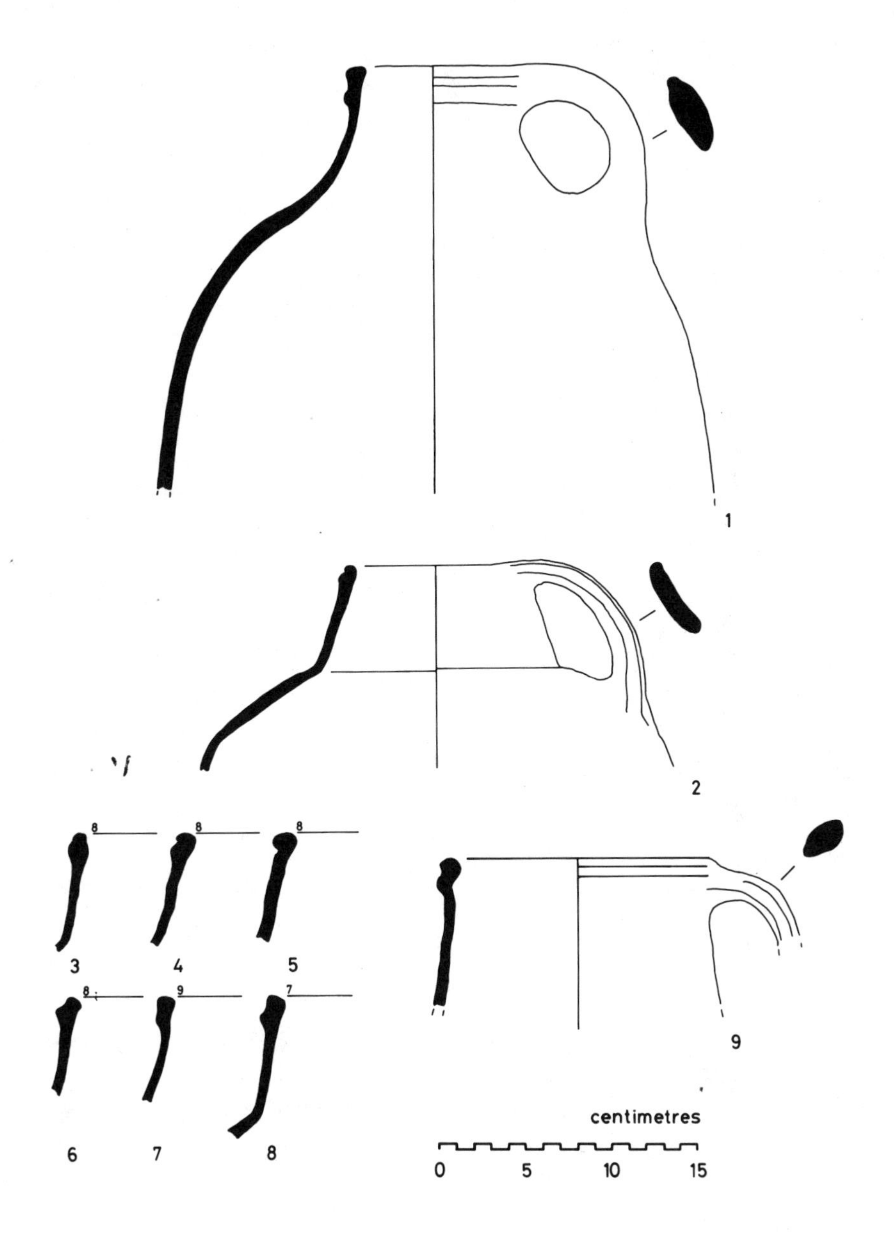

14. Large jugs with a ridged rim from Tawilan.

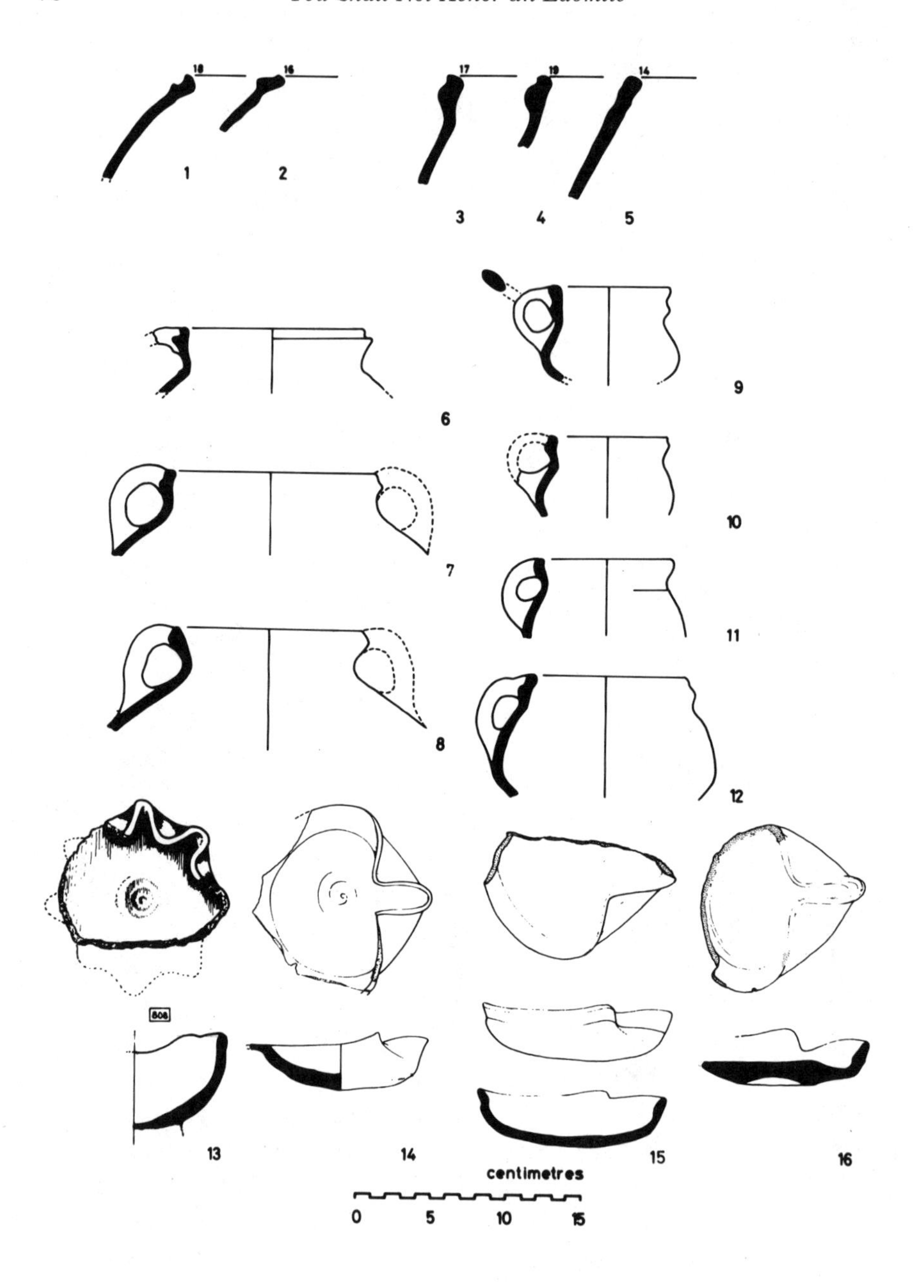

15. Cooking pots (1-12) and lamps (13-16) from Tawilan.

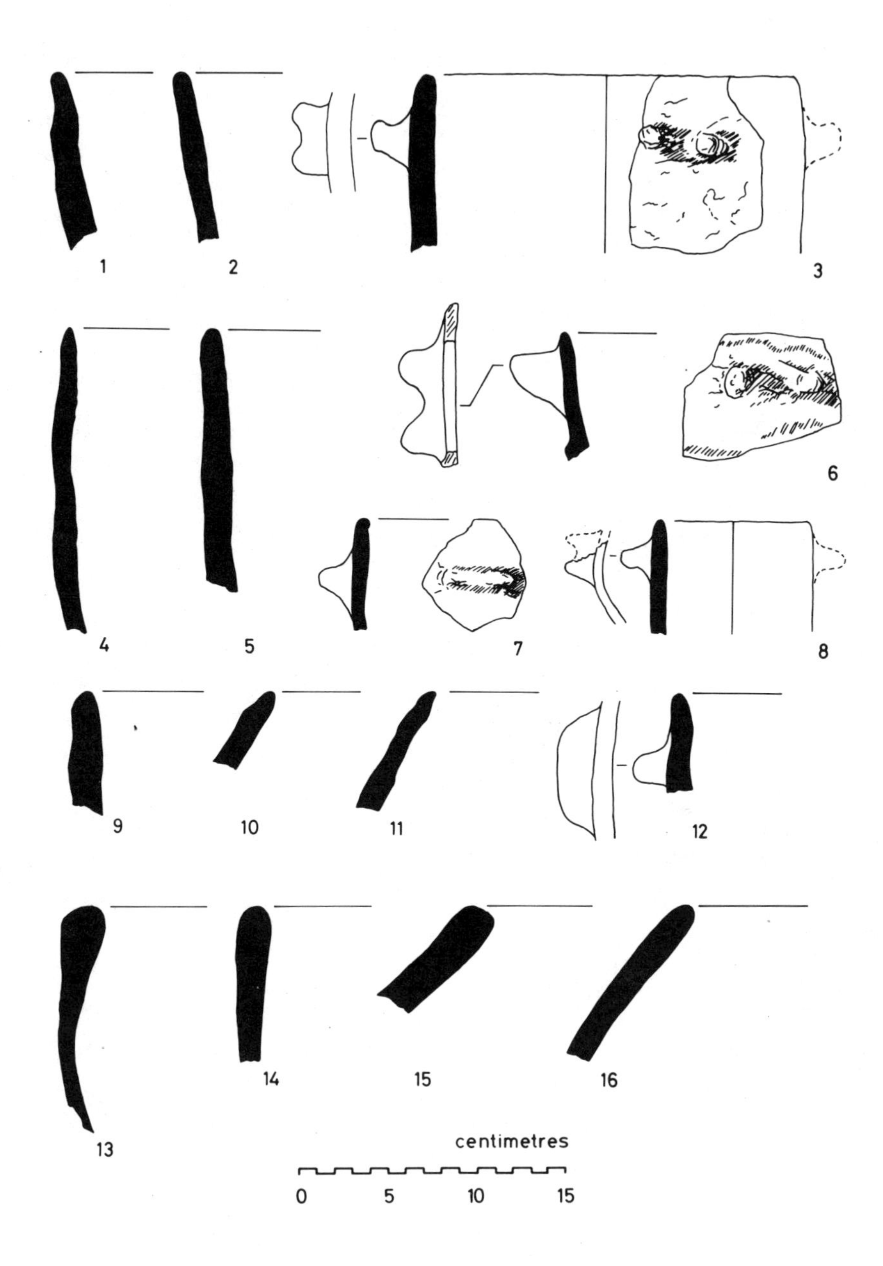

16. Negeb ware from Tawilan.

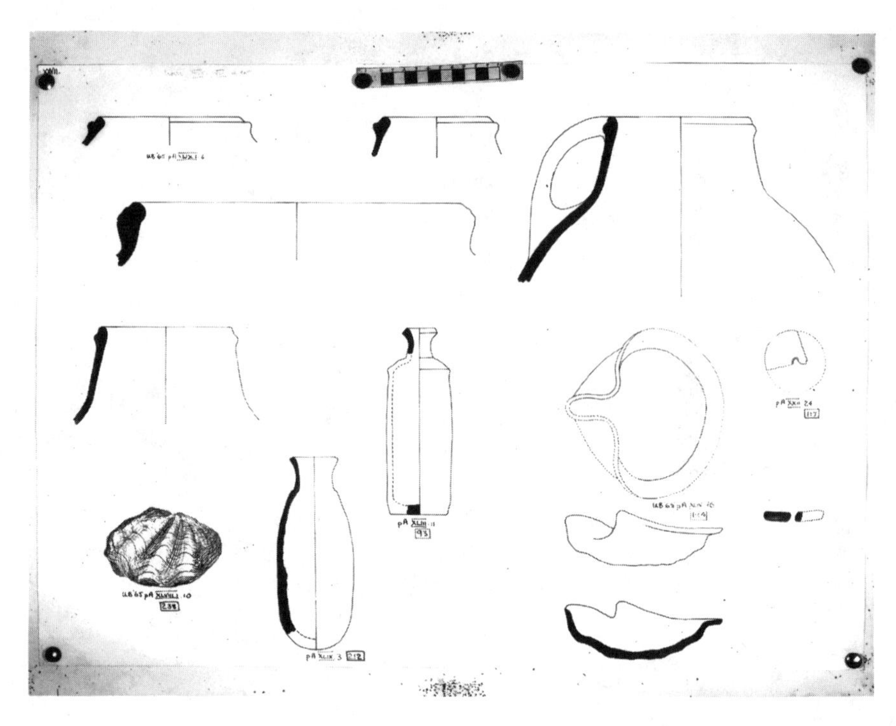

17. Pottery from Umm el-Biyara.

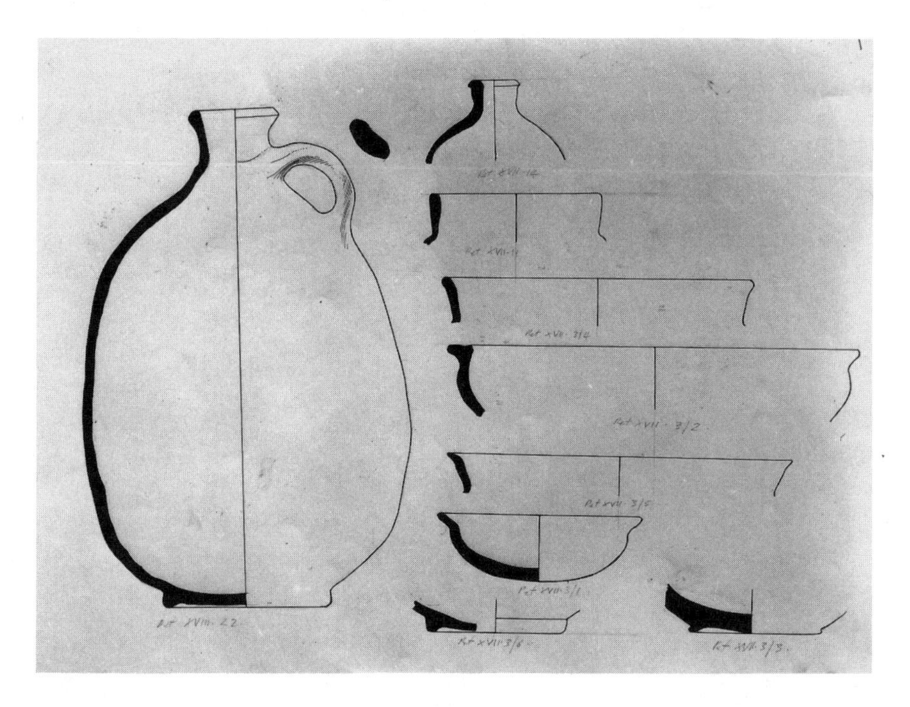

18. Pottery from Umm el-Biyara.

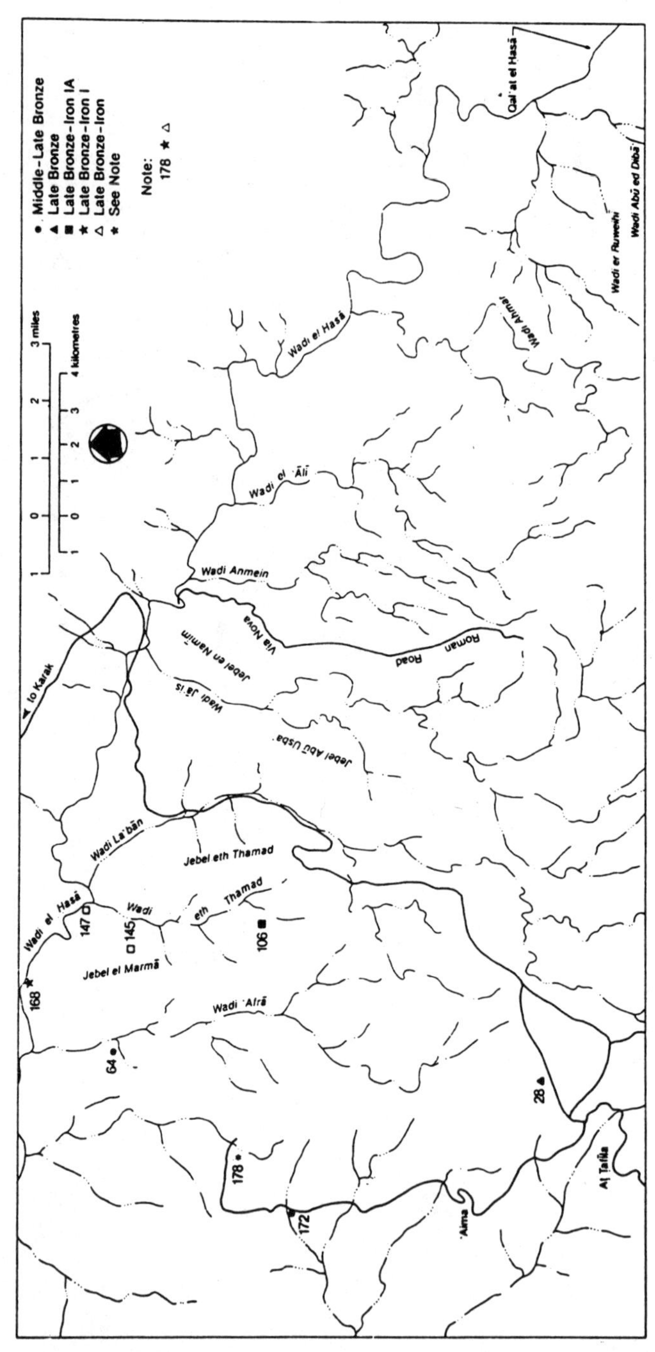

19. Middle-Late Bronze, Late Bronze, Late Bronze-Iron IA, Late Bronze-Iron I, and Late Bronze-Iron Age settlement pattern map for the Wadi el-Ḥasa Survey (from B. MacDonald, *The Wadi al Hasa Archaeological Survey 1979-1983* [Waterloo: Wilfrid Laurier University Press, 1988], fig. 47).

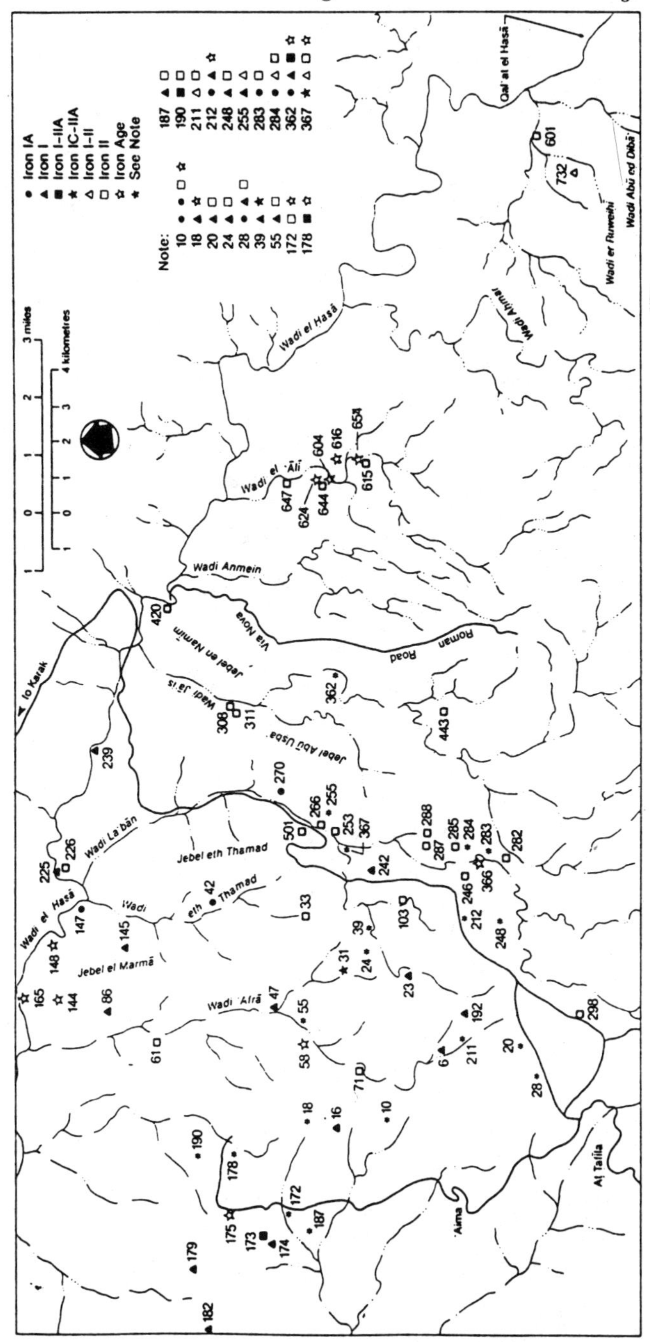

20. Iron IA, Iron I, Iron I-IIA, Iron IC-IIA, Iron I-II, Iron II, and Iron Age settlement pattern map for the Wadi el-Ḥasa Survey (from B. MacDonald, *The Wadi al Hasa Archaeological Survey 1979-1983* [Waterloo: Wilfrid Laurier University Press, 1988], fig. 48).

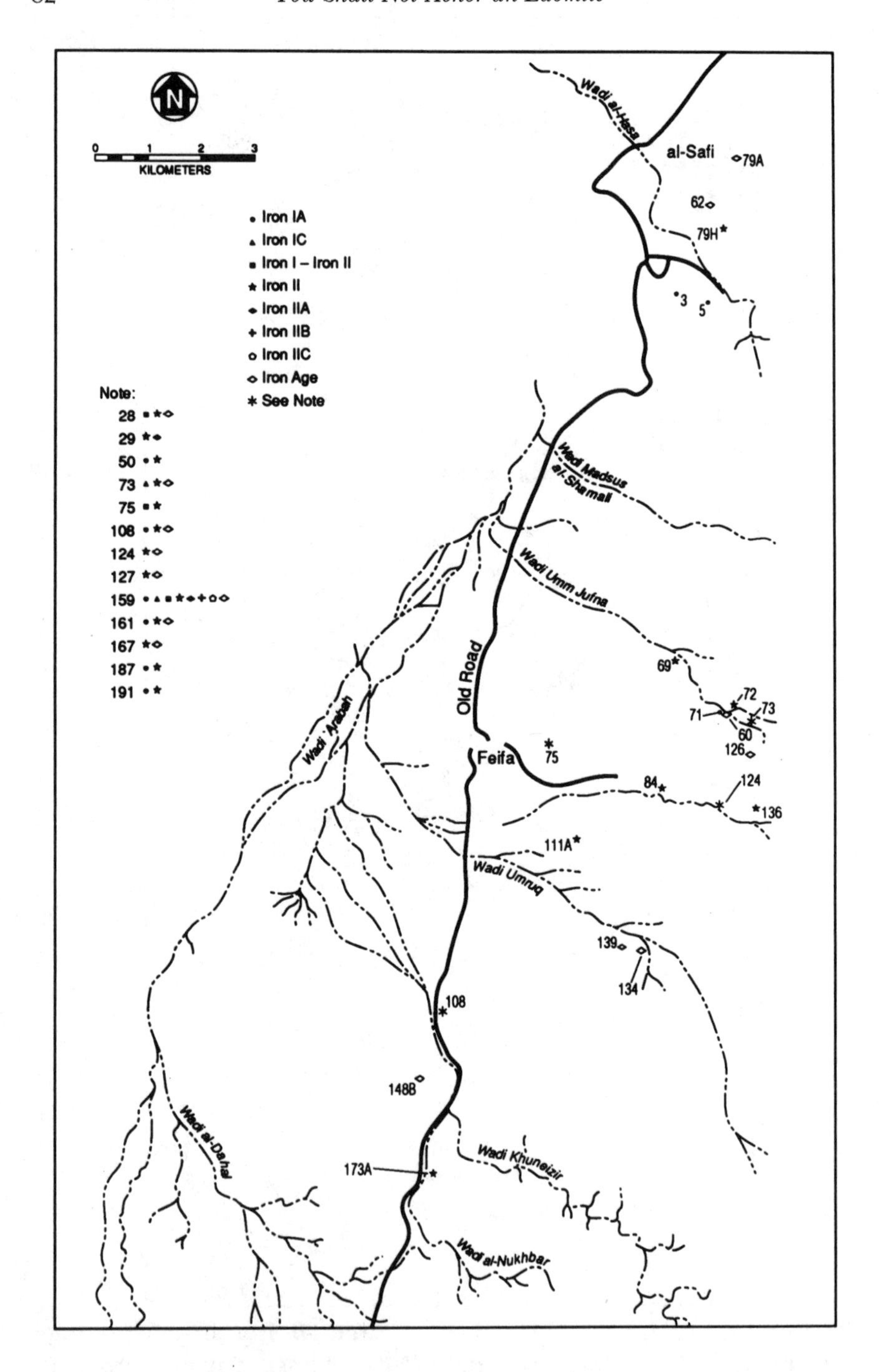

21. (See also facing page.) Iron IA, Iron IC, Iron I-II, Iron II, Iron IIA, Iron IIB, Iron IIC, and Iron Age settlement pattern map for the Southern

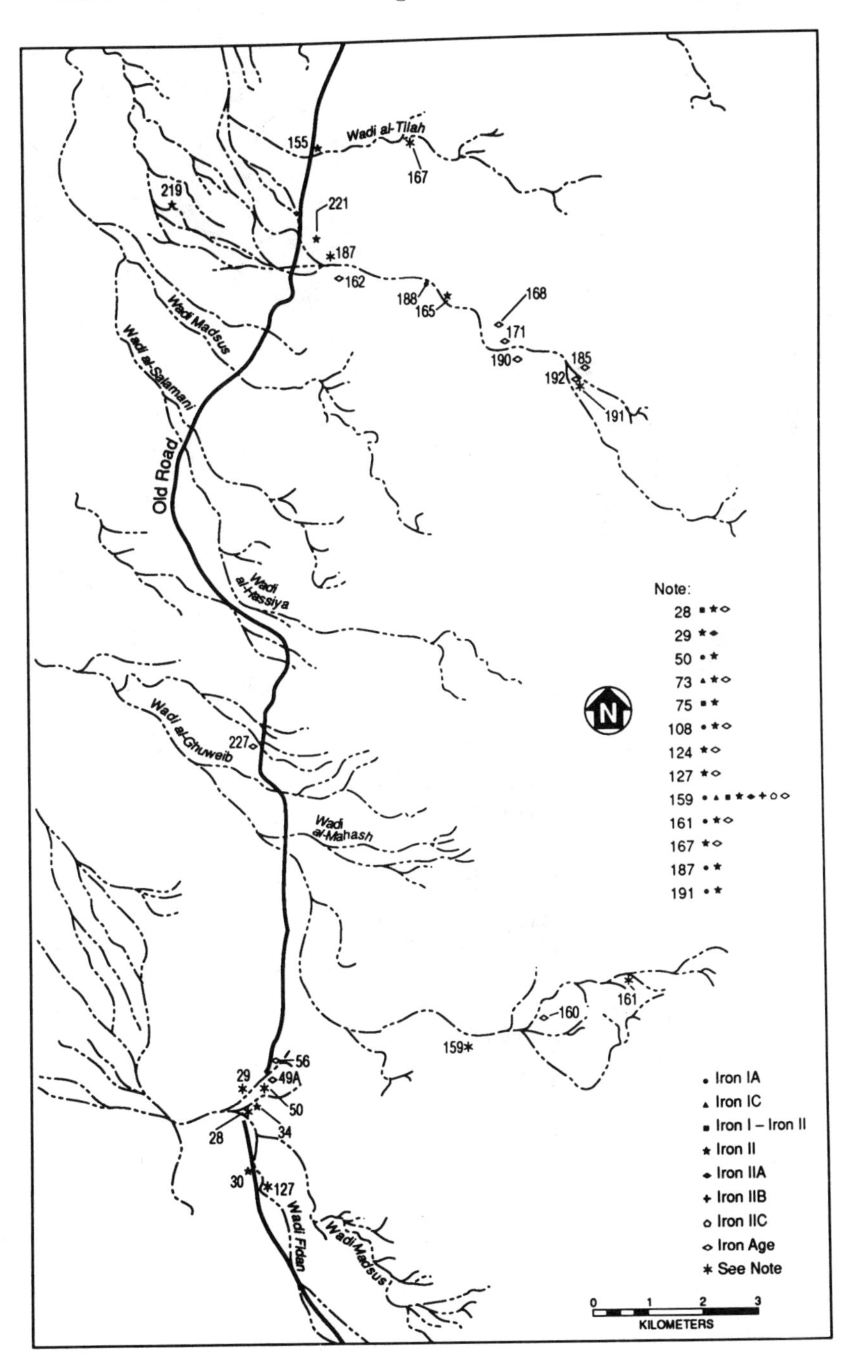

Ghors and Northeast ʿArabah Survey (northern and southern portions of map) (from B. MacDonald, *The Southern Ghors and Northeast ʿArabah Archaeological Survey* [Sheffield: J. R. Collis, 1992], fig. 14).

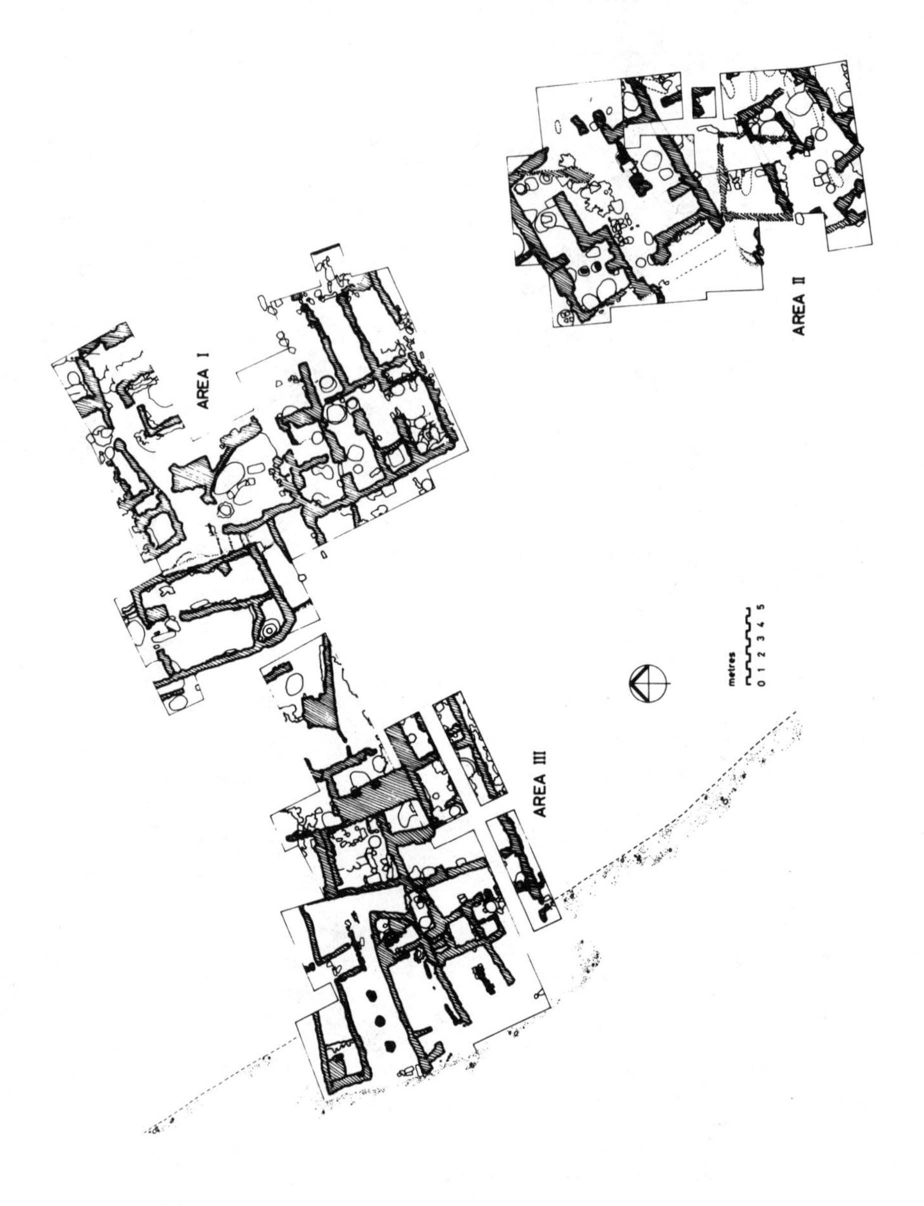

22. Overall plan of major areas at Tawilan.

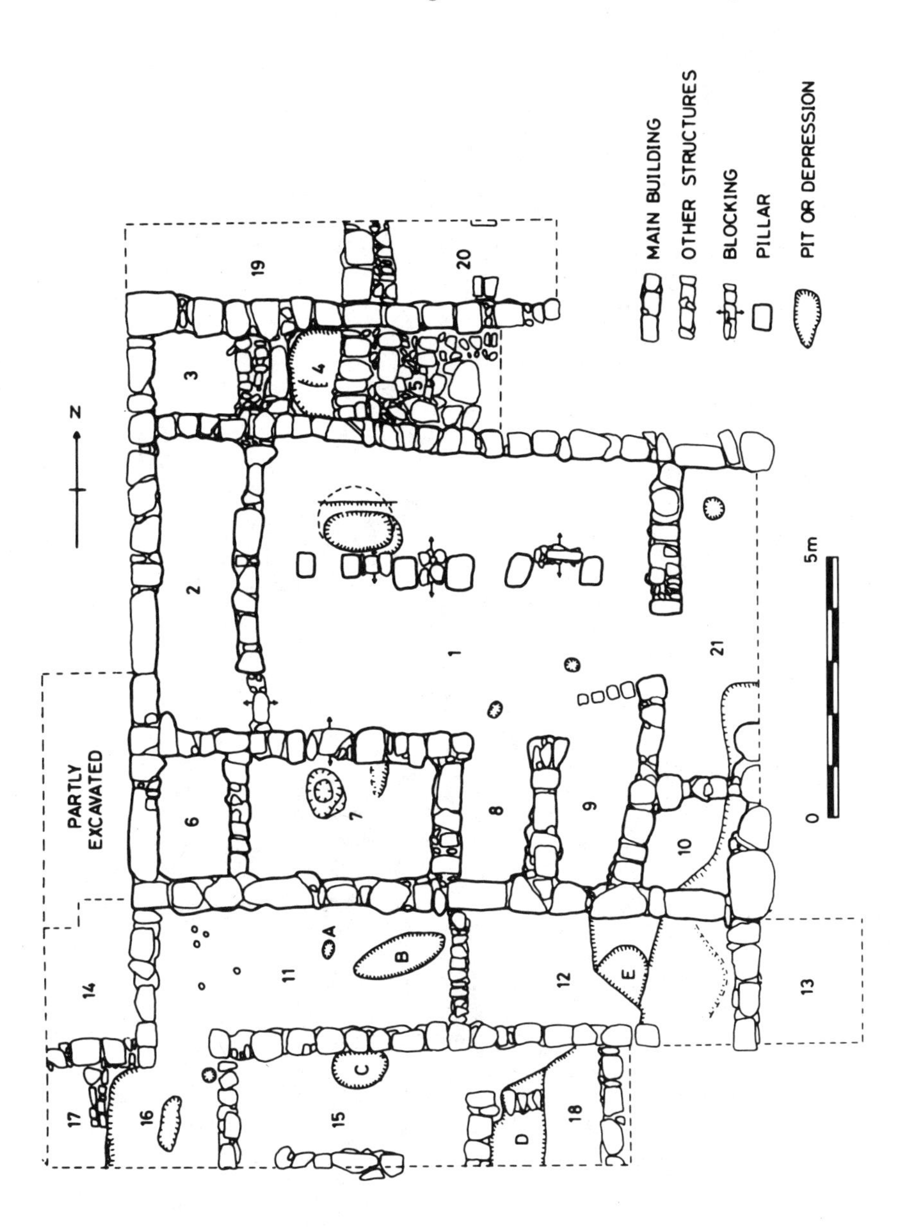

23. Ghrareh Area A (from S. Hart, *Levant* 20:92, fig. 3).

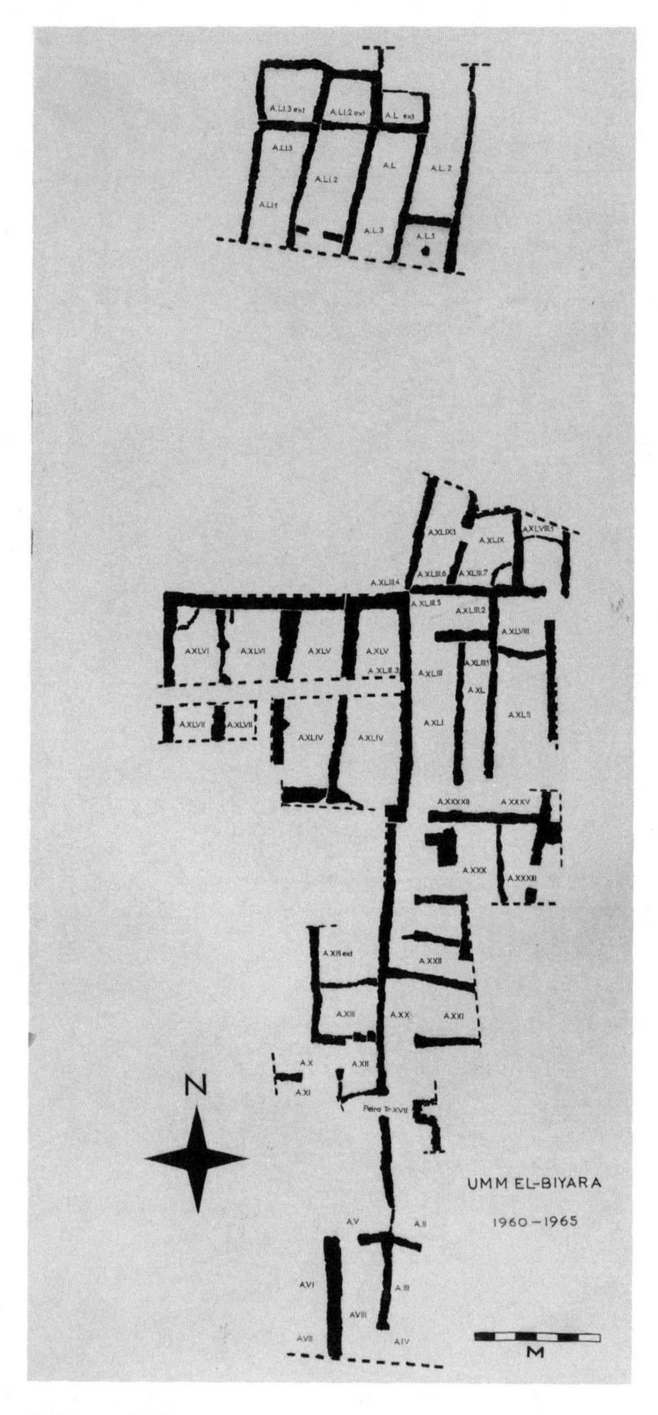

24. Plan of Umm el-Biyara.

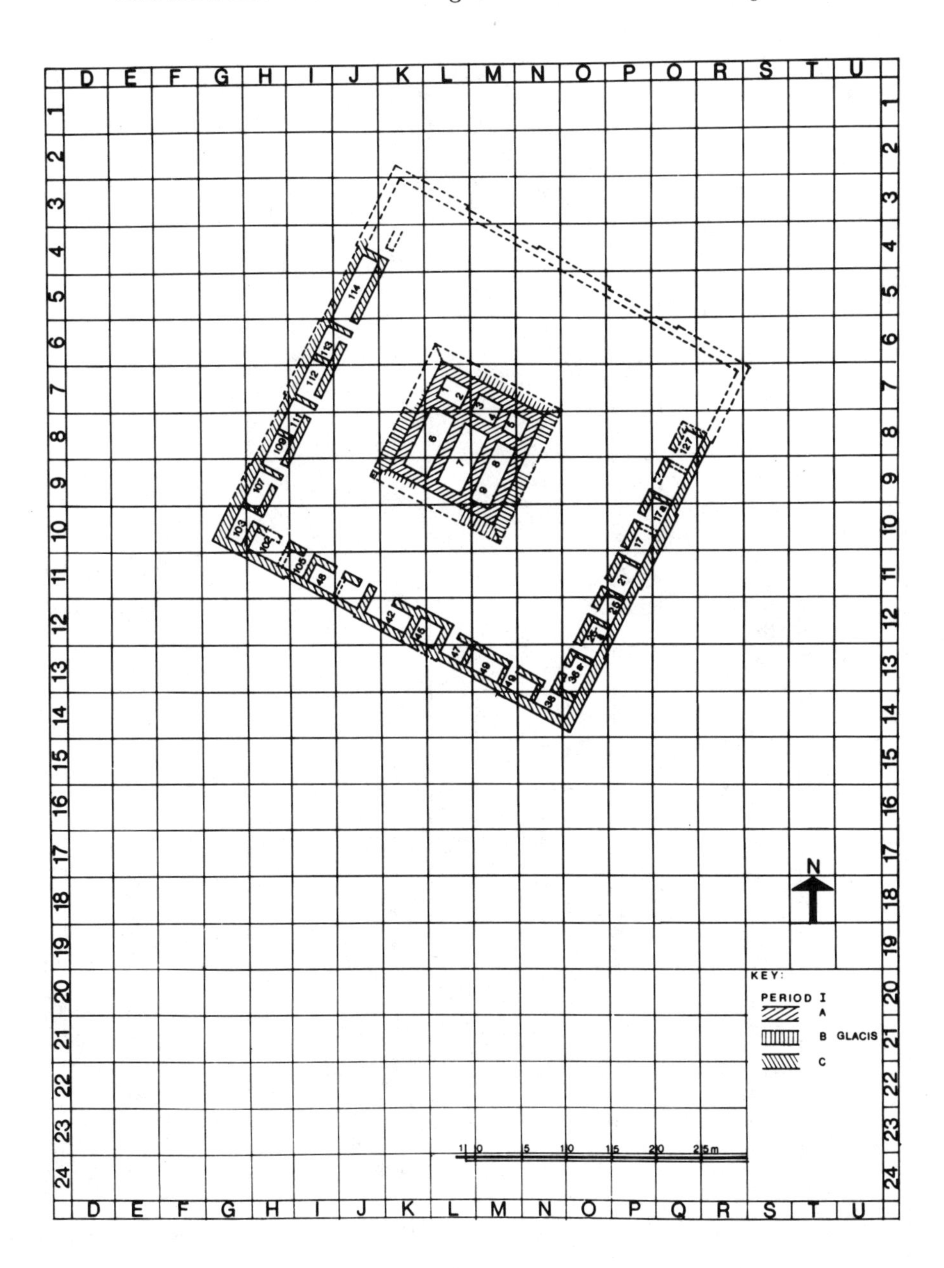

25. Tell el-Kheleifeh: the casemate fortress (from G. D. Pratico, *BASOR* 259:7, fig. 5).

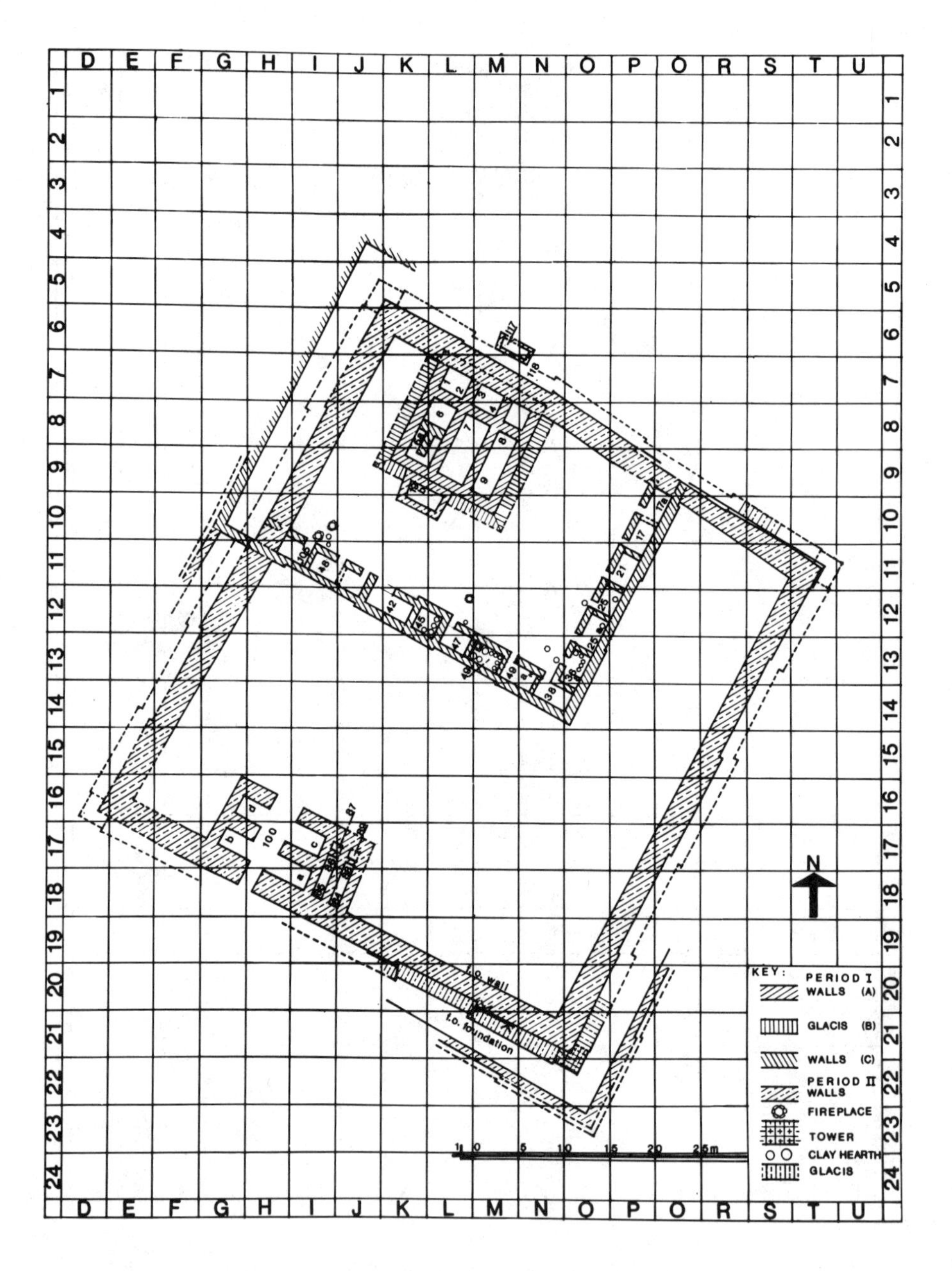

26. Tell el-Kheleifeh: the fortified settlement (from G. D. Pratico, *BASOR* 259:8, fig. 6).

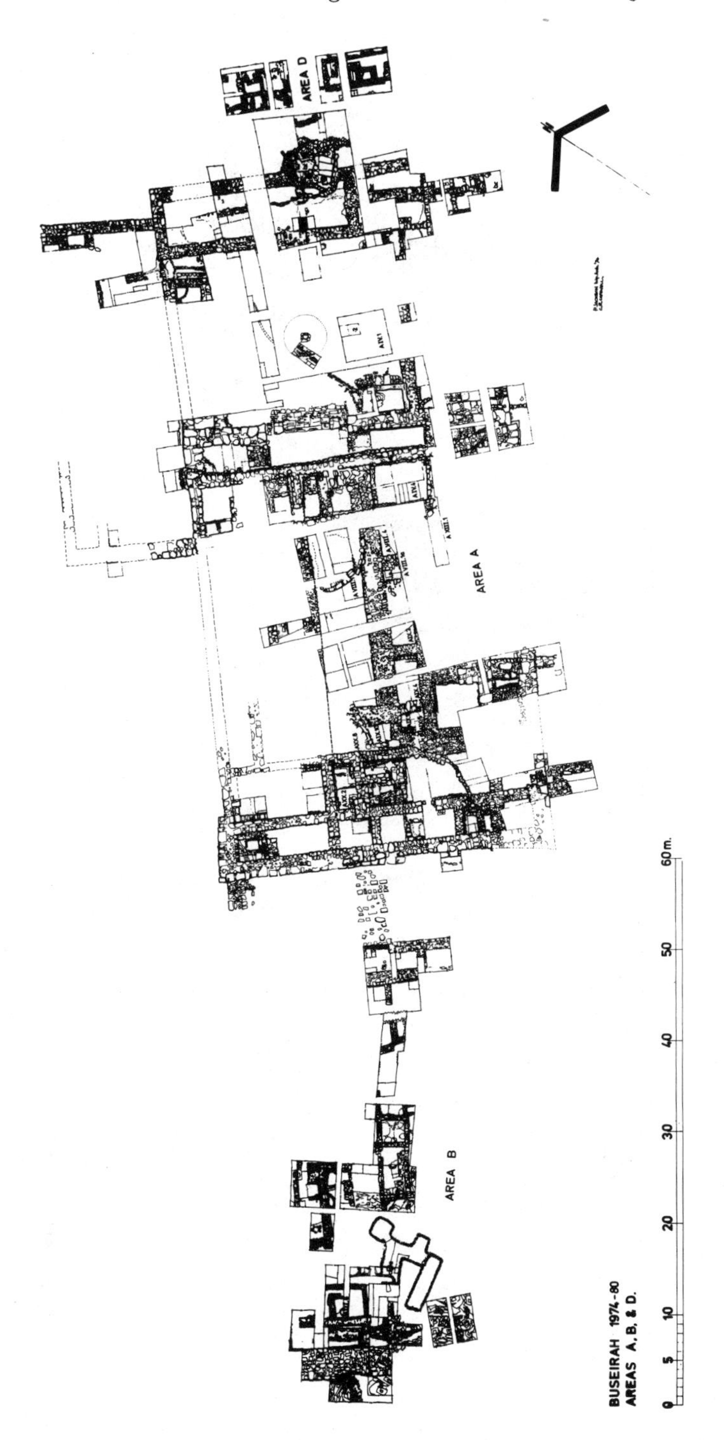

27. Buseirah Areas A, B and D.

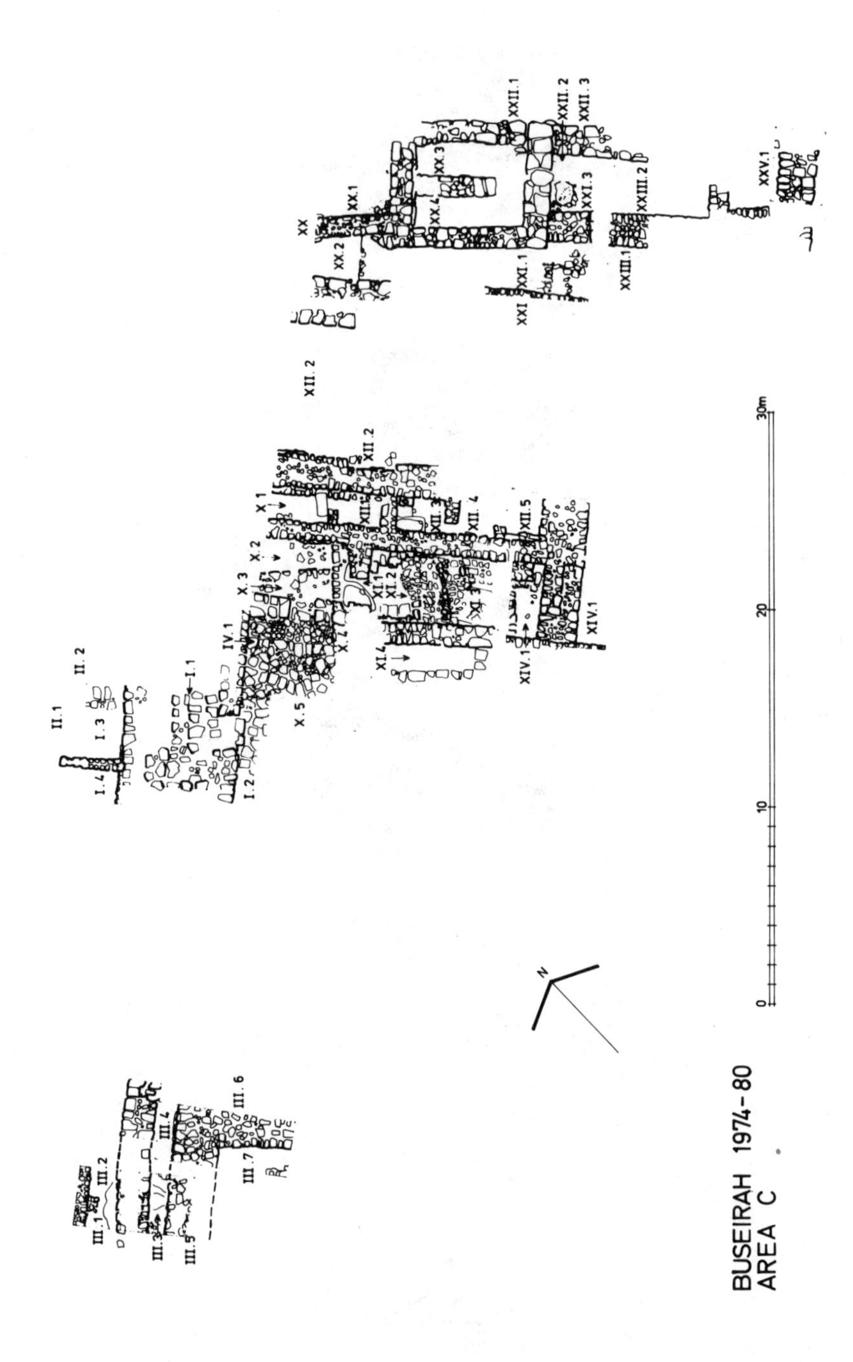

28. Buseirah Area C.

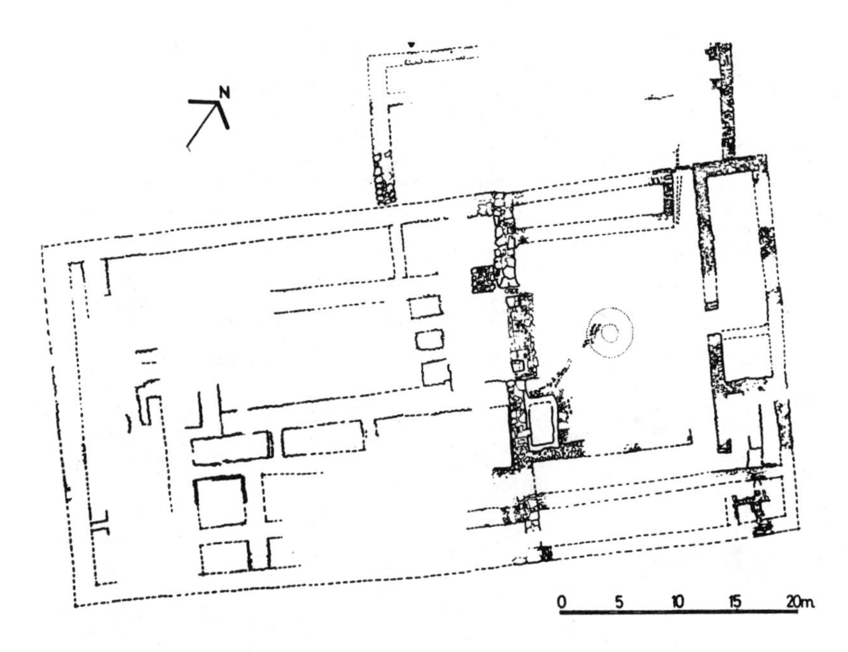

29. Buseirah Building B.

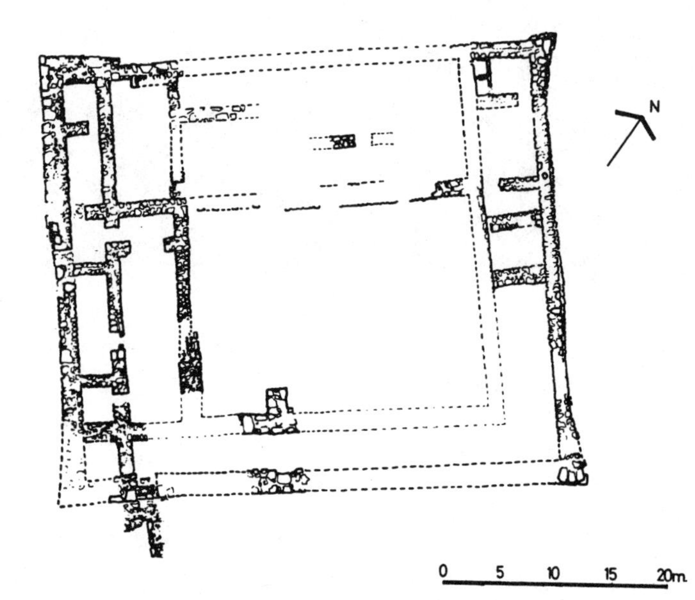

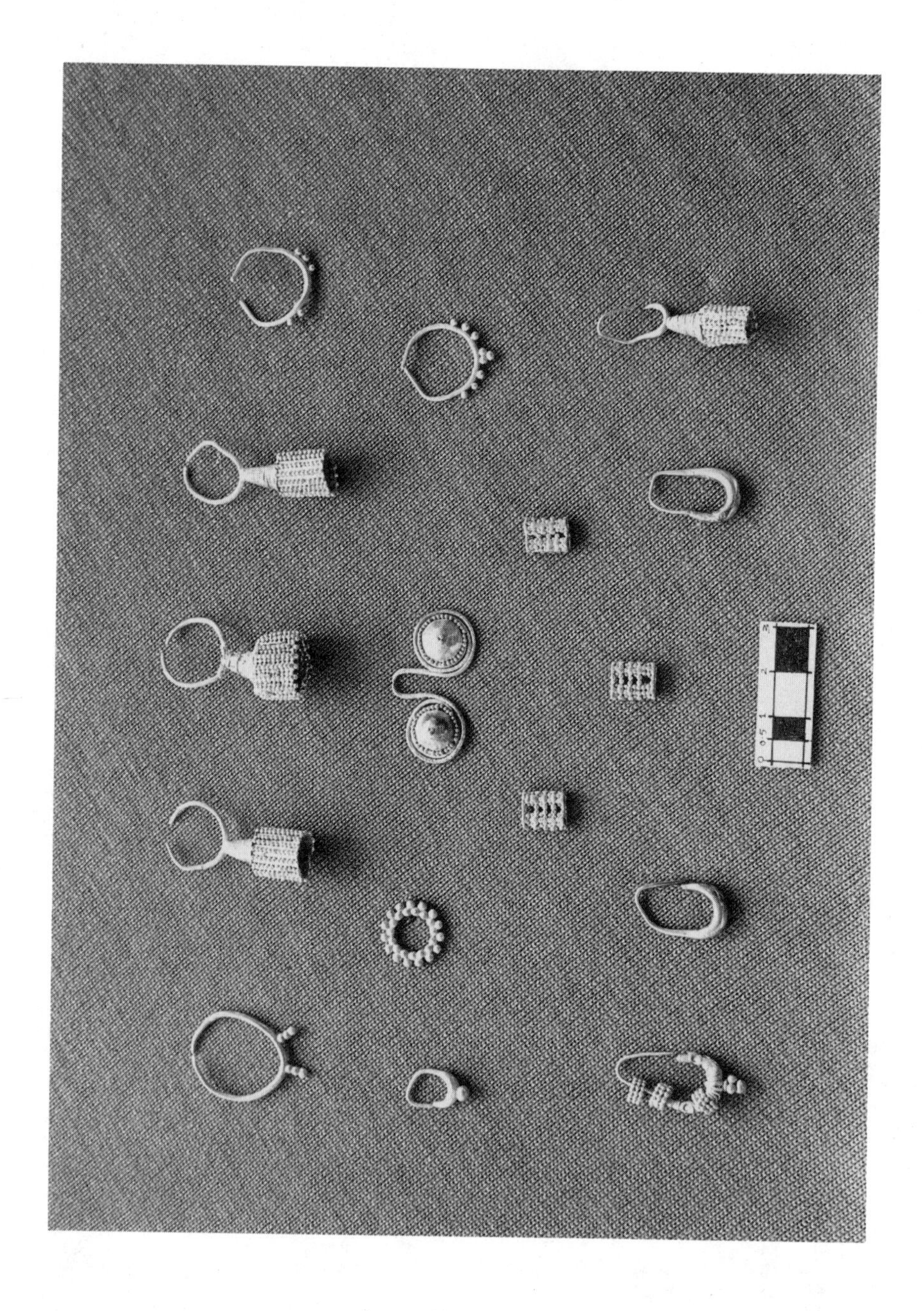

31. The gold jewellery from Tawilan.

EDOM: THE SOCIAL AND ECONOMIC HISTORY

Ernst Axel Knauf-Belleri

Recent authors seem to agree as far as the outlines of Edom's history are concerned.[1] Archaeological work through the past two decades has provided a sound foundation in space and time that previous reconstructions lacked. In light of Crystal M. Bennett's excavations and the surveys conducted by Steven Hart, Alistair Killick, David Graf, and Burton MacDonald, the textual references to Edom in the Egyptian, Assyrian, and biblical sources have achieved even more significance by being placed in a geographical, chronological and cultural-ecological context that now is more strictly defined.

In the Late Bronze Age, Edom was inhabited by bands and/or clans of nonsedentary or semisedentary agriculturalists and pastoralists, the *shasu* of the Egyptian sources, who became victims of the Egyptian "preventive punitive strikes" in the 13th and 12th centuries BCE. The attacks presumably were launched to protect Egyptian mining interests in the Wadi ʿArabah. Between the 12th and 9th centuries, the exact date of its onset not yet defined, village farming commenced in northern Edom along the southern bank of Wadi el-Ḥasa. A tribal system emerged, and Edom became subject to some form of Judahite suzerainty that did not, however, leave any architectural, epigraphical or ceramical traces on the ground.[2] Soon after Moab became independent of Israel (ca. 840 BCE), Edom threw off whatever Judahite yoke there was (2 Kgs 8:20-22). There are still no archaeological indications that the new Edomite tribal kingdom was a state; politically, it may be modelled after the Cherokee "kingdoms" of the early 18th century CE rather than the kingdom of Navarra in the 16th century. With the capture of Gaza in 734 BCE by Tiglath-Pileser III, Edom came within the Assyrian sphere

[1]E.g., E. A. Knauf, "Supplementa Ismaelitica 13. Edom und Arabien," *BN* 45 (1988) 62-81; J. R. Bartlett, *Edom and the Edomites* (JSOTSup 77; Sheffield: JSOT Press, 1989); P. Bienkowski, "Umm el-Biyara, Tawilan and Buseirah in Retrospect," *Levant* 22 (1990) 91-109; E. A. Knauf, "The Cultural Impact of Secondary State Formation: The Cases of the Edomites and Moabites," *Early Edom and Moab: The Beginning of the Iron Age in Southern Jordan* (ed. P. Bienkowski; SAM 7; Sheffield: JSOT Press, 1992) and the contributions by J. R. Bartlett, S. Hart and P. Bienkowski in the same volume.

[2]All the traces of Judah's claim to dominion over Edom are found in the Bible. Of these, the genealogical link between Isaac (= Judah, cf. Amos 7:9 and 16) and his "sons" Esau/Edom and Jacob/Israel can least easily be dismissed as postexilic in origin (Knauf, "Supplementa Ismaelitica 13," 69-70).

of influence and prospered.[3] Assyrian aid-in-development and the connection to the world market provided by Assyria furnished the Edomite tribal kingdom with the appurtenances of a state: a capital city (Bozrah/Buseirah), which was the first and only city ever built in Iron Age Edom, fortresses, and a bureaucracy, detectable by a handful of seals and sealings that derive from their activities. Assyrian-instigated trade and industry provided a market for Edomite agricultural production on a level previously unknown. With Assyrian and later Neo-Babylonian support, Edom expanded along the arteries of trade into north Arabia and towards the Mediterranean. Edom's prosperity came to a sudden end when Nabonidus annexed the kingdom in 552 BCE. The Neo-Babylonian attempt to run the profitable Arabian trade failed; in the Persian province of Arabia of which Edom formed a part, the oasis cities and bedouin sheikhs of north Arabia profited from Edom's downfall.[4] Parts of the Edomite tribes survived in southern Palestine, in Idumea, maintaining their ethnic identity and tribal structure. In Edom proper, the survivors returned to the economics and politics of the prestate period, until they became Nabateans and started another cycle of economic and political evolution and devolution that made them participants in the Roman empire's prosperity in the 2nd century CE and in the decline of its periphery in late antiquity.[5]

Two areas of recent controversy might briefly be mentioned in this context. (a) The dating of biblical references to Edom remains as controversial as anything in biblical studies. Suffice it to note that in the opinion of the present writer, hardly any OT reference to Edom predates the 7th century.[6] (b) The date of Iron Age pottery in Edom is only

---

[3]So M. Weippert, "Zur Syrienpolitik Tiglatpilesers III," *Mesopotamien und seine Nachbarn, II* (ed. H. J. Nissen and J. Renger; Berlin: Reimer, 1982) 395-408; idem, "The Relations of the States East of the Jordan with the Mesopotamian Powers during the First Millennium BC," *Studies in the History and Archaeology of Jordan III* (ed. A. Hadidi; Amman: Department of Antiquities, 1987) 97-105.

[4]So E. A. Knauf, "The Persian Administration in Arabia," *Transeuphratène* 3 (1990) 201-17.

[5]For Edomite-Nabataean continuity, see J. R. Bartlett, "From Edomites to Nabataeans. A Study in Continuity," *PEQ* 111 (1979) 53-66; E. A. Knauf, "Nabataen Origins," *Arabian Studies in Honour of Mahmud Ghul* (ed. M. Ibrahim; Wiesbaden: O. Harrassowitz, 1989) 56-61. Bartlett (*Edom and the Edomites,* 172-74) is still marred by the equation that is untenable on grounds both geographical and philological of the *Nabayāt* (the biblical Nebaioth) with the Nabataeans (**Nabaṭ*).

[6]A possible exception is provided by Amos 2:1 and an undisputable exception by Judg 5:4, where only a country called "Edom" is attested, but not a state or a nation. Many more references than commonly thought actually refer to postexilic Idumaea rather than to pre-exilic Edom (e.g., the names of Edomite origin in the genealogies of 1 Chronicles 2 and 4); see my articles "Hur," "Hori," "Manahath," "Manahathites," "Menuhoth," "Shalma," "Shobal," "Zur," *ABD.* Linguistically, it can be argued that the bulk of the Hebrew Bible was produced between the 7th and

partially clarified. The painted Edomite Iron IIC pottery was produced from ca. 700 BCE to ca. 450 BCE according to the excavations of C. M. Bennett and their subsequent processing. The unpainted wheel-thrown Iron IIC pottery and the handmade "Seirite" (=Pseudo-Negebite) ware, insofar as it shares Assyrianizing forms, can be roughly attributed to the same period. The date of the relatively few pieces of pottery found in northern Edom and in the Wadi ʿArabah that recall Palestinian Late Bronze, Iron I and Iron IIA/B forms is unknown, since no excavation in Edom has yet provided evidence to calibrate these forms. It is safe to assume that they are earlier than Edomite Iron IIC pottery and later than their Palestinian counterparts, but for the time being, it is impossible to tell how much earlier and how much later. Edom, on Palestine's periphery, always received Palestinian cultural innovations with some time lag and never received some innovations, such as the indented ware of the Persian period. "Iron IIC" starts in Edom 30-50 years later than in Samaria and lingers on in Edom some 100 years after being replaced in central Palestine by "Persian," which never penetrated into Edom.[7]

The following remarks focus on three aspects of ancient Edom's social and economic experience: (1) the fragility of agriculture and its

---

4th centuries BCE; the few texts—mostly fragments—that predate this period can usually be recognized by linguistic traits; see E. A. Knauf, "War Biblisch-Hebräisch eine Sprache?," *Zeitschrift für Althebraistik* 3 (1990) 11-23.

[7]The same time lag can be observed in Edomite linguistics; see E. A. Knauf, "Qaus," *UF* 16 (1984) 93-95; E. A. Knauf and S. Maáni, "On the Phonemes of Fringe Canaanite: The Cases of Zorah-Uḏruḥ and 'Kamâš̲attâ,'" *UF* 19 (1987) 91-94. Similar observations hold true for Edom in the early Islamic and later periods and for the world's favorite peripheries all over, be it Mexican missionary architecture or Bavarian forest votive painting. For J. A. Sauer's fallacious "shortcut" from cultural chronology to political chronology (e.g., in his "Transjordan in the Bronze and Iron Ages: A Critique of Glueck's Synthesis," *BASOR* 263 [1986] 1-26) that has yielded an erroneous dating of Edomite pottery types, see E. A. Knauf, "From History to Interpretation," *The Fabric of History: Text, Artifact and Israel's Past* (ed. D. Edelman; JSOTSup 127; Sheffield: JSOT Press, 1991) 26-64, esp. 45, n. 1. For a response to I. Finkelstein's attempt to identify Iron I pottery at Buseirah ("Edom in the Iron I," *Levant* 24 [1992] 159-66), see the remarks by P. Bienkowski ("The Date of Sedentary Occupation in Edom: Evidence from Umm el-Biyara, Tawilan and Buseirah," *Early Edom and Moab: The Beginning of the Iron Age in Southern* Jordan [ed. P. Bienkowski; SAM 7; Sheffield: JSOT Press, 1992] 99-112) and the unanimous rejection of Finkelstein's proposals among the participants of the Liverpool Colloquium, May, 1991, in the same volume. I agree with Burton MacDonald (*The Wadi al Hasa Archaeological Survey 1979-1983* [Waterloo, ON: Wilfrid Laurier University Press, 1988]) and M. Weippert ("Remarks on the History of Settlement in Southern Jordan during the the Early Iron Age," *Studies in the History and Archaeology of Jordan I* [ed. A. Hadidi; Amman: Department of Antiquities, 1982] 153-62) that some LB/Iron I pottery does exist in northern Edom, but I am unable, for the time being, to attribute a more precise date to it than the rather broad range indicated in the text, *supra.*

implications; (2) the transition from a tribal society to a state and back again; and (3) the role of trade and industry in a nonurban society.

1. Peasants and Pastoralists

Northern Edom (in Arabic, *al-Jibāl*), i.e. the region between Wadi el-Ḥasa and Wadi Ghuweir, forms an agricultural island in southern Jordan. Annual rainfall averages above 400 mm, which still implies that every third year insufficient rain for rainfed agriculture is to be expected. Soil quality is high; due to the variegated relief, wood and pasturage were (and partially still are) available in the immediate vicinity of the settlements. Rich copper ore deposits are located adjacent to that area along the lower courses of Wadi Ghuweir and its tributaries. Northern Edom allows a mixed Mediterranean economy of village-based horticulture, agriculture and stock-raising, if security for the producers and a market for their products are provided. The area also had supraregional significance if the copper ore in the neighboring Wadi ʿArabah were under its control.[8]

Although northern Edom belongs to those areas in Palestine where a Mediterranean rainfed economy is feasible, it is the most marginal of those areas. In addition to its unstable water supply, its economic development is further impeded by its logistic situation. Cut off from Palestine and central Jordan by considerable obstacles to traffic and commerce, the Wadi el-Ḥasa and the Wadi l-ʿArabah, Edom borders on the Syro-Arabian desert, which was without any political or commercial significance prior to the 8th century BCE. Being situated on the lower end of the rainfall average that allows Mediterranean village farming and facing formidable difficulties in exporting any agricultural (or other) surplus anywhere, it is easy to understand why northern Edom did not develop more than an agricultural subsistence economy. What needs explanation are those periods when northern Edom moved beyond subsistence economy or below settled agricultural life.

With the exception of some few, small and isolated village sites (like Wadi Musa and Badibdah), southern Edom, i.e. the region between Wadi Ghuweir and Ras en-Naqb, receives less than 250 mm rainfall per year. Only in very favorable years is agriculture at all possible. Here, village-based agriculture necessitates considerable investments in some kind of irrigation and in its maintenance. In the case of southern Edom, what needs explanation is any economic activity beyond the level of

[8]S. Hart, "Some Preliminary Thoughts on Settlement in Southern Jordan," *Levant* 18 (1986) 51-58; idem, "The Edom Survey Project 1984-85: The Iron Age," *Studies in the History and Archaeology of Jordan III* (ed. A. Hadidi; Amman: Dept. of Antiquities, 1987) 287-90; E. A. Knauf and C. J. Lenzen, "Edomite Copper Industry," *ibid.*, 83-88.

nonsedentary herders and part-time farmers. A considerable herding sector must also always have existed in northern Edomite peasant society, since goat breeding was the only low-rainfall insurance that was available in antiquity.[9]

For most of the 2nd millennium BCE, the absence of farming villages from northern Edom implies that Palestine in the MB and LB periods had no use for imports from that marginal agricultural area and that the area was too scarcely settled to urge its inhabitants to adopt modes of agricultural production more intensive than occasional part-time sowing and reaping by tent-dwellers. The incipient farming economy that can be observed along Edom's northern fringe at the very end of the 2nd millennium raises a question about the origin of the population pressure that induced village agriculture in Edom. It is safe to assume a connection with the Iron-I increase of settlements in the highlands of Palestine and northern Transjordan. This settlement activity may have foreclosed migration areas of a nomadic population centered in northern Edom and forced them to increase the intensity of production in their home area.[10] Alternatively, northern Edom may have been reached by an agricultural population displaced from Palestine or from a region closer to Edom by newcomers from Palestine.[11] For a variety

---

[9]Goats survive droughts that sheep and grain will not endure; so G. Dalman, *Arbeit und Sitte in Palästina, VI: Zeltleben, Vieh- und Milchwirschaft, Jagd, Fischfang* (Hildesheim: Olms, 1964; first pub. 1939) 182-84; 186-89; E. Wirth, *Syrien. Eine geographische Landeskunde* (Darmstadt: Wissenschaftliche Buchgesellschaft, 1971) 207-208; Ø. S. LaBianca, "Objectives, Procedures, and Findings of Ethnoarchaeological Research in the Vicinity of Hesban in Jordan," *ADAJ* 28 (1984) 277-79; E. B. Banning–I. Köhler-Rollefson, "Ethnoarchaeological Survey in the *Bēḍā* Area, Southern Jordan," *ZDPV* 102 (1986) 162-63.

[10]This is the model proposed for central Palestine by I. Finkelstein (*The Archaeology of the Israelite Settlement* [Jerusalem: Israel Exploration Society, 1988]). Even for Palestine, Finkelstein's original proposal hardly holds true; it is based on a *petitio principii* (first, the "Israelites" among the population of the highlands are defined as "nomads" who settled down and finally, it is concluded that the Israelites were nomads who settled down). In addition, Finkelstein's distinction between "Canaanite" villages and "nomadic" hamlets distorts an economic system of horticultural and agricultural cores with pastoral satellites that is distinctive for the Mediterranean mixed economy and which could only have functioned as an integrated system. For a more appropriate view of macro- and micro-histories of the LB/Iron I transition, see P. E. McGovern, *The Late Bronze and Early Iron Ages of Central Transjordan: The Baqʿah Valley Project, 1977-1981* (Philadelphia: University of Pennsylvania Museum, 1986) 335-44; R. B. Coote and K. Whitelam, *The Emergence of Ancient Israel in Historical Perspective* (SWBAS 5; Sheffield: Almond Press, 1987); R. B. Coote, *Early Israel: A New Horizon* (Minneapolis: Fortress, 1990); U. Hübner, *Die Ammoniter. Untersuchungen zur Geschichte, Kultur und Religion eines tranjordanischen Volkes im 1. Jahrtausend v. Chr.* (Wiesbaden: O. Harrassowitz, 1992) 164-65.

[11]So R. G. Boling, *The Early Biblical Community in Transjordan* (SWBAS 6; Sheffield, Almond, 1988). For a critique of Boling's use of the Bible, see E. A. Knauf, "Hesbon, Sihons Stadt," *ZDPV* 107 (1990 [1991]) 135-44.

of reasons, the second explanation is to be preferred. The *shasu*, as the tent-dwelling and stock-raising indigenous population of that area was called by the Egyptians, probably only migrated as far as the "chicken bedouin" of the contemporary Petra region—up to 2 km in a year and usually less.[12] As these nonsedentary farmers and herders without a tribal organization were already self-sufficient, no change in the pattern of international trade could have moved them toward a more intensive mode of production. Only immediate restriction of the territory available to them, a restriction exercised by newcomers with a more developed agricultural technique that would allow for the subsistence of a higher number of people within the same area, could have compelled them to adopt a more labor-intensive way of life. This fate they shared with innumerable nomadic groups in later periods all over the world.[13]

The agricultural colonization of southern Edom, an even more marginal area, commenced in the 7th century and did not last much more than 100 years. The enterprise must have responded to the sudden emergence of a local market that made it feasible. The sudden onset of settlement activity indicates that the factors that constituted the market emerged suddenly, in connection with the establishment of the *pax assyriaca*: the state, economically defined as the emergence of professional administration, i.e. a group of people who lived off the products of primary producers; the Edomite copper industry, which created a work force that had to be fed; and Edomite participation in long-distance trade, with traders and their animals that also had to be fed. As far as any statement about the identity of the settlers in southern Edom is possible, the new villagers comprised descendants of both the more agricultural Horite tribes (from northern Edom and partially originating from Palestine) and the more pastoralist Esavide tribes from Edom's east and south (see excursus *infra*). Due to the environmental

---

[12]For the "chicken nomads" of the Petra region, see Banning and Köhler-Rollefson, "Ethnoarchaeological Survey in the *Bēḍā* Area," 152-70. For the *shasu*, see M. Weippert, Semitische Nomaden des zweiten Jahrtausends," *Biblica* 55 (1974) 265-80; 427-33; E. A. Knauf, *Midian. Untersuchungen zur Geschichte Palästinas und Nordarabiens am Ende des 2. Jahrtausends v. Chr.* (Wiesbaden: O. Harrassowitz, 1988) 101-104; 110-14; 179.

[13]So N. N. Lewis, "The Frontier of Settlement in Syria, 1800-1950," *International Affairs* 31 (January, 1955) 48-60 = *The Economic History of the Middle East 1800-1914* (ed. C. Issawi; Chicago: University of Chicago Press, 1966) 258-68. To counteract exaggerated ideas about the role of nomads in settlement processes, the percentage of bedouin among the population of present-day Jerash is telling; see K. Hackstein, *Ethnizität und Situation. Ǧaraš—eine vorderorientalische Kleinstadt* (BTAVO 94; Wiesbaden: Reichert, 1989) 107. More elaborate arguments for a "Palestinian" origin of northern Edom's agricultural population at the beginning of the Iron Age may be found in Knauf, "The Cultural Impact of Secondary State Formation," 47-50.

constraints on agriculture in any region of 250 mm annual rainfall (or less), every tribe, if not every clan, village, and family, must have contained a pastoralist segment. It is not clear whether the increased market for food in the 7th century also gave rise to pastoral tribes without a farming segment. The first pastoralist nomadic tribes that are known in the ancient Near East were the protobedouin of the 9th-7th centuries BCE; earlier tribes contained both agricultural and pastoralist segments.[14] For the time being, it cannot be decided whether the proximity of these ancient Arabs instigated or prevented the formation of similar tribes in 7th-century Edom. For the Horite tribes, Gen 36:24 indicates that the labor of the agriculturalist was still divided inside the family, not between ethnic groups such as tribes.

Even at the peak of Edomite settled life in the 7th century BCE, not every Edomite was settled. Archaeological evidence for Edomite transhumant pastoralist may be provided by the handmade "Seirite ware" that shares Iron IIC forms and is attested both in the Wadi ʿArabah and at Tawilan (and other sites).[15] The nomadic segment of the Edomite peasant tribes helps to explain how Edomite ethnic identity and tribal structures were transported across the Wadi ʿArabah to survive among the Idumeans after the disappearance of the state and civilization from the Edomite plateau (cf. Manahath b. Shobal in Gen 36:23 and 1 Chron 2:52).

The Edomite plateau was never completely devoid of population. The vast majority of the people living on the Edomite plateau and in its adjacent regions prior to 500 BCE were neither specialized pastoralists nor specialized agriculturalists; most probably, they were compelled to practice some mixed economy. There were various degrees of settlement among them and significant degrees in the complexity of political organization (see Section 2, *infra*). At no point in history was the population of the Edomite plateau 100% subject to a state.

---

[14]So E. A. Knauf, *Ismael. Untersuchungen zur Geschichte Palästinas und Nordarabiens im 1. Jahrtausend v. Chr.* (2d ed.; Wiesbaden: O. Harrassowitz, 1989) 40-45; 142-43; idem, "Bedouin and Bedouin States," *ABD* 1.634-38; T. Staubli, *Das Image der Nomaden im Alten Israel und in der Ikonographie seiner sesshaften Nachbarn* (OBO 107; Fribourg: Universitätsverlag and Göttingen: Vandenhoeck & Ruprecht, 1991) 7-15.

[15] See H.-G. Bachmann and A. Hauptmann, "Zur alten Kupfergewinnung in Fenan und Hirbet en-Nahas in Wadi Arabah in Südjordanien," *Der Anschnitt* 36 (1984) 110-23, 121, fig. 17:5; A. Hauptmann, G. Weisgerber, and E. A. Knauf, "Archäometallurgische und bergbauarchäologische Untersuchungen im Gebiet vom Fenan, Wadi Arabah (Jordanien)," *Der Anschnitt* 37 (1985) 163-95, 188; 189, fig. 28:7; C. M. Bennett, Excavations at Tawilan in Southern Jordan," *Levant* 16 (1984) 1-19; 7, fig. 6.8.42.

Excursus: Horites, Esavides, Genealogy and Topography[16]

The only written source covering ancient Edom's social structure, if not social history, consists of the genealogies collected in Genesis 36. A historical interpretation of this laconic and uninviting document is made possible by pertinent evidence from the toponymic tradition in southern Jordan.

Genesis 36 presents Edom as being divided into two major population groups, the "sons of Esau" and the "sons of Seir," each of which consists of subtribes with several clans. One can argue for a 7th-century date for the source from which the biblical authors drew these ethnographic statistics.[17] Admittedly, the point at which the Edomite genealogies were committed into Hebrew writing provides only a *terminus ante quem* for the genealogies themselves. One also has to be aware of the possibility that ethnographic statistics were constantly updated and revised in the process of tradition. That this was the case in Genesis 36 has convincingly been argued by M. Weippert.[18] On the basis of Weippert's analysis, the following comments focus on the two primary lists contained in Genesis 36: the list of the "sons of Esau" (36:10-14) and the list of "the sons of Seir the Horite" (36:20-28). A third list, the *ʾallûpîm* of Edom (36:40-43), lacks any genealogical hierarchy. It contains names of tribes and/or places from both the Edom and the Hori lists and adds some new names. Weippert is obviously right in interpreting the list to reflect a later stage in the social and political development of Edom than is presupposed in the two earlier lists; how late a stage still needs to be determined.

The Esau list comprises three subtribes: 1.1. Eliphaz, 1.2. Reuel and 1.3. Oholibama, who together include 13 clans.[19] Oholibama bat Ana

---

[16]This excursus was first presented at the SBL/ASOR meetings in New Orleans, 1990. As some arguments in the previous section are based on that paper, which will not be published for the foreseeable future, a *précis* is inserted here.

[17]Knauf, *Ismael*, 61-63.

[18]M. Weippert, "Edom. Studien und Materialien zur Geschichte der Edomiter auf Grund schriftlicher und archäologischer Quellen" (Ph.D. dissertation, University of Tübingen, 1971).

[19]At least one clan name, 1.1.1 Teman, presumably was added by the Hebrew literary tradition, as Teman, "South," "Land of/in the South" was not a part of Edom, but another name for the whole territory of Edom or the whole of northern Edom (coined by her northern neighbors). In Amos 1:12, the fire that Yahweh is going to hurl on Teman will consume the palaces of Bozrah. It seems, then, that Teman was the name of the northern part of Edom with its capital at Bozrah (Buseirah). Ezek 25:13 threatens the Edomites "from Teman to Dedan," i.e., from the northern to the southern borders of their realm at the beginning of the 6th century BCE. In Jer 49:7, 20; Obad 9, Teman is used as a synonym for Edom. If Teman were the name of the region surrounding Bozrah/Buseirah, the capital of Edom, this broadening of the term's meaning becomes intelligible. It was this region where the formation of the

ben Zibeon (1.1) provides one of the three links between the Esau list and the Hori list: she is the daughter of Ana (2.3.2=2.4) and the granddaughter of Zibeon (2.3). The other two links are established by Nahat and Timna. Nahath (1.2.1) cannot be separated from Manahath (2.2.2.).[20] Timnaᶜ, the mother of Amaleq (1.1.6), is a daughter of Lotan (2.1.3.).[21] The sons of Esau contain a high percentage of personal names: Eliphaz, Omar, Reuel, Zerah, Jeush, Jaᶜlam and Korah (7 out of 17, i.e. 41.18%). There is only one regional name in the Esau list, Teman, of questionable origin, and one place name, Timnaᶜ. The original relevance of the remaining names is more or less unclear.

The structure of the list of the sons of Seir the Horite is much more complicated. It apparently reflects a longer period of change in the Seirite tribal system that repeatedly necessitated an updating of the genealogies. Hori appears twice (2.0 and 2.1.1), as do Ana (2.3.2 and 2.4) and Dishon (2.4.1 and 2.5). Furthermore, Dishon is merely a dialectical, if not purely orthographical, variant of Dishan (2.7). These multiple-entry listings of identical entities probably reflect the rise to prominence and subtribal status of some clans and the demise of others. All the names in the Hori list (with the exception of Hori) are possible place-names that end in *–ōn, –ān, –am*.[22] Only Lotan and Hemdan could also have been personal names.[23]

Edomite state started in the 9th century BCE and from where it penetrated further south in the following centuries. The references to Teman in Gen 36:15, 42 are derived from Gen 36:11; cf. Weippert, "Edom," 437-46. It is clear from all these references that Teman designated a region and, secondarily, a tribe; cf. R. de Vaux, "Téman, ville ou région d'Édom?" *RB* 76 (1969) 379-85. The identification of the archaeological site of Tawilan near Petra (thus N. Glueck, *Explorations in Eastern Palestine II* [AASOR 15; New Haven: American Schools of Oriental Research, 1935] 82-83) with Edomite Teman is untenable both on linguistic and philological grounds. Other possible Hebrew additions to the Edomite material in Genesis 36 are 1.1.5 Kenaz and 1.1.6 Amalek. 1.3 Oholibama is not easily conceivable as a personal and/or tribal name, although it also is rather opaque as a Hebrew fabrication.

[20]Tribes secondarily derived from or aggregated around other tribes frequently are designated by an M-derivative of the mother-tribe's name; e.g., Amîr and Muhaᶜmir in ancient South Arabia; cf. Knauf, *Ismael,* 69 and n. 342.

[21]It is difficult not to connect the tribal name "Lotan" (2.1) with the name of Abraham's nephew Lot, whose activities in Gen 13:18–19 center around the northern end of the Wadi ᶜArabah. Reuel (1.2) can also be traced on both sides of the Wadi ᶜArabah; see Knauf, *Midian,* 158-60.

[22] For Canaanite toponyms and their endings, see W. Borée, *Die alten Ortsnamen Palästinas* (2d ed.; Hildesheim: Olms, 1968) and A. F. Rainey, "The Toponymics of Eretz-Israel," *BASOR* 231 (1978) 1-17.

[23]If an early, i.e., pre-6th century date for the Hori-Seir list is accepted, Uz (2.7.1) must be a later addition, since Edom did not occupy the area of Uz in northwest Arabia before the late 7th or early 6th centuries; see E. A. Knauf, "Supplementa Ismaelitica 4. Hiobs Heimat," *BN* 22 (1983) 25-29; idem, "Hiobs Heimat," *WO* 19 (1988) 65-83. This observation would not apply if "Uz" is just a misvocalization,

The *ʾallûpîm* list seems to have been produced by ancient Hebrew scholars. Three of its names are of doubtful Edomite ancestry: Oholibama (3.4 = 1.3), Qenaz (3.7 = 1.1.5), and Teman (3.8 = 1.1.1) are all drawn from the Esau list. From the Hori-Seir list derive Timna (3.1 = 2.1.3) and Alwa (3.2 = Alwan, 2.2.1). The *ʾallûpîm* list adds Yetet/Yeter (3.3), Elah (3.5), Pinon (3.6), Mibsar (3.9), Magdiel (3.10) and *ʿīrām* (3.11). Most of the names are place names: Timnaʿ ("She protects," and cf. the name of the Qatabanian capital), Elah/Elath, Pinon (= Feinan),[24] Mibsar (= Bozrah or another "fortified" place?) and probably Iram (if *ʿīrām* "their city," then another reference to Bozrah/Buṣeirah). Only Yeter (if this should be read) and Magdiel are personal names.

Some additional information is provided by the editorial framework of the lists. Gen 36:9, the *tōlᵉdôt* introduction to the Esau list, qualifies Esau as the father of Edom on the mountain of Seir, thus linking the Esau list to the Hori-Seir list in terms of geography. In Gen 36:20, the sons of Seir the Horite are qualified as "the inhabitants of the country." It is not necessary to follow Deut 2:12 and conclude from Gen 36:20 and Gen 36:9 that the Seirites preceded the "sons of Esau" in the country of Edom. The late *ʾallûpîm* list still includes a contingent from the Horite list. The marital and other links between the Esau list and the Horite list would also contradict too violent a relationship between the two tribal groups. Presumably, Deuteronomy 2 projected the theory of "possession of the land by conquest," well established by the deuteronomistic history for Israel in Canaan (and proven wrong by scholarship in this century), on Israel's neighbors. If one interprets Gen 36:20 as originally referring to sedentary, agricultural tribes, one has Gen 36:40 on one's side: "These are the names of the tribal leaders of Edom according to their clans and their places, by their names." A sedentary interpretation of the Horite tribal system is also supported by the linguistic structure of the names themselves.[25]

The nature of the names listed in Gen 36:20-28 makes an investigation into the survival of some of these names feasible. The reference to the mountains of Seir circumscribes the area in which to look for possible survivors rather precisely.[26] Still, the well-known

---

induced by that famous Uz of Job, from an original *ʿēṣ or *ʿīs (see *infra*).

[24]For that name, see E. A. Knauf, "Supplementa Ismaelitica 9. Phinon–Feinan und das westarabische Ortsnamenkontinuum," *BN* 36 (1987) 37-50.

[25]Similarly, the names of the most prominent Israelite tribes derive from regional designations: Ephraim, Benjamin and Judah. For the formation of these tribes, see C. H. J. de Geus, *The Tribes of Israel. An investigation into some of the presuppositions of Martin Noth's amphictyony hypothesis* (Assen/Amsterdam: van Gorcum, 1976); Coote, *Early Israel.*

[26]Under such circumstances, blunders such as the one committed by Kamal

phenomenon of the ubiquity of Semitic place names will be encountered: there is not just one Mugheiyyir or one Khirbet el-Medeyyineh, but dozens of them.[27] The search for toponymical representations of the names listed in Genesis 36 is further encouraged by the observation that the rate of "Canaanite survivals" among present place names is rather high in marginal areas with a high agricultural potential.[28] A primary example for this survival is the name ash-Shaubak, derived from a Canaanite **śubk* (Hebrew *śōbe<u>k</u>*), "*macchia*, wilderness."

A case for toponymic survival can be made whenever a current place name has no Arabic genealogy but can be derived from a Canaanite name that may be supposed or attested by a sequence of sound changes that are known to have been operative in the area in question. This is the case with U<u>d</u>ruḥ, classical A<u>d</u>ruḥ, obviously a survival of Edomite Zerah (1.2.2),[29] and with ʿAin Saubalah, a survival of the Horite subtribe Shobal (2.2). Whereas recent maps[30] only show a spring under that name, in the days of Alois Musil[31] there was also a Khirbet Saubala near the spring. In addition, Jebel Saubala was the designation of the fertile plateau immediately south of the Wadi el-Ḥasa, which recent archaeological investigations have established as the core area of Edomite settlement activities, possibly as early as the late 13th century BCE.[32] By toponymic means, the tribal area of Shobal appears to be well established.

Nokha, on the same plateau, is another name without an Arabic etymology. Nokha recalls Nahat (1.2.1) and Manahath (2.2.2). The three names derive from the same root, NW<u>H</u>, "to rest."[33]

Salibi, who transposed ancient Palestine to southwestern Saudi Arabia, should be avoidable; for the basic pitfalls to which Salibi fell victim, see E. A. Knauf, "The West Arabian Place Name Province: Its Origin and Significance," *Proceedings of the Seminar for Arabian Studies* 18 (1988) 39-49.

[27]J. M. Miller, "Six Khirbet el Medeinehs in the Region East of the Dead Sea," *BASOR* 276 (1989) 25-28.

[28]E. A. Knauf, "Toponymy of the Kerak Plateau," *Archaeological Survey of the Kerak Plateau* (ed. J. M. Miller; ASOR Archaeological Reports 1; Atlanta: Scholars Press, 1991) 281-90.

[29]Knauf and Maáni, "On the Phonemes," 91-93.

[30]Jordan 1:100,000 (in Arabic) and the "Archaeological Map of Jordan," 1:250,000, in English.

[31]So A. Musil, *Arabia Petraea II. Edom. Topographischer Reisebericht* (2 vols.; Vienna: Alfred Hölder, 1907, 1908) 1.2, 313; 2.242.

[32]So MacDonald, *The Wadi al Hasa Archaeological Survey*; Weippert, "Remarks on the History of Settlement in Southern Jordan."

[33]As the Hebrew word *naḥat*, "calm," and the plural *menūḥōt* from *mānaḥat* indicate. Most commentators correct *ham-menūḥōt* in 1 Chron 2:52 to **ham-manaḥtî*. This correction, however, is unnecessary. Manahath can be derived from **Manâḥ*,

The last clear case for an Edomite tribal name in modern disguise is provided by the upper course of the Wadi Gharandal, called Wadi ʿAunah on the 1:250,000 map and Wadi ʿAunat (*sic!*) on the 1:100,000 map. The area was known to Musil as Naqb el-ʿAwnat.[34] One can confidently claim that this name reflects the name ʿAna (1.3; 2.3.2; 2.4) in Edomite, possibly ʿOna(t). Incidentally, *ʿanat* means "a herd of wild asses" in west Arabian,[35] which recalls the tradition of Gen 36:24: " . . . and Ana; this is the Ana who found the *yēmīm* in the desert when he pastured the asses of Zibeon, his father."

In most cases, however, inherited names are reshaped and reinterpreted by the receiving language. It would not be suspected that Jbeil, meaning a "small mountain" in Lebanese Arabic, actually continues a toponymic tradition that started some 5000 years ago if there were not ancient sources that mention Gubla and indicate that it should be sought in approximately the same region where Jbeil is located. In cases such as this, additional evidence is needed in order to connect a present toponym with an ancient predecessor. Recent re-etymologization may be ruled out in cases where only ancient and classical Arabic, but not contemporary standard or vernacular Arabic, provide etymologies. *ʿĪṣ* means "wood" in ancient west Arabian.[36] This could explain the name of Khirbet ʿIs near Ṭafileh, which has been equated with Uz (2.7.1) by various scholars.[37] Khirbet ʿIs cannot have been the Uz of Job, nor can the events mentioned in Job 1 conceivably have happened near Ṭafileh. It is possible, however, that ʿIs reflects a Canaanite *ʿēṣ*, "tree" or "trees."[38] It is also possible that Horite ʿṣ is to be connected with that *khirbeh* indeed, but is to be separated from Job's Uz (a connection then established by the biblical tradition).

---

in Hebrew, *Mānôaḥ*. Menuhoth is a plural formation of the same name: **Manāḥāt* becomes **Menōḥôt* in Canaanite and finally, by dissimilation, *Menūḥôt* in Hebrew (as in *megûrôt*, plural of *māgôr*, and in similar cases). It is perfectly possible that Nahath represents a Hebrew revocalization of the Edomite name, which may well have been **Nōḥat* originally.

[34]Musil, *Arabia Petraea II*, 2, 193. The spelling of the 1:100,000 map indicates that the name did not appear to be Arabic to, at least, the native speaker responsible for the legends. Arabic *ʿaunah*, "forced labor, corvee," does not provide a feasible etymology either.

[35]B. Lewin, *A Vocabulary of the Huḏailian Poems* (Göteborg: Kungl. Vetenskaps- och Vitterhets-Samhället, 1978) 307.

[36]Lewin, *Vocabulary*, 308. It is likely that this word for "wood" is a Canaanite loanword in West Arabian; see *infra*, n. 38.

[37]Musil, *Arabia Petraea II*, 1, 339. The Uz of Job is derived from Arabic *ʿAuḍ*; cf. Knauf, "Hiobs Heimat," 68, 71.

[38]The root is ʿḌ; see T. Nöldeke, *Neue Beiträge zur semitischen Sprachwissenschaft* (Strasbourg: Trübner, 1910 = Amsterdam: APA-Philo Press, 1982) 144-45.

Seil ad-Dathnah was the name under which the Wadi Shobak-Wadi el-Ghuweith system was known to Musil.[39] The name may be translated as "waterflow of the waterflow," *dathnah* being a rare classical word of the same meaning as *sail.* If Dishon (2.4.1; 2.5), a noun designating a kind of antelope (Deut 14:5), can be connected with Amorite (hence Akkadian) *ditanu(m)*, the root must have been DṮN.[40] In this case, the Edomite name is probably preserved in the redundant *dathnah.* Since *ᶜilyan* is not attested in contemporary Arabic, Khirbet el-ᶜIlyan, "the ruin of the tall beast or person," is a better candidate for Alwa (3.2)/Alwan (3.2.1) than Khirbet ᶜIlawah, "the ruin of the increase," a word in contemporary use and quite appropriate for a site near Ras en-Naqb.

As is the case with the "waterflow of the waterflow," awkward semantics may serve as an indicator for names received from another language. Khaur-al-Manaᶜiyyin, "the flat valley plain of those belonging to the impediment," provides a case for the localization of Timna (2.1.3, 1.1.6, 3.1). Musil mentions a Khirbet es-Serabit in this plain.[41] On the other hand, since Khirbet el-Hama means "ruin of the summit," which accurately describes its location, it is doubtful that the site can be connected with Hemam (2.1.2), even if *hāmah* does not frequently produce toponyms. In addition, Standard Arabic *–ah* should have been recorded as *–e* by Musil; **hāamā* or**hāma* (the forms corresponding in written Arabic to colloquial *hāma*) do not match the noun formations possible in Arabic, a fact that may indicate an inherited name. Another obstacle to the antiquity of that name, however, is provided by the current maps that have Majdal instead, unknown to Musil or his guide, and clearly a rendering of Canaanite *migdōl.*[42]

Majādil recalls Magdiel (3.10). There is, however, the plural *majādīl* of *mijdāl,* "flagstone, ashlar," a name not inappropriate for an ancient site used for stone robbery. The place name is always recorded with a short vowel in its last syllable, a fact that does not enhance the probability that the name derives from "flagstones." *Majdal* would lead to a plural *majādil,* but *majdal* seems to be restricted to toponyms where the noun replaces Canaanite *migdōl* or Aramaic *magdal*; it is not an Arabic noun in common use that would habitually produce a plural. Instead of

---

[39]Musil, *Arabia Petraea II,* 1, 323.

[40]Cf. H. B. Huffmon, *Amorite Personal Names in the Mari Texts* (Baltimore: Johns Hopkins University Press, 1965) 184; W. von Soden, *Akkadisches Handwörterbuch* (3 vols.; Wiesbaden: O. Harrassowitz, 1965-1981) 3.173b. For the preservation of the interdentals in Edomite, see Knauf and Maáni, "On the Phonemes," 91-93.

[41]Musil, *Arabia Petraea II,* 1, 32. I have not been able to trace the present name of that ruin nor its periods of occupation.

[42]Musil, *Arabia Petraea II,* 1, 282. The map 1:250,000 has Majdal, and the map 1:100,000 Khirbet Majdal.

Majadil, Musil recorded Khirbet el-Mqeir, "ruin of the small stone-made trough."[43] *ʿAbr*, plural *ʿubūr* (colloquially, *ʿabūr* means "ford, crossing"), perfectly explains the name of the spring near Buṣeirah, less perfectly the same name further to the northeast. The concentration of ʿBR names within a relatively small area is surprising. Therefore, the names can be marked as possible, by no means probable, survivors of Ebal (2.2.3).[44]

Needless to say, there are hundreds, if not thousands, of ʿAin eḍ-Ḍabʿ, Ḍibaʿ, etc. They are as ubiquitous as hyenas used to be. Two of the numerous ḌBʿ-names of southern Jordan are included here because, surprisingly, they are located near or within the western slopes, and not, as similar names in ancient Moab and Edom used to be, along the eastern desert fringe. Furthermore, the name Zibeon (1.3; 2.3) refers to the same root and the same animal. Also, there is a striking proximity of one of the Hyena springs to what survived of Ana (2.3.2), Zibeon's son.

Keeping all the limitations raised by the various degrees of possibility and probability in the identification of names from Genesis 36 with recent place names in southern Jordan in mind, are there still significant spatial distributions of the places with connections to Edomite tribes and clans? Surprisingly, there are. First, there is a clear-cut east-west stratification between Horites to the west and Esavides to the east in spite of the fact that ancient Edom was a narrow strip of fertile soil running north-south along the edge of the plateau.[45] The prime of Edom's main agricultural area was occupied by the Horite subtribe of Shobal (2.2). The location of possible candidates for Shobal's clans Ebal (2.2.3) and Alwan (2.2.1)[46] may indicate that the process of Edomite agricultural expansion was partially fed and probably initiated by colonists from the agricultural core area who migrated south in order to found new villages. Village-based agricultural colonization was one of the main factors in the resettlement of Jordan in the second half of the 19th century CE.[47] For Lotan (2.1), the data base is too small. There is a good case for Thimna (2.1.3), but a bad case for Hemam

---

[43]Musil, *Arabia Petraea II*, 2, 242-43. For *miqr* or *muqr*, cf. C. Denizeau, *Dictionnaire des parlers arabes de Syrie, Liban et Paléstine* (Paris: G.-P. Maisonneuve, 1960) 501. As I am not familiar with this site, I cannot decide whether it provides the archaeological potential for stone-robbery.

[44]The sound changes *ā* to *ū* (via *ō*) and *l* > *r* are rather trivial.

[45]Edom basically had neither east nor west, being land squeezed between the desert and the wilderness of the western slopes (Seir); so E. A. Knauf, "Edom und Seir," *Neues Bibel-Lexicon* (ed. M. Görg and B. Lang; Zürich: Benziger, 1990) 467-68; idem, "Seir," *ABD* 5.1072-73.

[46]In each case, the northern variants are more probable than the southern variants, solely on linguistic grounds (see *supra*).

[47]So Lewis, "Frontier of Settlement"; Hackstein, *Ethnizität*, 21-31; B. Mershen and E. A. Knauf, "From Ǧadar to Umm Qais," *ZDPV* 104 (1988) 128-45.

(2.1.2). Taken together, the distribution of the two Lotan sites may indicate the fragmentation of a tribe that had passed into oblivion when these two settled segments survived.[48] The Zibeon (2.3)–Ana (2.4)–Dishon (2.4.1) group is located not on the Edomite plateau, but in the valleys of the western slopes, where recent explorations south of Petra have revealed some agricultural sites from the late Iron Age.[49] The one (but reliable) Esau site that is not also a Shobal or Lotan site, Zerah (1.2.2), is situated far east of the Hori sites (and of the 350 mm-rainfall line) in an area of agricultural colonization where, based on modern analogies, nomads probably joined the settlement process that was instigated by landlords and peasants. Two Horite clans, Timna (1.1.6 and 2.1.3) and Nahath (1.2.1)–Mahanath (2.2.2), may have joined Esau when Esau rose to power with the formation of the Edomite state. Esau's "nomadic" prehistory and subsequent dominance in that state is documented by the editorial framework of the lists in Genesis 36, the structure of the Esavide tribal names, and the history of the Edomite national deity, Qos.[50] Contrary to the clustering of Horite and Esavide sites, sites from the *ʾallûpîm* list are evenly distributed over Edom. Their arrangement is indicative of a central power's attempt to organize and control the whole country. It cannot be decided, however, whether this central administration was Edomite, Assyrian, Babylonian, or even Persian.

Genesis 36 is one of those texts that traditional historians do not like: it exhibits all the literary charm of a telephone directory in which the numbers are missing. But maybe it is the task of the modern historian to start searching for those missing numbers and establish a connection. It is in biblical texts like Genesis 36 where historians who want to base their research not on accounts, but on accounting books find some source material for descriptive historiography.

---

[48]This is a speculation based on very meager data and influenced by the assumption that the Lot tradition of the Hebrew Bible reflects glimpses of LB/Iron I history; on fragmentation, see E. R. Service, *Origins of the State and Civilization. The Process of Cultural Evolution* (New York: W. W. Norton, 1975) 66-68.

[49]M. Lindner, "Edom outside the Famous Excavations: Evidence from Surveys in the Greater Petra Area," *The Beginning of the Iron Age in Southern Jordan* (ed. P. Bienkowski; SAM 7; Sheffield: J. R. Collis, 1992) 143-66. The identification of sites as belonging to this group is highly probable for Ana, probable for Dishon, and perhaps likely for the southern variant for Zibeon.

[50]See supra, and previously Weippert, "Edom"; idem, "Edom und Israel," *Theologische Realenzyklopädie* (21 vols.; ed. G. Krause and G. Müller; Berlin and New York: W. de Gruyter, 1971-1991) 9.291-99; for Qos, see Knauf, "Qaus"; idem, "Qaus in Aegypten," *Göttinger Miszellen* 73 (1984) 33-36.

2. *Kinship and Kingship*

Edomite state formation was not a process "from kinship to kingship." There was a short period, comprising the 7th century and the first half of the 6th century, when a thin veneer of statehood was added to Edomite tribal society without changing the texture of Edomite society very deeply.

Like state formation, the formation of tribes in Edom was due to confrontations with the outside world.[51] The confrontation that led to Edomite tribes started with the incipient settlement of Edom in the Iron I period and culminated with Edom's exposure to Judahite rule in the 10th and 9th centuries. The confrontation that produced a short-lived Edomite state commenced with the establishment of Assyrian indirect rule over Edom in 734 BCE or shortly thereafter and ended with the establishment of Neo-Babylonian direct rule in 552 BCE.[52]

Edom's *shasu* population of the LB period was pretribal: in the Egyptian sources, the *shasu* are always specified according to "countries," i.e. areas. Their highest order of political organization was the *mhwt*, "family" or "clan."[53] The absence of any political entity such as a state or a tribe/chiefdom from the Edomite plateau in the Iron I period can be deduced from the fact that the Feinan copper mines were clearly controlled by people from the west by then (see *infra*, Section 3).

Tribal organization usually is the political response of a non-state population to a state expanding into their territory. The state's pressure may be exerted directly by military means or colonization or indirectly by "opening" the "underdeveloped" areas to trade, i.e. the mechanics of the state-run world economic system. It is unclear whether the process of Edomite tribal formation could already have started in the 13th century BCE as a response to Egyptian "preventive punitive campaigns" into Seir.[54] Archaeologically, pre-Iron IIC Edom, as yet not clearly datable, consists of a handful of villages and hamlets between Tafileh and the Wadi el-Ḥasa, centered around the largest of these sites from where one can see them all, Khirbet Mashmil. This spatial organization, a two-level hierarchy of settlements, is indicative of a simple

---

[51] B. J. Price, "Secondary State Formation: An Explanatory Model," *The Origins of State: The Anthropology of Political Evolution* (ed. R. Cohen and E. R. Service; Philadelphia: Institute for the Study of Human Issues, 1978) 161-86.

[52] For more detail, see Knauf, "The Cultural Impact."

[53] H.-W. Fischer-Elfert, *Die satirische Streitschrift des Papyrus Anastasi I. Übersetzung und Kommentar* (Wiesbaden: O. Harrassowitz, 1986) 168.

[54] Knauf, *Midian*, 110-14.

chiefdom.[55] If the Hadad who fled Solomon (1 Kgs 11:14-22) was indeed an Edomite,[56] this was his entire realm.

The state is a cultural import on the Edomite plateau, as is indicated by its sudden appearance and its sudden disappearance when its outside support collapsed. Chronologically, the appearance of those material culture remains that can be interpreted as indicative of a state society—urbanism, writing, a certain density of luxury items[57]—is restricted in Edom to ca. 700-650 BCE, i.e., the period of Assyrian and Neo-Babylonian indirect rule. Whereas indirect rule usually precedes state formation,[58] in the case of Edom and other secondary states, the state produced the only urban site that ever existed in Edom, Bozrah, with an architecture as imported as the institution itself.[59] Besides Bozrah, there were no cities in Edom, not even towns.

While the Assyrian-induced state affected Edom's economy (see *supra*), it did not affect Edom's society very much. Edom's tribal statistics as reflected in Gen 36:10-14, 20-28 were collected in the 7th century, i.e. at the same time as the Edomite state flourished.[60] Needless to say, the tribal system survived the state. After the exile, the Edomite

---

[55]For the socio-political interpretation of archaeology, see C. S. Steele, "Early Bronze Age Socio-Political Organization in Southwestern Jordan," *ZDPV* 106 (1990) 1-33.

[56]For the view that Hadad was an Aramaean, a view that has much to commend it, see A. Lemaire, "Hadad l'Édomite ou Hadad l'Araméen?," *BN* 43 (1988) 14-18.

[57]For these items and their significance, see D. W. Jamieson-Drake, *Scribes and Schools in Monarchic Judah: A Socio-Archeological Approach* (SWBAS 9; Sheffield: Almond Press, 1991).

[58]W. Dostal, *Egalität und Klassengesellschaft in Südarabien. Anthropologische Untersuchungen zur sozialen Evolution* (Horn-Vienne: Ferd. Berger & Sons, 1985) 363-66; H. J. Nissen, *Grundzüge einer Geschichte der Früzeit des vorderen Orients* (Darmstadt: Wissenschaftliche Buchgesellschaft, 1983) 41-70. Service's view to the contrary (*Origin*, 280-82) may be modified if the civilizations of Egypt and Meso-America are no longer regarded as pristine civilizations.

[59]So C. M. Bennett, "Neo-Assyrian Influence in Transjordan," *Studies in the History and Archaeology of Jordan I* (ed. A. Hadidi; Amman: Department of Antiquities, 1992) 181-87; idem, Excavations at Buseirah (Ancient Bozrah)," *Midian, Moab and Edom. The History and Archaeology of Late Bronze and Iron Age Jordan and North-West Arabia* (ed. J. F. A. Sawyer and D. J. A. Clines; JSOTSup 24; Sheffield: JSOT Press, 1983) 9-17; P. Bienkowski, "Umm el-Biyara, Tawilan and Buseirah in Retrospect."

[60]See *supra*, n. 17. This dating is even more valid if these statistics were originally compiled at the Edomite court and not in Jerusalem. Since such a compilation would be the work of a central administration, it cannot predate the establishment of such an administration. The possibility that these genealogies were collected by the Judahites in the 9th century can be ruled out by the observation of the considerable amount of change and mobility that the lists exhibit (see *supra*, excursus): too much change for the short period of Judahite rule. Alternatively, the genealogies were collected among the postexilic Idumaeans in the Negeb. In this case, however, the editorial framework would be wholly anachronistic.

tribe of Shobal is encountered at Kirjath-Jearim together with its clan Manahath (cf. 1 Chron 2:52 with Gen 36:23).

When Qos-Gabr ruled at Bozrah[61] the Edomite farmers on top of Umm el-Biyara did not rely on walls or moats or on any kind of police force for their protection, but on the sheer inaccessibility of their dwelling. It is hard to conceive of a more nonurban way of life. The inconvenience of getting up and down their rock fortress cannot have been less in antiquity than it is today. It is not quite clear from whom these Edomites sought protection: was it perhaps their neighbors, or maybe even the claim of the king and his administration?[62] Umm el-Biyara is not an isolated phenomenon. Three comparable sites have recently been discovered,[63] and more may still be found in future surveys and excavations. By using a natural fortress for protection, the people of Umm el-Biyara carried typical prestate modes of defense into the Edomite state. It should not be argued that Selaᶜ (2 Kgs 14:7) could not be identical with es-Silᶜ north of Buseirah because the site, another natural fortress, lacks indications of occupation from the 9th/8th centuries BCE.[64] A prestate society would typically use a mountain refuge in times of need, especially war. Such occasional occupation would not necessarily produce remains of architecture and domestic pottery.

The dependency of Edomite statehood on outside support is well demonstrated by the failure of the attempt by Nabonidus to turn the vassal principality into a province within his empire. Once there was no more need for Edom's copper (due to the close cooperation between

[61]For the structure of Edomite kingship, the "Edomite King List" in Gen 36:31-39 is rather irrelevant. None of these "kings" bears an unmistakably Edomite name or appears in any Assyrian or Babylonian document dealing with Edom. These "kings" were either bedouin and village chiefs from Edom after 550 BCE (thus, E. A. Knauf, "Alter und Herkunft der edomitischen Königsliste Gen 36,31-39," *ZAW* 97 [1985] 245-53) or, more likely, Aramean kings of the 11th century BCE (thus Lemaire, "Hadad l'Édomite," 14, n. 3). Bartlett (*Edom,* 94-102) fails to recognize the linguistic problems involved.

[62]In this case, the sealing of Qos-Gabr from Umm el-Biyara (Bartlett, *Edom,* 213) may represent a trade item or even a piece of booty. One cannot, of course, rule out the possibility that the farmers of Umm el-Biyara regarded the king who resided at Bozrah as their tribal chief, whereas the king may or may not have tended his fellow tribesmen as subjects. For the Assyrians, they were certainly subjects of a vassal king; cf. Knauf, *Ismael,* 100-101 and n. 553.

[63]At least one neighboring civilization regarded these mountain retreats as typical of the Edomite way of dwelling: Obad 3–4. For these sites, see Lindner, "Edom outside the Famous Excavations," 143-66; idem, *Petra. Neue Ausgrabungen und Entdeckungen* (Munich and Bad Weisheim: Delp, 1986) 121-27; idem *et al.,* "Es-Sadeh—A Lithic – Early Bronze – Iron II (Edomite) – Nabataean Site in Southern Jordan," *ADAJ* 34 (1990) 193-237.

[64]S. Hart, "Selaᶜ: The Rock of Edom?," *PEQ* 118 (1986) 91-95.

Cyprus, the Phoenicians and the Persian empire based on mutual benefit) and once the revenues of the caravan trade were harvested by another agency (that also was dependent on the market provided by the empire), the ruling class lost its financial base. The agricultural potential of the country was not high enough to enable the maintenance of an imperial administration, as it had never been high enough to carry the burden of an independent state.[65] After the disappearance of the state and settled civilization, however, a population with an Edomite ethnic identity persisted[66] and endured long enough to hand the Edomite state's national deity Qos down to the Nabateans.[67]

3. Trade and Industry

The copper ore deposits of the central Wadi ʿArabah were vigorously exploited in the 12th/11th and 7th centuries BCE.[68] The Feinan copper ore had one severe disadvantage in comparison with its Cypriote competition: for the industrial centers of Palestine-Syria, it was nearly inaccessible for logistical reasons. Therefore, it was only in periods when the Cypriote supply did not function well or did not function at all that efforts were made to produce copper at Feinan and its vicinity against all odds.

There is no evidence that connects Early Iron Age Feinan with the Edomite plateau, or vice versa. There are, however, some indications of connections between Early Iron Age Feinan and the contemporary Negeb. It is my impression that Feinan's Iron Age I pottery has close connections with Khirbet el-Mshash.[69] In any case, Khirbet el-Mshash was

---

[65]The maintenance of the Roman province of Arabia was due to a large extent to the capital flow from the empire to this specific periphery in the course of the establishment and maintenance of the limes.

[66]So H. J. de Geus, "Idumaea," *JEOL* 26 (1980) 53-74; I. Ephʿal, *The Ancient Arabs. Nomads on the Borders of the Fertile Crescent, 9th-5th Centuries BC* (Jerusalem: Magnes and Leiden: Brill, 1982) 199-201.

[67]See Knauf, *Ismael,* 110-11; idem, "Dushara and Shaiʿ al-Qaum," *Aram* 2:1&2 (1990) 175-83.

[68]See Hauptmann *et al.*, "Archäometallurgische und bergbauarchäologische Untersuchungen"; idem, "Chronique archéologique: Feinan, 1984," *RB* 93 (1986) 236-38; idem, "Fainān 1984," *AfO* 33 (1986) 256-59; Knauf and Lenzen, "Edomite Copper Industry."

[69]See Hauptmann *et al.*, "Archäometallurgische und bergbauarchäologische Untersuchungen," 190 and nn. 82-86; 191, pl. 29:2-6. The pottery plates in the Bochum reports were drawn and controlled by staff not familiar with Palestinian pottery forms and were never seen by the staff member responsible for pottery reading before publication; in some cases the drawings—e.g., the "Assyrian bowls"—bear no resemblance to the actual piece. My comments are based on the sherds, not on their drawings as published. V. Fritz, who seems best qualified to test the Mshash connection further, is presently working on that pottery.

a copper processing and trading site. I. Finkelstein is right that the Mshash-phenomenon can only be explained by trade. He is wrong, however, in assuming that it was part of the "Arabian trade" network prior to the 8th century BCE.[70] There was a large copper-producing center in the Wadi ᶜArabah and a trading center in the Negeb, on the route from the Wadi ᶜArabah to the Palestinian market of that copper. The most viable conclusion about the relationship between the two areas is that Mshash controlled the Feinan copper production in the 12th/11th centuries and prospered from that trade.[71] Early Iron Age Feinan was exploited by the west, not by the east. Feinan established some kind of contact between the land of Edom and the rest of Palestine. This contact may have contributed to the movement of people from southern Palestine to Edom. The modes of production around Iron I Feinan have not yet been investigated. A "tribal metallurgical industry" is by no means a singular phenomenon. Tribal industries may be characterized by the production of small quantities with a high amount of time and manpower; it is feasible whenever tribal labor is cheap enough in comparison with other sources, or if there is no competition.[72]

The Feinan copper works of the early Iron age were a consequence of the breakdown of the first Mediterranean world economic system[73]

---

[70]I. Finkelstein, "Arabian Trade and Socio-Political Conditions in the Negev in the Twelfth-Eleventh Centuries BCE," *JNES* 47 (1988) 241-52; for a different position, cf. C. Edens and G. Bawden, "History of Taymaʾ and Hejazi Trade During the First Millennium B.C.," *JESHO* 32 (1988) 48-103; Knauf, *Midian*, 26-31; idem, "The Migration of the Script, and the Formation of the State in South Arabia," *Proceedings of the Seminar for Arabian Studies* 19 (1989) 79-91; P. Bienkowski, "The Date of Sedentary Occupation in Edom: Evidence from Umm el-Biyara, Tawilan and Buseirah," *Early Edom and Moab: The Beginning of the Iron Age in Jordan* (ed. P. Bienkowski; SAM 7; Sheffield: J. R. Collis, 1992) 99-112.

[71]Similarly, Arad controlled that region in the EB I-II periods; so A. Kempinski, "Urbanization and Metallurgy in Southern Canaan," *L'urbanisation de la Palestine à l'âge du Bronze ancien* (ed. P. de Miroschedji; *BAR* 527; Oxford: BAR, 1989) 163-68; Lindner *et al.*, "Es-Sadeh," 199-204. For the nonurban character of EB Arad, see also I. Finkelstein, "Early Arad—Urbanism of the Nomads," *ZDPV* 106 (1990) 34-50. A more adequate model for understanding that site than Finkelstein's "nomadic urbanism" is provided by Steele, "Socio-Political Organization."

[72]So N. van der Merwe, "The Advent of Iron in Africa," *The Coming of the Age of Iron* (ed. T. A. Wertime and J. D. Muhly; New Haven and London: Yale University Press, 1980) 463-506; R. L. Gordon *et al.*, "Antiker Eisenbergbau und alte Eisenverhüttung im ᶜAğlūn," *AfO* 33 (1986) 282-83; E. A. Knauf, "King Solomon's Copper Supply," *Phoenicia and the Bible* (ed. E. Lipínski; OLA 44; Leuven: Peeters, 1991) 167-86, esp. 184-85.

[73]For world economic systems, see I. Wallerstein, *The Capitalist World-Economy: Essays* (Cambridge: Cambridge University Press, 1979); for the ancient Mediterranean, A. B. Knapp, *The History and Culture of Ancient Western Asia and Egypt* (Chicago: Dorsey, 1988); for Palestine, Coote and Whitelam, *Emergence.*

ca. 1200 BCE that resulted in the temporary absence of copper from Cyprus. The resuscitation of the Feinan industry on an even larger scale in the 7th century BCE was a consequence of Edom's integration into the second Mediterranean system that started to emerge in the late 11th century, reached Israel in the 9th century, Spain and south Arabia by the end of the 8th century,[74] and was Assyrian-controlled by the time it reached Edom. Since Cypriote copper was controlled by the Phoenician port cities[75] and Assyrian-Phoenician relations were strained at some times and openly hostile at other times, Assyria's interest in Edom can be explained primarily as an interest in Edom's copper. The association of Edomite "painted palace ware" with mining and smelting sites[76] leaves no doubt that now it was Edom, the new polity from the plateau, that controlled the production.

Edom's new capital, Buseirah, was built further south than any previous Edomite central place (Khirbet Mashmil, es-Silᶜ). This shift of the political center is another indication of the growth of Edomite statehood from north to south. This shift may also have been prompted by the copper mining area. Little is as yet known about the organization of labor in 7th century BCE Feinan and Khirbet en-Nahas. The available evidence suggests that no permanent installations were erected (as the Romans did some centuries later); rather, Edomite mining and smelting expeditions arrived from time to time from the plateau and worked in the middle of the debris and the ruins that their predecessors had left. This procedure, which recalls the Egyptian mining expeditions of the Bronze Age, would indicate that even to the inhabitants of the Edomite plateau, the section of the Wadi ᶜArabah that was situated at their doorstep was a forbidding, foreign region where no Edomite in his or her right mind volunteered to spend more time than was absolutely necessary. Edom's technological skill in producing copper was "Edom's wisdom" to which Jer 49:7 and Obad 8 allude.[77]

---

[74]Knauf, *Midian*, 31; idem, "The Migration of the Script"; idem, "King Solomon's Copper Supply."

[75]The Assyrians could claim suzerainty over Cyprus, but they could never claim expertise in seafaring.

[76]Bachmann and Hauptmann, "Zur alten Kupfergewinnung," 110-23, 120 fig. 16:4; Hauptmann *et al.*, "Archäometallurgische und bergbauarchäologische Untersuchungen," 191 fig. 29:10, 13 (Assyrian bowl!), 14. In addition to the wheel-thrown "fine ware," there is also handmade "Seirite peasant ware" to be found (Bachmann and Hauptmann, "Zur alten Kupfergewinnung," 121 fig. 17:5; Hauptmann *et al.*, "Archäometallurgische und bergbauarchäologische Untersuchungen," 188, 189 fig. 28:7), another illustration of the coexistence of an "urban" and a tribal sector in ancient Edom's society (cf. *supra*, section 2).

[77]Knauf and Lenzen, "Edomite Copper Industry," 87. There is no need to invent another set of "lost books" or to look for remnants of Edomite sapiential writings in the Hebrew Bible.

In addition to industrial production, 7th century Edom also profited from the Arabian trade that had commenced in the 8th century: long-distance trade in small quantities of highly treasured substances, not just incense. By virtue of geography, both Edom and its successor, the Nabateans, controlled the outlet of the west Arabian "incense route" to the Mediterranean port city of Gaza. Edom's trading interests are attested textually in Ezek 27:16 and archaeologically by camel statuettes from Buseirah. In all likelihood, the statuettes were votive offerings of long-distance traders.[78] As long-distance trade in the ancient Near East was state-controlled, if not directly state-organized, the loss of Edom's independence (or semi-independence) induced an immediate and severe recession of Edom's GNP. The recession quickly desolated a countryside that never produced a large agricultural surplus in spite of numerous agricultural installations and which now lacked the instigation to produce any surplus at all.

Conclusions

The ups and downs of Edom's social and economic development in the Iron Age reflect the typical fate of a third-world country. Edom's prosperity began when Tiglath-Pileser III wisely decided to rule Edom indirectly rather than directly, to take his share out of Edom's surplus (after making sure that there was a surplus), and to leave the remainder to the cooperating Edomite elite. Edom's prosperity ended abruptly when Nabonidus foolishly thought the time had come for annexation. This time did not come until 106 CE, when the Romans successfully integrated into the civilized world what by now had become Nabataea. The Edomites, or at least the Edomite ruling circles, had played their cards well when they got a chance; finally, however, their fate was decided by powers beyond their grasp.

---

[78] E. A. Knauf, "Supplementa Ismaelitica 12. Camels in Late Bronze and Iron Age Jordan: The Archaeological Evidence," *BN* 40 (1987) 20-23.

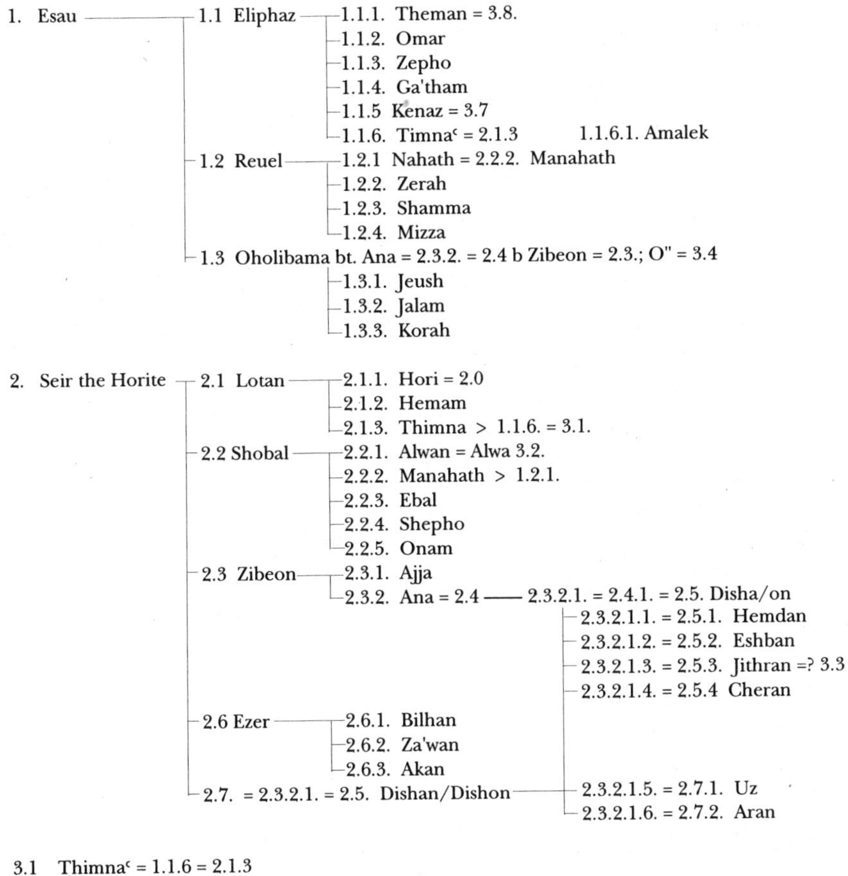

3.1 Thimnaᶜ = 1.1.6 = 2.1.3
3.2 Alwah = Alwam .2.1
3.3 Yetet/Yeter =? Yitran 2.3.2.1.3. = 2.5.3
3.4 Oholibama - 1.3.
3.5 Elah
3.6 Pinon
3.7 Qenaz = 1.1.5.
3.8 Theman = 1.1.1.
3.9 Mibzar
3.10 Magdiel
3.11 Iram

Figure 1. The Genealogies of "the sons of Esau" and the Horites, and the list of the *ʾallûpîm.*

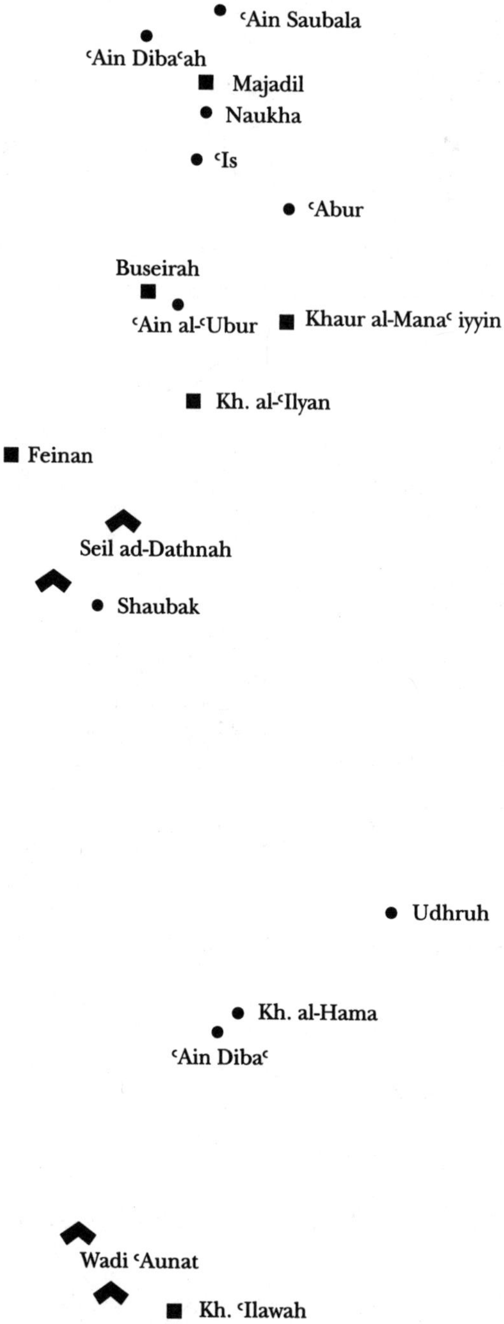

ʿAin Saubala

ʿAin Dibaʿah

Majadil

Naukha

ʿIs

ʿAbur

Buseirah

ʿAin al-ʿUbur

Khaur al-Manaʿ iyyin

Kh. al-ʿIlyan

Feinan

Seil ad-Dathnah

Shaubak

Udhruh

Kh. al-Hama

ʿAin Dibaʿ

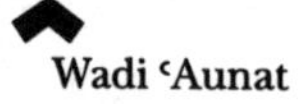

Wadi ʿAunat

Kh. ʿIlawah

Figure 2. South Jordanian places with names that are probably or possibly Edomite.

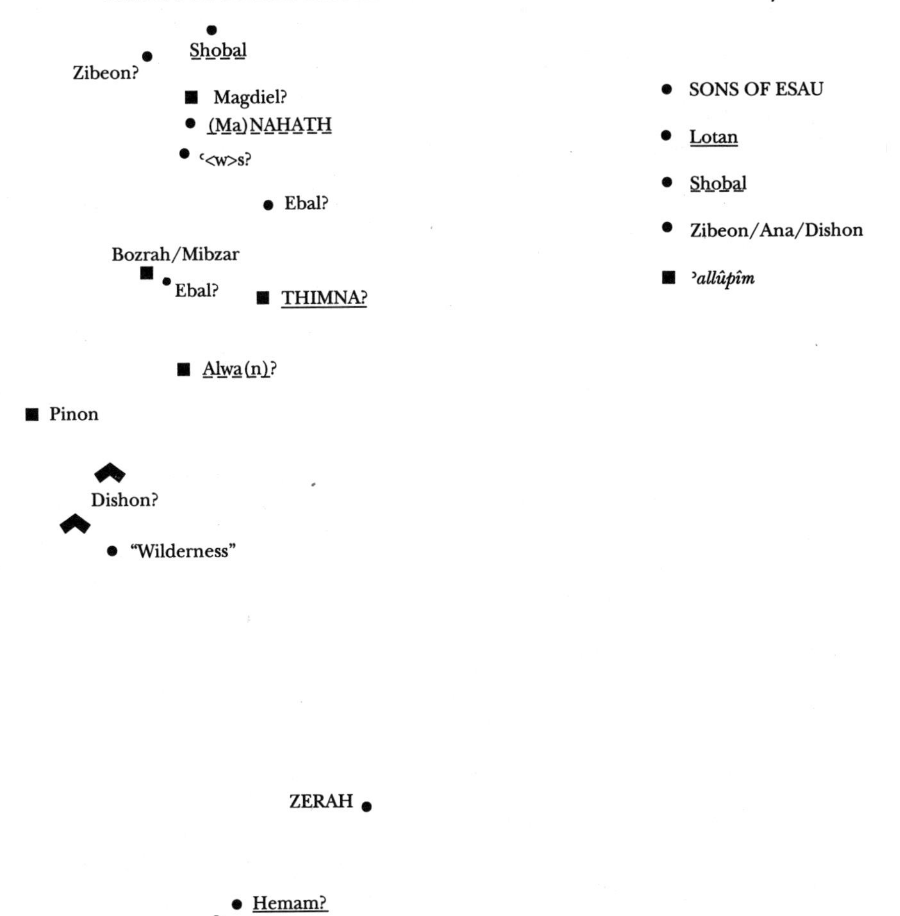

Figure 3. The distribution of Esavide and Horite sites.

EDOMITE RELIGION. A SURVEY AND AN EXAMINATION OF SOME RECENT CONTRIBUTIONS

J. Andrew Dearman

There are several problems involved in an analysis of Edomite religion. They include the wide geographical area included at one historical moment or another under the name Edom, the paucity of written sources, especially Edomite texts, and a general unclarity concerning the criteria used to determine what makes a religious term or practice "Edomite." Nevertheless, the recent contributions by Knauf (1984A + B; 1985B: 108-11; 1988A: 55-57; 1988B; Bartlett (1989: 187-207) and Beit Arieh (1991; and also 33-40 in this volume) provide relevant bibliography and welcome discussion in light of these problems. Bartlett, in particular, gives a good overview of the subject matter. This essay is intended to provide additional analysis of some of their conclusions in a critically constructive fashion and, where it seems feasible, to attempt to build on their results.

Defining Edomite Religion

Edomite religion can be understood in national (political), cultural, or territorial terms. These senses are not mutually exclusive, but it is often necessary to specify which sense of the term is being used. What might be called group cultural self-awareness can be more important to self-understanding than the terminology of nationalism or the bond of shared terrain. For example, members of a pastoral clan in southern Jordan or northern Sinai of the Iron Age may have derived their primary cultural and religious identity from the clan itself. Any allegiance to a king of an Edomite state or adherence to a national cult may have been of secondary significance to them. If a considerable variety of religious expression existed among different tribes and clans in these regions, then describing their cultic practices as "Edomite" may be primarily a territorial reference; i.e., they celebrate their cult in the region of Edom. Perhaps only in a secondary sense would "Edomite" apply as a cultural or a national designation for their cult. Indeed, understood primarily in a national or cultural sense, it might be misleading to describe the religious phenomena as Edomite.

Geography and settlement patterns play particularly important roles in defining the subject matter and classifying the relevant data. As Edelman (1-11 in this volume) makes clear, the Late Bronze and Iron Age sources that use the name Edom or a related designation (e.g., Seir) differ over its territorial extent. Edom is, first of all, a geographical term, probably reflecting the reddish sandstone cliffs in southern Jordan. If the area between the Wadi el-Ḥasa and the Wadi Ḥisma in southern Jordan is the heart of Edom, then the lands south (to ʿAqaba) and west (parts of the Negeb and northern Sinai) were also, at times, considered Edomite. In the cases of these latter territories, Edelman, Bartlett (1989: 33-54) and others have pointed out that it is not clear whether they were known early on in some sources as Edom, or whether over time these regions became more Edomite due to shifting political control and habitation trends. Bienkowski (1990; 1992; and 41-92 in this volume) and others have shown that the settlement patterns in southern Jordan reflect little, long-term sedentary occupation; instead, the population was primarily pastoral and mobile, with an "Edomite" urban population apparently beginning in Iron Age II(C). In varying degrees this observation about shifting habitation trends (with relatively sparse sedentary occupation) is also true of the Negeb.[1] The Sinai region has never supported much of a sedentary population.

For the reasons cited above, it is impossible to deal adequately with the origins of Edomite religion and difficult even to say which practices can be considered indigenous to it. These issues are better left aside and attention given first to southern Transjordan in Iron II and to Neo-Assyrian texts that refer to three Edomite kings of the period with whom the Assyrian rulers dealt (Bartlett, 1989: 122-45, 204).[2] As noted above, these contacts coincide with a developing urban culture in southern Jordan. Two of the Edomite kings have theophoric names, Qos-malaku and Qos-gabr, both of which preserve the name of a deity Qaus/Qos. The same divine name in "Edomite" (קוס) is preserved on a few seals and seal impressions (Bartlett, 1989; 204-5) from southern Jordan. These textual references are evidence for a veneration of Qos that can be called Edomite religion in all three of the senses named above, regardless of earlier forms of Edomite religion or of other cultic practices contemporary with the veneration of Qos. In fact, Qos-veneration is a primary indicator of Edomite religion for scholars, even

---

[1] The Negeb region experienced an increase in sedentary activity in the early Iron Age (Finkelstein, 1988; Naʾaman, 1992). Part of the reason may have been the trading links with the "Midianites" of northwest Arabia (Cross, 1988: 57-63; Knauf, 1988; Edens and Bawden, 1989). Population groups in the Negeb at this time may well have included Edomites. Naʾaman, for example, believes that the Edomite Hadad, Solomon's adversary (1 Kings 11), was a chieftain in this area.

[2] This approach also leaves aside the question of the early development of an Edomite state. The Edomite territories (east and west of the ʿArabah) were certainly capable of supporting tribal occupation, as well as the claim of territorial sovereignty by local rulers before the 8th century BCE. See previous footnote.

though the equation of Qos and Edom is essentially part of a circular argument (Qos=Edom; Edomite=Qos veneration).

With all due caution, the theophoric names with Qos in the Neo-Assyrian references probably confirm the religion of the Edomite royal line(s)[3] and thus, the name of a deity worshipped in the national cult of Edom. Rose's objections to these conclusions about the state cult seem unduly skeptical (Rose, 1977). In his defense, it is true that these few texts are meager resources from which to draw sweeping conclusions; they reveal little about other aspects of either the political structure of the Edomite state or other cult(s) it may have sponsored, and it is possible that the primacy of Qos may not have held true for earlier periods in Edom. Nevertheless, as Bartlett has pointed out (1978), it is most unlikely that Qos entered Edom as late as the 8th century as Rose has conjectured, and it is virtually certain that the 8th and 7th centuries were not a time of political decline in Edom as he has claimed.[4]

Rose has rightly called attention to the surprising silence of the Hebrew Bible concerning the cult of Qos, unlike its references to the deities of Edom's northern neighbors, Milkom, the god of the Ammonites, and Kemosh, the god of the Moabites. A postexilic personal name, Barqos (Ezra 2:52; Neh 7:55), is all that is preserved.[5] Whether Rose is correct or not that a primitive Yahwistic cult preceded the worship of Qos in Edom and that the memory of this cult lies behind the biblical references to the "brotherhood of Edom" will be discussed below.

The material culture of southern Jordan in the Iron Age contributes very little data to the understanding of Edomite religion. There are no temples firmly identified from the partially excavated sites of Buseirah (biblical Bozrah), Tawilan, and Umm el Biyara, and the pottery vessels often labelled as "cultic" (e.g., fertility figurines) are part of a common cultural heritage of Syria-Palestine. Thus, the more recent finds at the cultic site of Qitmit in the Negeb, which the excavator Beit Arieh has concluded are Edomite (1991; and 35-36 in this volume), are potentially quite significant for an increased understanding of Edomite religion.

---

[3] A Lihyanite inscription from al ʿUlā (= ancient Dedan; JS 83:7) refers to a ruler named *GLTQS.* It is additional evidence of Qos' association with a ruling dynasty. Edomite contact with Dedan is presupposed in Jer 49:8.

[4] Rose depends on the older reconstruction of Glueck in making his claim for Edom's declining fortune in the 8th century BCE. As Bartlett has pointed out in response, this is exactly the opposite of what has been concluded from more recent surveys and excavations in Edom.

[5] G. W. Ahlström (1993: 734, n. 2) has proposed that 2 Chron 25:24 gives evidence of an Edomite temple in Jerusalem. The reference to ʿEbed-Edom is insufficient reason for such a conclusion (cf. 1 Chron 26:15).

Beit Arieh's treatment leaves no doubt concerning the cultic nature of Qitmit. What, however, makes the cultic materials Edomite, and if they are Edomite, are they Edomite in all three senses noted above? The excavator's conclusion that the cultic materials are Edomite is based on significant evidence. Among other things, the painted wares, decorated vessels, and some cooking pots have strong affinities with ceramics known from excavated Edomite sites in southern Jordan, and two fragmentary inscriptions preserve the letters *qoph, waw* and *samek* (קוס), probably part of a theophoric name or title. The presence of Edomites in the Negeb in the 7th/6th centuries BCE is well-known.[6] An "Edomite" ostracon was discovered at Ḥorvat ʿUza (Beit Arieh and Cresson, 1985), a site close to Qitmit. There are also the famous references to Edom/ Edomites in the Arad ostraca (Aharoni, 1981: no. 3, 21, 24; Bartlett, 1989: 141-43), discovered some 10 km north of Qitmit. Neutron activated analysis of several decorated vessels from Qitmit demonstrates, however, that they were manufactured locally in the Beersheba-Arad basin. Thus, if the patrons of Qitmit were Edomite, the gentilic label should be understood primarily as a cultural designation.

Unfortunately, it is unknown to what extent an explicitly Edomite cultural influence is true of the remarkable anthropomorphic figures from Qitmit such as the three-horned goddess and the cult stand/jar decorated as a bearded male. Both pieces have parallels from the Eastern Mediterranean and Phoenician cultures.[7] It is also not known if the anthropomorphic figures represent deities worshipped in the state cult of Edom (below). The *bamâ* or cultic complex has three rooms and an altar enclosure, and Beit Arieh has cogently proposed that separate cultic acts (e.g., sacrifice, consumption of food, prayers) were performed in the different parts of the complex. No close parallels exist to the architecture of the complex either, although Beit Arieh notes in passing (1991: 113-14) that analogies exist in Transjordan (T. Mazar), at (Idumean) Marissa in the Shephelah and in Cyprus.

Other intriguing questions remain concerning the cult at Qitmit. If the site does not represent Edomite religion in a political sense (which remains unclear), who then were the patrons of the cult? Perhaps the materials represent forms of religious expression associated with several clans or population groups who traversed the area, a mixture of

---

[6] See note 1 above concerning possible earlier Edomite activity in the Negeb. Ahlström (1993: 722-727) has proposed that there had been a strong Edomite presence in the Negeb since the campaign of Sennacherib against Judah in 701 BCE, when Judahite sovereignty over outlying areas was sharply reduced. This presence may have included control of Arad, stratum VII, and Beersheba, stratum II.

[7] According to Beit Arieh (1991: 95, 112-13), his colleague P. Beck is completing a monograph on the anthropomorphic pottery vessels and figurines from Qitmit.

Edomite, Amalekite, Arab, Qedarite, and Kenite religious traditions. Qitmit is situated near two different routes used by travelers and trading groups. Like Kuntillet ʿAjrud in the northern Sinai and its eclectic cult (Meshel, 1978; Weinfeld, 1984), Qitmit may have been a stopping-point that also served as a cultic way-station for several groups. In the case of Qitmit, Edomite was an appropriate cultural term of self-identity for some of the clients. It cannot be determined if the cultic clients of Qitmit considered the site to be a part of Edom in a geographical sense.

The Identity of Qos

The discussions by Milik (1958: 237-41; 1960), Vriezen (1965), Rose (1977), Bartlett (1978; 1989: 200-207), Oded (1971), Knauf (1984A+B), Graf (1990:50-51) and Klingbeil (1992: 80) preserve the various references to Qos in ancient sources. These references are found in a variety of languages and population groups and demonstrate the appeal of the deity Qos. They may also reflect the ability of Qos to assimilate and to combine the characteristics of other deities (below) or may simply illustrate his conception in terms of one or more of the established categories for deity in the ancient Near East (e.g., storm deity, "high god").

As noted above, Neo-Assyrian annals and a few "Edomite" epigraphic texts (8th-7th centuries BCE) preserve the earliest firm references to Qos, and they remain the primary indicator of Edomite religion during Iron II. Little is known about an Edomite state or religion before these references (that coincide with the rise of an urban population segment in Edom). Both Oded and Knauf (1984B) have concluded that an Egyptian topographical list at Karnak from the time of Ramses II[8] (and apparently reused at Medinet Habu during the period of Ramses III) preserves references to Qos in a few toponyms or clan names. References to Qos in the 13th century BCE are plausible, although these would be the earliest preserved references by several centuries. If they refer to Qos, they would be contemporary with early references in Egyptian texts to the regions of Edom and Seir (e.g., Pap Anastasi VI, 54-6; Pap Harris I, 76: 9-11). The names in question, however, are obscure; no conclusive evidence exists to link them with Edom or Seir, and both scholars acknowledge that Egyptologists have usually interpreted them differently. Bartlett declined to discuss them in his recent monograph.

---

[8] Oded refers to list xxiii in Simons (1937: 158). Knauf rejects no 8, *qṯiśr*, but accepts Oded's interpretation of the other four names as formed with Qos (nos. 7 = *qśrʿ*, 9 = *qśśpt*, 13 = *qśnrm*, and 21 = *qśrbn*). Given the peculiarities of rendering foreign terms in Egyptian syllabic orthography, perhaps all that can be said about these four names is that the interpretation proposed by Oded and Knauf is grammatically possible.

Even after the decline of the Edomite state in the 6th century BCE, the name Qos is known from Nabatean texts, pre-Islamic Arabian sources, and a few widely scattered references preserved in Greek inscriptions. Most of the references are preserved in theophoric names. This chronology and range of references raises several questions. Was Qos originally Edomite, originally Arabian, or another example of a religious phenomenon shared among neighbors that survived political changes? An Arabian origin for the deity appears to be the predominant view among scholars, but that conclusion is complicated by questions of the political relationship and ethnic ties between Edom and its neighbors/successors (Arabs, Nabateans; cf. Knauf, 1988B; Bartlett, 1990; Graf, 1990; Healey, 1989) as well as the paucity of relevant texts. Hammond (1973: 98), for example, has resorted to a description of Qos as simply an "Edomite-Arabian-Nabataean deity."

Knauf has provided the most detailed discussion of Qos' *Heimat* and identity. First, he proposes that the name of the Nabatean deity Dushara (dwšrʾ, דושרא, Δουσάρης) is really the cognomen of Qos; that is, whatever the historical relationship between the Edomites and the Arabs/Nabateans (Bartlett, 1990; Graf, 1990), the national deity of Edom and the chief Nabatean deity share a common identity. Secondly, he suggests that the name Dushara, which is actually an epithet (*du Šara* = the one of *Šara*), originally referred to Qos. The epithet is similar to the description of YHWH as "the One of Sinai" (*zeh sînay*) in Judg 5:5. Thirdly, he argues that *Šara* is the semantic and geographical equivalent of Seir and shows the rootedness of Qos in the hill country of Jordan south of the Wadi al-Ghuweir, known even today as esh Shera. Perhaps the site of Jebel al Qos in the Ḥisma (coordinates 221.887) even preserves a reflection of his home. Fourthly, Knauf concludes that the name Qos is proto-Arabic and derived from the Semitic term "(war/hunting) bow."

All four of these proposals are open to debate, with the fourth having the strongest foundations. Knauf acknowledges that if the name Qaus/Qos is proto-Arabic, it is not excluded that the deity was indigenous to Edom (or at least older than the Iron Age Edomite state), since he concludes that a part of the population in Edom from at least the 13th century BCE was proto-Arabic (1988B: 66). Perhaps Qos took center stage in Edom sometime between the 10th and 8th centuries BCE as the incipient Edomite state began to expand.

The proposed identification of Qos with Nabatean Dushara is based on circumstantial evidence, but it is plausible. On the one hand, some continuity between Edomite and Nabatean religion is expected. The two had chronological proximity and considerable geographical overlap. Furthermore, it is logical to expect a proper name in addition to an epithet for the deity widely described as the chief Nabatean god. Dushara has been described as the patron deity of Nabatean rulers (Kammerer, 1929: 404-05), a characteristic frequently proposed for Qos and Edomite kings in light of the Neo-Assyrian preserved royal names Qos-malaku and Qos-gabr. On the other hand, Dushara has an eclectic identity, combining Arabian elements in his veneration (e.g., crude, "seeing eye" cult stones)[9] with characteristics of Hadad, Baʿal Shamayim, and even Zeus. Since the name Qos continued to be used in the Nabatean/Roman period, it is just as likely that Qos and Dushara were originally two separate deities, with Dushara gradually assimilating Qos' identity as his popularity increased.

What requires continued reflection in light of the analyses of Vriezen and Knauf is the nature and function of a divine "name" like Qos (= the Bow). The older treatment by Vriezen lacks the linguistic sophistication of that by Knauf, yet he demonstrates forcefully that the "name" of Qos follows the pattern of identifying a deity through a representative inanimate object. "The Bow" not only represents and identifies a particular deity; this kind of "name," which in some respects is the functional equivalent of an epithet, also suggests the possibility that another proper name existed for Qos.[10] For example, Milkom (< Malikum? mimation?), the "name" of an Ammonite deity, rarely appears in Ammonite theophoric names (and like the references to Qos, these are all Iron II or later). The primary theophoric element in Ammonite is *ʾel*. Nevertheless, there is no conclusive evidence that two different deities are evoked by these "names," since *ʾel* may be the name of the Canaanite high deity or a generic reference to deity ("god"). Perhaps Milkom (= the king) and the Canaanite high deity *ʾel* are one deity (Tigay, 1986: 19-20; Younker, 1985: 178-79); or *ʾel* and *milkom* refer to "god" and "king" respectively and indicate a deity with yet another "name." There is evidence from the Hellenistic period that suggests Qos was worshipped in bi-name form. A dedication to Πακειδοκώσῳ in Delos (IG xl, 2311) presupposes Semitic *paqîd-qôs*. Either Qos himself is the divine "inspector," or perhaps his name was combined with an epithet for Dushara, who may be the divine "inspector" or "guardian"

---

[9] Perhaps Dushara also assimilated some of the cultic features of the worship of *ʿAttar* or *Ruḍāʾ*, two of the most prominent north Arabian deities (for references, see Knauf 1985: 81-88).

[10] For the widespread use of archery and bow imagery in the ancient world, see Brown (1993). Resheph, for example, was known as the "Archer" at Ugarit and among Phoenicians (cf. KAI 32:3-4 and Dahood, 1958: 70; Fulco, 1976: 49). Qos could be the Edomite assimilation of Resheph, the "Archer" or "Bowman." There are established connections between Resheph and Idumean culture in Palestine (see Teixidor, 1972: 419-20 [no. 47]), but conclusive evidence is lacking to identify the two.

(Πακειδᾶ) worshipped in Jerash (Vincent, 1940; Milik, 1960) .[11] Qos, then, possibly had other "names" or epithets, whether or not the later identification with Dushara proves firm.

Vriezen describes Edomite Qos, the divine Bow, as a warlike and nationalistic deity. The aggressive hunting nature of Esau (=Edom) in the ancestral accounts of Genesis is consistent with this description. Knauf (1984; 1988: 51, 56) would add that Qos seemingly fits the typology of a Hadad-type deity, what he describes as the "syrisch-arabischen Wettergottes." Additional possibilities present themselves; perhaps Qos is Hadad in classical Edomite form and not an independent deity, or perhaps Qos is the "bow" identification of Hadad that hypostasized and developed independently. Neither of the latter possibilities can be evaluated successfully due to the lack of primary evidence, but suggestive evidence exists that Hadad was venerated by a royal line in Edom. The divine element Hadad appears in the name of one of Esau's descendants in Gen 36:35-36 (cf. 1 Chron 1:46-50; Bartlett, 1989: 83-102; contrast Knauf, 1985A). According to 1 Kgs 11:14-22, an Edomite prince named Hadad was an adversary to Solomon. Much remains obscure about this figure, not least his identity and sphere of influence. Na'aman (1992: 74-79) believes that he was a chief or tribal leader in the Negeb; Lemaire (1988) has suggested the possibility that he was an Aramean, in which case he is irrelevant to an investigation of Edom. Edelman (1995) has questioned his historicity altogether, proposing he may be a "bad-guy" character. Multiple epithets for Hadad and his conflations with other deities in the ancient Near East are such that an identification of Hadad with Qos cannot be ruled out. The sculptures at Khirbet Tannur show that the iconography of Nabatean Dushara is an Arabic and Hellenistic appropriation of Baʿal Shamayim/Hadad (Savignac, 1937; Glueck, 1965: 195-199). If Qos is not another name or epithet for Hadad, then he occupied the place of a Hadad-type deity, manifesting many of Hadad's characteristics.

Rose (1977) has raised the possibility that a cult of YHW(H) was known in Edom before that of Qos, an Arabian deity who arrived there no earlier than the 8th century BCE. According to him, before the arrival of Qos both (southern) Judahite and Edomite clans worshipped an *ʾel* deity. In a process of development this *ʾel* deity became YHW in Israel and later YHWH. Also, YHW was subsequently identified in Edom with Qos, the new deity, whose name and character submerged

---

[11] Two inscriptions from Jerash that refer to a deity named Πακειδᾶ (no. 17-18 in Kraeling, 1938) are associated with a Nabatean presence in the city. There are also a few inscriptions from Jerash that refer to a "holy Arabian God" (cf. nos. 19-21). The "Arabian deity" could be an epithet for Dushara or Qos.

much of the earlier cultic heritage shared with Judahite clans. Thus, the "brotherhood" language for Edom in the Hebrew Bible (e.g., Deut 2:2-8; Amos 1:11) and its lack of references to Edom's deity are faint recollections of this cultic heritage.

On the one hand, it seems unlikely that Qos became Edomite as late as the 8th century. Rose's theory that an Arabizing wave swept through Edom at this time simply lacks evidence, although cultural contact, if not a measure of cultural overlap between Edom and Arabia, was common throughout the Iron Age. More likely options are that Qos was also known by other names or epithets from the major categories for deities (Hadad, Baal [cf. Gen 36:38; 1 Chron 1:46-50], ʾEl, YHWH, Rešep, ʿAttar, Ruḍāʾ); or that Qos, perhaps a local mountain deity, rose to prominence with the expansion of a national identity in Edom, assimilating characteristics of one or more of these deities. The region of Edom had strong contacts with both the classical Canaanite cultures and the pre-Islamic cultures of Arabia. A fully developed Qos may have possessed both Canaanite (e.g., *ʾel,* Hadad) and Arabian (e.g., ʿAttar, Ruḍāʾ) characteristics. On the other hand, Rose's proposal for a pre-Israelite form of Yahwism in Sinai/southern Jordan is very likely. On the basis of Deut 33:2, Judg 5:4-5, and Hab 3:3, scholars have long suggested roots for primitive Yahwism south and/or southeast of the monarchical borders of Judah. In more recent years the theory has made a comeback, based in part on possible Egyptian topographical references to a Yahweh toponym in the *shasu* land (Soleb IV a 2 and Amarah West 96 = Giveon, 1971: doc. 6a and 16a; cf. Axelsson, 1987: 57-61; Knauf, 1988: 43-63) and in part, in reaction to newer theories about the emergence of Israel in Canaan that have stressed Israel's indigenous identity (Cross, 1988: 57-63; Mettinger, 1990: 404-13; Staubli, 1991: 166-67, 230-32).

As with the question of identifying Hadad and Qos, the precise relationship between Qos and YHWH in Edom remains unanswered. Again, various possibilities present themselves: perhaps a pre-Israelite YHWH in Seir or Midian assimilated with Qos as the latter became known in Edom, or at an earlier stage the two names referred to the same deity. Both the pre-Israelite YHWH and the later Edomite Qos may have been south Canaanite or proto-Arabic identities of Hadad, or if originally separate deities, they may have possessed similar Hadad-type characteristics. In light of present knowledge, it can be concluded that at certain stages in their development Hadad, YHWH and Qos shared the *Gestalt* of a militant weather deity, whatever other characteristics were affirmed for them by their worshippers, and that it is impossible to untangle the lines that intersect their identities.

Evidence for an Edomite Pantheon

Vriezen comments that from the late Assyrian age until the Persian period Qos "dominates the Edomitic pantheon" (1965: 332). The fact is that for the period in question there is no firm evidence for other members of the Edomite pantheon (2 Chron 25:20?); Vriezen has simply assumed by analogy with other states that such a pantheon existed for the national cult. If the term pantheon is understood simply as a synonym for Edomite polytheism, then undoubtedly there was an Edomite pantheon. Polytheism existed in every state of the ancient Near East. If, however, "Edomite pantheon" is understood to designate the cult sponsored by the royal house that expressed national identity, then Qos is the only name preserved in the meager sources, and great care should be used in the choice of other state cults for analogies. Analogies can be drawn to the Phoenician city states, each of which supported sophisticated pantheons, to nation states dominated by a capital like Aram-Damascus and Judah-Jerusalem, to an Arab tribal alliance like the confederation of ʿAttaršamain (texts in Ephʿal, 1982: 162-63; Knauf, 1985: 9, note 41, 82-83), or to the later Nabateans, Edom's successors, whose eclectic culture portrays the veneration of a wide assortment of deities (Zayadine, 1990).

An underlying presumption should be that a symbiotic relationship existed between the Edomite polity and the national cult, regardless of other cults that may have been Edomite in a geographic or cultural sense. Politics and religion provided mutual support at an institutional level. Secondly, the land of Edom supported a tribal-pastoral economy that, given the opportunity, could also support economic specialization and an urban elite. In the Neo-Assyrian period an Edomite king would require both the support of his particular clan/tribe and the allegiance of the newly-emerged, urban elite in order to become "first" among other tribal rulers. Qos possibly played a role similar to his human counterpart, giving expression to Edomite identity by being both the god of the ruling house and the divine symbol of the state polity. The forms of political organization to use as analogies, therefore, are first the nation states and secondly, the Arab tribal confederations. Just as Hadad supported Damascus and Aram or YHWH Judah and Jerusalem, so Qos supported Edom (and Bozrah). Just as ʿAttaršamain symbolized an Arab tribal confederation, even though each tribe had its own deities, so Qos represented an Edomite polity for its tribal constituents.[12]

---

[12] Discussion continues over the gender(s) of ʿAttar (šamain) in south Canaan and among the various Arab tribes and over the question whether two different deities existed (one masculine and one feminine) or whether there was one deity whose identity developed over time and through cultural diffusion. These issues complicate

Serious consideration should be given to the possibility that the Edomite state cult was monolatrous, regardless of the cultic affinities of individual tribes and other clients of the state. The evidence is not decisive, but a plausible case can be made for monolatrous state cults in Judah, Aram-Damascus, Ammon and Moab. F. M. Cross has expressed this point of view well (1983: 36-37):

> "In the Phoenician and Aramaean city states there are city gods, triads of city gods, patron gods of the king who often differ from the chief city gods, but in both documentary evidence and in the onomastica, we find multiple state deities and personal deities. On the contrary, the onomastica of Israel, Ammon, Moab, and Edom are dominated to a remarkable degree by the name or epithet of the national deity: in Israel by Yahweh or ʾEl (of which Yahweh is the characteristic league epithet), Moab by Chemōš, an epithet of ʿAṯtar, Edom by Qôs, probably an epithet of Hadad, and Ammon by ʾEl (almost exclusively, although his epithet Milcom is well known)."[13]

The problems with this conclusion are also well known. Onomastica provide selective evidence for the cultic affinities of population groups, and without other indigenous texts (e.g., sacrificial lists, national myths) important elements for reconstructing a national cult can easily be missed. It is difficult, therefore, to know how much weight to place on

---

any discussion about a possible identification between ʿAṯtar/ʿAštar and Qos. Among Arab tribes ʿAttar was associated with the morning star Venus, and it is a well-known phenomenon in the ancient Near East that the gender of deities identified with astral phenomena could vary between population groups (e.g., the sun deity was feminine at Ugarit and masculine in Babylon). Among the south Arabian tribes especially, ʿAttar was masculine and a supranational or supratribal deity. Possibly, however, ʿAttar was feminine among some north Arabian tribes. ʿAttaršamain is identified in the Neo-Assyrian texts as a goddess, but this could be due to the similarity of the name with Ištar. In addition to the references to Knauf already cited, see Caskel (1958: 100-106) and Ryckmans (1989: 160-62) for the identification(s) of ʿAttar. Apparently Kemosh was identified with ʿAštar/ʿAṯtar in Moab (see note 13 below), and it has been suggested that Kemosh and Milkom are both epithets of ʿAttar (Gray, 1949:77-79).

[13] See also Cross (1988: 62) for similar comments. Although this is not the place for a full debate of particulars in Cross' reconstruction, I would hesitate to include Aram-Damascus in the city state model (with the Phoenicians) as he does. What little evidence exists for the Aramean state cult in Damascus in Iron Age II seems to reflect the dominance of Hadad in a manner analogous to that suggested for Qos in Edom. Also, I agree with Cross that the reference to ʿAštar Kemoš in line 17 of the Moabite Inscription from Dhiban is to a single (masculine) deity, but I am inclined to read it as a dual name rather than interpreting Kemosh as an epithet for ʿAttar. Admittedly, the difference between an epithet and a name can be inconsequential in these cases. A masculine ʿAttar (and Kamis/Kemoš) is consistent with the Canaanite (i.e. Moabite and not Arabian) sphere and is attested already among Bronze Age sources (Caquot, 1958; Archi, 1980: 167-72; 1993: 6-16; Müller, 1980: 10-15; Stieglitz, 1990: 82-84) in the 3rd millennium BCE. Both Archi (1980: 171) and Müller (1980: 14-15) note the relative popularity of personal names formed with ʿAttar at Ebla.

the onomastica. Evidence for so-called "popular" or "folk religion" is even more difficult to recover, quantify, and to evaluate in its relation to a state cult. Nevertheless, the monolatry of the state cult in Ammon or Moab is suggested by the references to "high places" constructed in Jerusalem by Solomon for his Ammonite and Moabite wives (1 Kgs 11:7-8). One *bamâ* is for Chemosh and the other for Molek (a slur on the name Milkom; cf. 2 Kgs 23:13). In both cases, the *bamâ* represents a Transjordanian ruling house (and a corresponding state polity), as did the two princesses married to Solomon.

It is possible, nevertheless, that the Edomite national cult acknowledged a pantheon, even while concentrating on the veneration of Qos. This would seem to be Vriezen's view, although it is unclear whether Qos' "domination" of the Edomite pantheon is understood by him to mean that Qos was also worshipped as the "high deity," like ʿAttar among the South Arabian tribes, or whether Qos was understood as the national guardian (*paqîd*?) but a deity still in a subordinate role to the "high deity" (= head of the pantheon). Possibly the role of "high deity" in Edom accrued to a south-Canaanite form of ʾEl rather than to an Arabian ʿAttar. Decisive evidence is lacking, in spite of the claim by Knauf (1988B: 66) that "there should be no doubt that for Deut 32:8f. Qos was a son of El and a brother of Yahweh, like the Ammonite Milkom and the Moabite Chemosh."[14]

Perhaps Qos was understood in a henotheistic sense by some in Edom—as a deity granted the role of care for the land of Edom as part of the order of the pantheon. As noted above, Qos may have been a local deity dwelling on Jebel al Qōs before developing into the national god of Edom. Milik's careful description of Qos as the "national god of the land of Edom" can be understood in a henotheistic sense,[15] although this is not a necessary conclusion. Theophoric names using Qos among Nabateans and Arabs, however, occur in diverse regions and do not seem to reflect any henotheistic tendencies. Thus, if the veneration of Qos was limited earlier to the area of Edom, his cult eventually expanded among Nabatean and Arab worshippers.

The possibility also needs to be considered that the cultic materials from Qitmit reflect an Edomite pantheon. If this is true, it is impossible

---

[14] "Es kann aber kein Zweifel bestehen, dass für Dt. 32,8f Qaus wie der ammonitische Milkom und der moabitische Kamoš ein Sohn Els und Bruder Yahwes war." Again, this is not the place for a full debate of particulars. I think that the reference to ʿ*elyon* in Deut 32:8 is understood as an epithet of YHWH by the Deuteronomistic editor/writer and that it is by no means certain that the *Vorlage* of the text presupposed a pantheon with ʾEl at the head and YHWH (or Qos) in a subordinate position.

[15] "Dieu national du pays d'Edom" (Milik, 1960: 95).

to tell whether or not Qos is represented among the anthropomorphic figures. Perhaps Qos is the bearded male figure who decorates a storage jar? If Qos is the bearded figure, then who does the three horned "goddess" represent? Perhaps she is a consort for Qos, the Edomite equivalent of Asherah or Ashtarte, or of the Arabian ʿAttaršamain.[16] The later Nabateans worshipped ʿAtargatis as the consort of Dushara, along with other goddesses (e.g., ʾlt, al ʿUza, al Kutba and Manawat). Any of these deities could find an earlier counterpart in the Qitmit goddess.

As noted above, the location and eclectic nature of the cultic materials at Qitmit seem to rule out an easy association with the national Edomite cult. Granted that a significant percentage of the materials is Edomite in a cultural sense, it cannot be determined if this is true as well in a political sense. All that can be said at present is that a relationship between them is plausible. If the Qitmit materials portray an Edomite pantheon, then the term pantheon is best understood in this instance as a synonym for polytheism and not as a reference to the state cult, whose existence at Qitmit cannot be established for certain.

In conclusion, it can be said that there is less evidence for a pantheon in the Edomite state cult than is often assumed. No final judgment can be made because the evidence is too meager. If an official Edomite pantheon existed, it—like the identity of Qos and most everything Edomite—largely remains a mystery.

---

[16] As discussed above (notes 12 and 13), the gender of ʿAttarsamain is not clear.

Bibliography

Aharoni, Y.
1981 *Arad Inscriptions* (Jerusalem: Israel Exploration Society).

Ahlström, G.
1993 *The History of Ancient Palestine* (Minneapolis: Fortress).

Archi, A.
1980 "Les dieux d'Ebla au IIIe millenaire avant J.C. et les dieux d'Ugarit." *Les Annales Archeologiques Arabes Syriennes: Revue d'Archeologie et d'Histoire* 29-30: 167-72.
1993 "How a Pantheon forms. The cases of Hattian-hittite Anatolia and Ebla of the 3rd millennium B.C." Pp. 1-18 in *Religionsgeschichtliche Beziehungen zwischen Kleinasien, Nordsyrien und dem Alten Testament* (ed. B. Janowski *et al.*; OBO 129; Göttingen: Vandenhoeck und Ruprecht).

Axelsson, L. E.
1987 *The Lord rose up from Seir. Studies in the history and traditions of the Negev and southern Judah* (ConBOT 25; Lund: Gleerup).

Bartlett, J.
1978 "Yahweh and Qaus: Response to Martin Rose (*JSOT* 4 [1977] 28-34)." *JSOT* 5: 29-38.
1989 *Edom and the Edomites* (JSOTSup 77; Sheffield: JSOT Press).
1990 "From Edomites to Nabateans: the Problem of Continuity." *Aram* 2: 25-34.

Beit Arieh, I.
1991 "The Edomite Shrine at Ḥorvat Qitmit in the Judean Desert. Preliminary Excavation Report." *TA* 18:93-116.

Beit Arieh, I. and Cresson, B.
1985 "An Edomite Ostracon from Ḥorvat ʿUza." *TA* 12: 96-101.

Bienkowski, P.
1990 "Umm el-Biyara, Tawilan and Buseirah in Retrospect." *Levant* 16:91-109.
1992 "The Date of Sedentary Occupation in Edom: Evidence from Umm el-Biyara, Tawilan and Buseirah." Pp. 99-112 in *Early Edom and Moab. The Beginning of the Iron Age in Southern Jordan* (ed. P. Bienkowski; SAM 7; Sheffield: J. R. Collis).

Brown, J. P.
1993 "Archery in the Ancient World: 'Its Name is Life, its Work is Death.'" *BZ* 37: 26-42.

Caquot, A.
1958 Le dieu ʿAthtar et les textes des Ras Shamra." *Syria* 35: 45-60.

Caskel, W.
1958 "Die alten semitischen Gottheiten in Arabien." Pp. 95-118 in *Le antiche divinità semitiche* (ed. S. Moscati; Roma: Centro di studi semitici).

Cross, F. M.
1983 "The Epic Traditions of Early Israel: Epic Narrative and the Reconstruction of Early Israelite Institutions." Pp. 13-39 in *The Poet and the Historian. Essays in Literary and Historical Biblical Criticism* (ed. R. E. Friedman; Chico: Scholars Press).
1988 "Reuben, First Born of Jacob." *ZAW* Sup 100: 46-65.

Dahood, M. J.
1958 "Ancient Semitic Deities in Syria and Palestine." Pp. 65-94 in *Le antiche divinità semitiche* (ed. S. Moscati; Roma: Centro di studi semitici).

Edelman, D. V.
1995 "Solomon's Adversaries Hadad, Rezon and Jeroboam: A Trio of 'Bad-Guy' Characters Illustrating the Theology of Immediate Retribution." Pp. 166–91 in *The Pitcher is Broken: Memorial Essays for Gösta W. Ahlström* (ed. L. Handy and S. W. Holloway; JSOTSup 190; Sheffield: JSOT Press).

Edens, C. and Bawden, G.
1989 "History of Taymāʾ and Hejazi Trade During the First Millennium B.C." *JESHO* 32: 48-103.

Ephʿal, I.
1982 *The Ancient Arabs. Nomads on the Borders of the Fertile Crescent, 9th-5th Centuries B.C.* (Jerusalem: Magnes Press).

Finkelstein, I.
1988 "Arabian Trade and Socio-Political Conditions in the Negev in the Twelfth-Eleventh Centuries B.C.E." *JNES* 47: 241-52.

Fulco, W. J.
1976 *The Canaanite God Rešep* (AOS 8; New Haven: American Oriental Society).

Giveon, R.
1971 *Les bédouins shosou des documents égyptiens* (Leiden: E. J. Brill).

Glueck, N.
1965 *Deities and Dolphins* (New York: Farrer, Straus and Giroux).

Graf, D.
1990 "The Origin of the Nabateans." *ARAM* 2: 45-75.

Gray, J.
1949 "The Desert God ʿAttar in the Literature and Religion of Canaan." *JNES* 8: 72-83.

Hammond, P.
1973 *The Nabataeans—Their History, Culture and Archaeology* (Gothenburg: P. Åströms).

Healey, J.
1989 "Were the Nabataeans Arabs?" *ARAM* 1: 38-44.

Kammerer, A.
1929 *Pétra et la Nabatène* (Paris: P. Geuthner).

Klingbeil, G. A.
1992 "The Onomasticon of the Aramaic Inscriptions of Syria-Palestine during the Persian Period." *JNSL* 18: 67-94.

Knauf, E. A.
1984A "Qaus." *UF* 16: 93-95.
1984B "Qaus in Ägypten." *GM* 73: 33-36.
1985A "Alter und Herkunft der edomitischen Königsliste Gen. 36,31-39." *ZAW* 97: 243-53.
1985B *Ismael. Untersuchungen zur Geschichte Palästinas und Nordarabiens im 1. Jahrtausend v. Chr.* (Wiesbaden: Otto Harrassowitz).
1988A *Midian. Untersuchungen zur Geschichte Palästinas und Nordarabiens am Ende des 2. Jahrtausends v. Chr.* (Wiesbaden: Otto Harrassowitz).
1988B "Supplementa Ismaelitica 13. Edom und Arabien." *BN* 45: 62-81.

Kraeling, C. H.
1938 *Gerasa. City of the Decapolis* (New Haven: ASOR).

Lemaire, A.
1988 "Hadad l'Edomite ou Hadad l'Araméen?" *BN* 43: 14-18.

Meshel, Z.
1978 *Kuntillet Ajrud. A Religious Centre from the Time of the Judaean Monarchy on the Border of Sinai* (cat. no. 175; Jerusalem: Israel Museum).

Mettinger, T. N. D.
1990 "The Elusive Essence. Yahweh, El and Baal and the Distinctiveness of Israelite Faith." Pp. 393-417 in *Die Hebräische Bibel und ihre zweifach Nachgeschichte. Festschrift für Rolf Rendtorff* (ed. E. Blum, *et al.*; Neukirchen-Vluyn: Neukirchener Verlag).

Milik, J. T.
1958 Nouvelles inscriptions nabatéenes." *Syria* 35: 227-51.
1960 "Notes d'épigraphie orientale: 2. A propos du dieu édomite Qôs." *Syria* 37: 95-96.

Müller, H. P.
1980 "Religionsgeschichtliche Beobachtungen zu den Texten von Ebla." *ZDPV* 96: 1-19.

Na'aman, N.
1992 "Israel, Edom and Egypt in the 10th Century B.C.E." *TA* 19: 71-93.

Oded, B.
1971 "Egyptian References to the Edomite Deity Qaus." *AUSS* 9: 47-50.

Rose, M.
1977 "Yahweh in Israel-Qaus in Edom?" *JSOT* 4: 28-34.

Ryckmans, J.
1989 "Le Panthéon de l'Arabie du Sud préislamique. Etat des problèmes et brève synthèse." *RHR* 206: 151-69.

Savignac, R.
1937 "Le dieu nabatéen de La'aban et son temple." *RB* 46: 401-16.

Simons, J. J.
1937 *Handbook for the Study of Egyptian Topographical Lists Relating to Western Asia* (Leiden: E. J. Brill).

Staubli, T.
1991 *Das Image der Nomaden im Alten Israel und der Ikonographie seiner sesshaften Nachbarn* (OBO 107; Göttingen: Vandenhoeck und Ruprecht).

Stieglitz, R.
1990 "Ebla and the Gods of Canaan." Pp. 79-89 in *Eblaitica: Essays on the Ebla Archives and Eblaite Language* (vol 2; ed. C. H. Gordon, G. Rendsburg; Winona Lake: Eisenbrauns).

Teixidor, J.
1972 "Bulletin d'épigraphie sémitique 1972." *Syria* 49:419-20.

Tigay, J.
1986 *You Shall Have No Other Gods. Israelite Religion in the Light of Hebrew Inscriptions* (HSM 31; Atlanta: Scholars Press).

Vincent, L. H.
1940 "Le dieu Saint Paqeidas à Gérasa." *RB* 49: 98-129.

Vriezen, T.
1965 "The Edomitic Deity Qaus." *OTS* 14: 330-53.

Weinfeld, M.
1984 "Kuntillet Ajrud inscriptions and their significance." *SEL* 1: 121-30.

Younker, R.
1985 "Israel, Judah, and Ammon and the Motifs on the Baalis Seal from Tell el-ʿUmeiri." *BA* 48: 173-80.

Zayadine, F.
1990 "The Pantheon of the Nabataean Inscriptions in Egypt and the Sinai." *ARAM* 2: 151-74.

THE EDOMITE DIALECT AND SCRIPT: A REVIEW OF THE EVIDENCE[1]

David S. Vanderhooft

Introduction

While the history and archaeology of the Edomites in the Iron Age (and the Idumeans after that) undergo clarification and refinement, the language of the Edomites remains obscure. The paucity of written materials limits efforts to understand it and renders even a schematic grammar impossible. The present essay has two aims: to review the evidence for the existence of an Edomite dialect and to isolate idiosyncratic characteristics of the script associated with "Edomite" texts. The temporal frame, dictated by the dates of the extant inscriptions, is roughly the 7th and 6th centuries BCE; later evidence is brought in occasionally where this may prove helpful.[2] The few diagnostic linguistic features evident in the texts justify the inclusion of Edomite in the Canaanite linguistic group. The question whether Edomite is an independent dialect remains more uncertain.[3]

Several recent studies attempt to classify Edomite within the northwest Semitic language group on the basis of the epigraphic data; the most important for present purposes are those of F. Israel[4] and W. R. Garr.[5] In his 1979 study, Israel catalogued the corpus of possible

[1]Research for the present study was conducted with the help of a Social Sciences and Humanities Research Council of Canada doctoral fellowship. I am grateful for the advice offered by Professors Frank Moore Cross, Jo Ann Hackett, and John Huehnergard. Of course, they bear no responsibility for any errors.

[2]I follow F. Israel ("Supplementum Idumeum," *Rivista biblica italiana* 35 [1987] 346–47) in recognizing two phases when speaking of the history of the dialect (without prejudice at this point as to the independent status of the dialect): the first phase is contemporary with the existence of the Edomite kingdom (8th through 6th centuries) and is the focus of the present discussion; the second (5th through 2nd centuries) is more difficult to categorize and is attested only indirectly in Aramaic and Greek epigraphs. The second phase generally falls outside the scope of the present study except where comparative materials can illuminate the earlier period.

[3]The classification of the Semitic languages adopted here is that of J. Huehnergard, "Languages (Introductory)," *ABD* 4.155–70.

[4]"Miscellenea Idumea," *Rivista biblica italiana* 27 (1979) 171–205; idem, "Supplementum Idumeum," 337–56.

[5]*Dialect Geography of Syria-Palestine, 1000–586 B.C.E.* (Philadelphia: University of Pennsylvania Press, 1985).

Edomite texts and, based on a few diagnostic phonological and morphological features, concluded that it is "un dialetto semitico nordoccidentale di tipo cananeo" and that it may be considered "conservative."[6] At the same time, J. Naveh published a collection of Aramaic ostraca from Beer–sheba, many of which possess names with the theophoric element Qaus/Qos, the Edomite national deity. Naveh also characterized Edomite as a dialect with Canaanite linguistic features.[7] Garr's reconstruction of a Syro-Palestinian dialect geography in the first half of the first millennium BCE includes evidence for Edomite derived primarily from Israel's 1979 study. He ultimately places Edomite closest to Hebrew and Moabite on the dialect continuum. In 1987 Israel augmented his first study with evidence from the Ḥorvat ʿUza ostracon.[8] Based on the ostracon's verbal morphology, the existence of the prefixed definite article *h–* (already known), and the use of the relative pronoun *ʾšr,* he seconded Garr's view of the position of Edomite relative to Hebrew and Moabite.[9] None of the above conclusions require fundamental revision. It remains to analyze the evidence for the existence of an independent Edomite dialect, taking into account the Ḥorvat ʿUza ostracon, and to consider the nature of the extreme south cursive script of the period.

"Edomite"

Before surveying the actual corpus of texts, it is necessary to review the criteria for identifying an inscription as Edomite. The three primary criteria are: provenance, the appearance either independently or in personal names (PNs) of the divine name (DN) Qaus/Qôs, and paleography. None is sufficient alone, and strictly speaking, as Huehnergard has argued, none is linguistic.[10]

Only inscriptions from the Edomite heartland, including Buseirah, Umm el–Biyara and Tawilan, were likely composed in a local dialect. The texts known from these sites, however, are very brief or fragmentary and include almost exclusively proper names, in a few cases titles or commodities. Since there are inherent difficulties in using proper names as sources for the grammar of a dialect (and the onomasticon is

---

[6]Israel, "Miscellanea Idumea," 180–85. His characterization of the dialect as conservative should be abandoned in view of the evidence. This will be discussed below.

[7]"The Aramaic Ostraca from Beer–Sheba (Seasons 1971–1976)," *TA* 6 (1979) 194.

[8]I. Beit Arieh and B. Cresson, "An Edomite Ostracon from Ḥorvat ʿUza," *TA* 12 (1985) 96–101.

[9]Israel, "Supplementum Idumeum," 346.

[10]J. Huehnergard, Review of Garr, *Dialect Geography, JBL* 106 (1987) 531.

comparatively small anyway), texts from Edom proper are of little linguistic value. The language at sites adjacent to the Edomite heartland, which may or may not have been directly influenced by Edom (e.g., the southern Negeb of Israel[11]), cannot definitely be identified as Edomite, not even in the early 6th century. Inscriptions from these regions can only be identified as Edomite on the basis of the other criteria, as with the Tell el-Kheleifeh and Ḥorvat ʿUza epigraphs (see below). The situation is analogous to that of the Hebrew Yavneh-Yam letter: the status of Meṣad Ḥashavyahu as part of the Judahite kingdom in the late 7th century is in doubt,[12] but the presence of at least some Judahites and a Hebrew letter (and thus scribe) is not. The unquestioned presence of Edomites in the eastern Negeb during the late Iron Age says nothing, then, about the primary local dialect.

The second criterion is the onomasticon. The inclusion in an epigraph of the DN Qaus/Qos or a PN containing that theophoric element is a possible but not definite indication of the dialect of the inscription. Many names containing the element Qos have appeared in Akkadian, Aramaic and other inscriptions.[13]

Paleography is the third criterion, though again problematic. Naveh has done pioneering work in isolating distinctive elements of the Edomite script,[14] and the appearance of the Ḥorvat ʿUza ostracon has further clarified distinctive aspects of the cursive. It is likely that the south Transjordanian scripts diverged from the Hebrew, with which they were initially identical, about 700 BCE.[15] After this divergence, however, the influence of the Aramaic scripts in these regions makes clear differentiation of the local script from the Aramaic problematic.

---

[11]For the view that Edom directly controlled or annexed parts of Judah adjacent to the ʿArabah early in the 6th century, see I. Beit Arieh and B. Cresson, "Ḥorvat ʿUza: A Fortified Outpost on the Eastern Negev Border," *BA* 54 (1991) 134; for another recent interpretation of the Edomite presence in this region in the late 7th and 6th centuries, see I. Finkelstein, "*Ḥorvat Qiṭmīt* and the Southern Trade in the Late Iron Age II," *ZDPV* 108 (1992) 156–70.

[12]N. Naʾaman, "The Kingdom of Judah under Josiah," *TA* 18 (1991) 3–71.

[13]For convenient catalogues of the known Qos names, see Israel, "Miscellenea Idumea"; "Supplementum Idumeum."

[14]J. Naveh, "The Scripts of Two Ostraca from Elath," *BASOR* 183 (1966) 27–30. See earlier, W. F. Albright, "Ostracon No. 6043 from Ezion-Geber," *BASOR* 82 (1941) 11–15. Glueck accepts the judgments of Naveh ("Tell el-Kheleifeh Inscriptions," *Near Eastern Studies in Honor of W. F. Albright* [ed. Hans Goedicke; Baltimore: Johns Hopkins, 1971] 225–42), as does L. Herr in the main (*The Scripts of Ancient Northwest Semitic Seals* [HSM 18; Missoula: Scholars, 1978] 161; idem, "The Formal Scripts of Iron Age Transjordan," *BASOR* 238 [1980] 21–34).

[15]Naveh, "The Scripts of Two Ostraca," 28–30; idem, *The Early History of the Alphabet* (Jerusalem: Magnes, 1982) 100–105; idem, "Aramaic Script," *ABD* 1.342–45.

The mere presence of one or another of these three criteria thus cannot confirm an inscription as Edomite. Still, some inscriptions do possess them in permutations that disqualify the texts as Hebrew, Ammonite, Phoenician or Aramaic. Therefore, though the linguist must recognize the tenuousness and nonlinguistic nature of the criteria for establishing the database, it is still useful to employ the historical designation "Edomite" for this group of inscriptions. Whether the texts finally provide enough linguistic data to isolate a dialect, though, is a question that must be posed anew.

Texts

The following texts have been considered Edomite by at least one scholar.[16] My discussion will focus on the material readings and the criteria for identifying particular texts as Edomite.

I. Ostraca

1. Milik reads an ostracon excavated by C. M. Bennett at Umm el–Biyara as follows:

šmn . *ṙ*[
mʿdṙ . *m*[
bd . ooo . *ḃn* o[[17]

Milik's reading is based on infrared photos and so cannot be checked against the published plate, in which some of the letters identified by him are not legible. Based on the photograph, I tentatively propose the following reading:

šmn · *r*[
mʿr[..] *n*[
br · *ḃ*[.] *ṫ*[

---

[16]For lists of texts considered Edomite, see especially Glueck ("Tell el–Kheleifeh Inscriptions"), though not all of his texts are Edomite; E. Puech, "Documents épigraphiques de Buseirah," *Levant* 9 (1977) 11–20; Herr, *Scripts of Ancient Northwest Semitic Seals,* 161–70; Israel, "Miscellanea Idumea"; J. Bartlett (*Edom and the Edomites,* [JSOT Sup 77; Sheffield: Academic, 1989] 209–228), who discusses "inscriptions from Edom," though not all are from Edom, nor are they all Edomite. See also A. Lemaire, "Epigraphy, Transjordanian," *ABD* 2.563–5 and R. A. DiVito, "The Tell el–Kheleifeh Inscriptions," *Nelson Glueck's 1938–1940 Excavations at Tell el–Kheleifeh: A Reappraisal* (ed. by G. D. Pratico; ASOR Archaeological Reports 3; Atlanta: Scholars, 1993) 51-63.

[17]Communication in C. M. Bennett, "Fouilles d'Umm El–Biyara," *RB* 73 (1966) 399, pl. XXIIa.

If the second word of the first line should be completed *rḥṣ*, it would be identical to the Hebrew designation for virgin oil. The second line is unclear; even if Milik's reading is correct it is uncertain whether the interpretation *m(n)* plus geographical name (GN) is valid. His reading *bd* in the third line is doubtful. The second letter is identical to the *reš* of the first line. This is probably the Aramaic term *br*, "son," and specifies the sender or recipient of the oil. The reading *bn* in the last line is unclear at best, and there may be traces of a *taw* following.

Bennett classifies the letter forms of the ostracon as "phéniciens semi-cursifs" and dates them to the 7th century. The archaeological context makes the date likely, but the script is Aramaic cursive and not Phoenician. The open *ʿayin* is unknown before the 5th century in the Phoenician cursive, and *reš* (or *dalet* for that matter) similarly does not open in the Phoenician cursive before the 5th, and even then it does not open on top.[18] The double looped head of *mem* is unknown in the Phoenician sequence, but it is characteristic of the Aramaic and other Transjordanian scripts. Provenance, then, is the only evidence for labelling the ostracon Edomite, for neither the legible words nor the script proves the ostracon is anything other than Aramaic.

2. Puech published a fragmentary ostracon from Buseirah (registry no. 816) that preserves five letters:

] *ḣkrkb* [?[19]

He ascribes it tentatively to about 700 BCE. The meaning of the word is obscure. Puech suggests this might be the same as Biblical *krkb*, a quadriliteral root that designates the "border" or "rim" of an altar (Exod 27:5; 38:4), here perhaps with the prefixed definite article. At the suggestion of A. Malamat, Bartlett wondered whether the word might be *kdkd*, a precious stone associated with Edom in Ezek 27:16 and also attested in Isa 54:12.[20] Puech's reading is to be preferred, for if *kdkd* is correct, *dalet* possesses an impossibly long downstroke. It exhibits such length only in the Aramaic cursive, where the head is, however, open. Puech compares the script with that of the Deir ʿAlla plaster inscription from about the early 7th century, which is acceptable.[21]

---

[18]See, for example, pls. VII–XI in J. B. Peckham, *The Development of the Late Phoenician Scripts* (Cambridge: Harvard University, 1968) 104–13.

[19]Puech, "Documents épigraphiques," 17, Pl. V-B.

[20]Bartlett, *Edom and the Edomites*, 216.

[21]J. Hoftijzer and G. van der Kooij, *Aramaic Texts from Deir ʿAlla* (DMOA; Leiden: E. J. Brill, 1976); on the paleography, see especially Jo Ann Hackett, *The Balaam Text from Deir ʿAllā* (HSM 31; Chico: Scholars, 1984) 9–19.

3. Another fragmentary ostracon from Buseirah preserves a few letters, which Puech reads as follows:

]*n kd/r 1* (?) (symbole).[22]

Apparently the ostracon preserves notice of a shipment of produce. Puech dates it about 700 BCE. The text is too badly preserved to allow further comment.

4. The most significant addition to the corpus of ostraca is the Ḥorvat ʿUza ostracon, dated stratigraphically to the late 7th or early 6th century. The following reading was proposed by the publishers:

1.	*ʾm̊r̊ · lmlk · ʾmr · lblbl ·*	(Thus) said Lumalak: Say to Blbl
2.	*hšlm · ʾt · whbrktk*	Are you well? I bless you
3.	*lqws · wʿt · tn · ʾt hʾkl*	by Qos. And now give the food (grain)
4.	*ʾšr · ʿmd · ʾḥʾmh [ ]*	that Aḥiʾma/o ...
5.	*whrm ʿ[z]ʾl · ʿl mż[bḥ (?) ...]*	And may U[z]iel lift [it] up upon (the altar?)
6.	*[ ] ḥmr · hʾkl*[23]	[lest] the food become leavened (?)

The reading of the first three lines is relatively sure, and the beginnings of lines 4 and 5 are clear. I suggest the following reading, historical vocalization, and translation:[24]

1.	*ʾm̊r · lmlk̇ · ʾmr · lblbl ·*	ʾimr Limilk[25] ʾi/umur la–Blbl
2.	*hšlm · ʾt · whbrktk*	haš–šalōm ʾatt wa–hibriktī–kā[26]
3.	*lqws · wʿt · tn · ʾt · hʾkl*	la–Qaws wa–ʿatt[27] tin ʾit ha–ʾukl
4.	*ʾšr · ʿmd · ʾḥ̊ʾmh · w[..*	ʾašr ʿimmad[28] ʾAḥi–ʾim–ô[29]

[22]Puech, "Documents épigraphiques," 20.

[23]Beit Arieh and Cresson, "An Edomite Ostracon," 97; see also Israel, "Supplementum Idumeum," 339–42, and W. Zwickel, "Das 'edomitischen' Ostrakon aus Ḫirbet Ġazza (Ḥorvat ʿUza)," *BN* 41 (1988) 36–40.

[24]Based on the published photograph alone. I have not had the opportunity to examine the ostracon.

[25]For names of the type *l*+ DN, see M. Noth, *Die Israelitischen Personennamen im Rahmen der gemeinsemitischen Namengebung* (Stuttgart: Kohlhammer, 1928) 153 and J. K. Stark, *Personal Names in the Palmyrene Inscriptions* (Oxford: Clarendon, 1971) 29, 93. Examples include: *lʾl, lšmš, lrmn, lmklʾ*.

[26]I concur with the editors in reading the otherwise unattested causative of *brk*. This formula (with the *piʿēl* of *brk*) is well attested in NWS epistolography. Zwickel proposes reading the *he* as interrogative, but this destroys the formula and produces an awkward phrase at best. On the possible short form of the suffix, see F. M. Cross and D. N. Freedman, *Early Hebrew Orthography* (AOS 36; New Haven: American Oriental Society, 1952) 65–67. On the two *i*–class vowels of the causative suffix conjugation, see J. Huehnergard, "Historical Phonology and the Hebrew Piel," *Linguistics and Biblical Hebrew* (ed. Walter Bodine; Winona Lake: Eisenbrauns, 1993).

[27]On this form, which is extremely common in Hebrew epistolography, see Cross and Freedman, *Early Hebrew Orthography*, 52–3.

[28]Although it would represent another lexical peculiarity, this form could perhaps be taken as the absolute form of the preposition, related to the inflected Hebrew form

5. *whrm* ʿ*[..]l*· ʿ*lmż[...* wa–hirim PN ʿal miz[biḥ ..
6. ʿ*mṙ* · *h*ʾ*kl* ʿumr ha–ʾukl[30]

1. Word of Limilk, say to Blbl,
2. Are you well? I bless you
3. by Qos. Now then, deliver the grain
4. which is in the possession of ʾAḥiʾimo and[?
5. and [PN] will offer upon the al[tar ..
6. a sheaf of grain.

Since Ḥorvat ʿUza is in the eastern Negeb of Judah provenance does not prove that the text is Edomite. The editors instead point to two of the other three criteria outlined above to support the ascription: presence of the DN Qaus/Qos and paleography. Certainly, the invocation of a blessing by the Edomite deity suggests an Edomite sender and recipient.

The cursive script is idiosyncratic and is systematically reviewed below in conjunction with ostracon 6043 from Tell el–Kheleifeh.

5. A number of ostraca were excavated at Tell el–Kheleifeh, most containing lists of names or commodities and all dating from the 7th century and later.[31] Provenance in many cases is the only indication that they might be Edomite. The majority are clearly Aramaic or Phoenician. One, registry number 6043, has received considerable attention. It belongs to Level IV and thus dates, according to Glueck, to the 7th–6th centuries. Both the script and the onomasticon suggest the possibility that the text is Edomite. The beginnings of ten lines of text are preserved. The following represents Glueck's reading:

ʿ*immādī.* F. M. Cross reads ʿ*immādî* and emends the text by prefixing *lamed* to the following PN, though it should be noted that the text is difficult to read at this point anyway. I am grateful to Prof. Cross for sharing his reading of the ostracon, which is to appear in an essay by him titled, "A papyrus recording a Divine legal decision: the root *rḥq* in Biblical and Near Eastern legal usage," for the M. Haran volume of *Eretz Israel* . A suggestion similar to mine was recorded by H. Misgav ("Two Notes on the Ostracon from Ḥorvat ʿUza," *IEJ* 40 [1990] 216).

[29]"His mother's brother." The name is known from a Hebrew seal of the 7th century, *ʾḥʾmh bn yqmyhw* (P. Bordreuil and A. Lemaire, "Noveaux sceaux hébreux, araméens, et ammonites," *Semitica* 26 [1976] 48, pl. IV:8) and also from the late Iron Age hoard of bullae from Jerusalem, *lpšḥr bn ʾḥʾmh* (N. Avigad, *Hebrew Bullae From the Time of Jeremiah* [Jerusalem: Israel Exploration Society, 1986] 97, no. 151). The final *he* is a *mater* for the third masculine singular possessive suffix.

[30]Cross suggests the following reading after *ʾḥʾmh*: *y*ʿ*l / whrm šʾl* ʿ*lmz[bḥ . qw]s /* ʿ*mr hʾkl*, "let Saul bring up and offer on Qos's altar a sheaf of grain." I am unable to detect the traces of *samek* at the end of line 5, but the reading ʿ*mr hʾkl*, "sheaf of grain," is superior to the problematic *ḥmr hʾkl* of the editors. Given the reading *whrm* ... ʿ*lmz*[, and the common usage of *hrym* in biblical Hebrew in connection with offerings, *mz*[*bḥ*] seems likely.

[31]Glueck, "Tell el–Kheleifeh Inscriptions" and DiVito, "Inscriptions."

1. *rʾl*
2. *bdqw(s)*
3. *šlm*
4. *qwsb(nh)*
5. *pgʿqws*
6. *nʿm*
7. *škk*
8. *rpʾ/h*
9. *pgʿq(w)s*
10. *qwsny*[32]

On this reading, five of the ten names preserve the theophoric element *qws*. Naveh has argued that the script should be considered Edomite.[33] This observation can now be taken further based on comparison with the Ḥorvat ʿUza ostracon. I propose the following reading of ostracon 6043 from Kheleifeh. A discussion of the cursive script follows the summary of the ostraca.

1. *ʿdʾl̇*[34]
2. *brq[ws?*[35]
3. *šlm*
4. *q̇wsb[nh?*
5. *ṣdqẇ[.*
6. *[.]ʿm*
7. *[.]kk*
8. *rpʾ*
9. *ḥdq[ws]*[36]
10. *qwsny* or *qwss[..*

6. Glueck recognized two letters, *ḥm*, on another ostracon from Tell el-Kheleifeh and thought it to be Edomite.[37] The sherd came from the debris of Level V and was dated to the 5th–4th centuries. DiVito, following a suggestion of F. M. Cross, argues that the script is actually

[32]Glueck, "Tell el-Kheleifeh Inscriptions," 229. Earlier proposals are tabulated by Bartlett (*Edom and the Edomites*, 219). The best photo of the ostracon is available in G. D. Pratico, ed., *Nelson Glueck's 1938–1940 Excavations at Tell el-Kheleifeh: A Reappraisal* (ASOR Archaeological Reports 3; Atlanta: Scholars, 1993) pl. 82.

[33]"The Scripts of Two Ostraca," 14.

[34]*ʿAdīʾel*, "an ornament is El," or *ʿIdīʾel*, "my witness is El." Three persons are so named in the Bible (1 Chr 4:36; 9:12; 27:25), and the name is attested on two seals, the second of which is given below as a possible Edomite example (II.10).

[35]The name is attested in Ezra 2:53//Neh 7:55 and might also be present in ostracon 37 from Beer-sheba (Naveh, "Aramaic Ostraca," 188, pl. 27); see also Israel, "Supplementum Idumeum," 188, n. 126.

[36]*Ḥadīqaus*, "my joy is Qos." Names based on the verbal root *ḥdy* are known in the Bible: *yaḥdîʾēl* (1 Chr 5:24) and *yeḥdĕyāhû* (1 Chr 24:20; 27:30). An early Phoenician seal bears the related hypocoristicon *ḥdy* (see most recently, P. Bordreuil, *Catalogue des sceaux ouest-sémitiques inscrits* [Paris: Bibliotèque nationale, 1986] 19–20, no. 1).

[37]"Tell el-Kheleifeh Inscriptions," 237.

Aramaic.[38] The *ḥet,* however, is comparable to the first letter of the ninth line of ostracon 6043 from Tell el-Kheleifeh, so it could be placed in the earlier Edomite tradition.

7. Naveh has classified a lone ostracon from Tel ʿAroer as Edomite. He does not offer a reading for the poorly preserved ostracon, but argues that the identifiable letters exhibit a mixture of Hebrew and Aramaic features.[39] He is correct that the *ʾalep* is not of the "star" type characteristic of the Aramaic sequence from the mid–7th century onward. It is closer to the form known from the Ḥorvat ʿUza ostracon. On the other hand, the *he* and especially the *mem* without a right "shoulder" are good Aramaic or Transjordanian forms, while the *dalet,* if correctly identified, is not like that of ostraca 4 and 5 above. Rather than suggest a mixture of Hebrew and Aramaic influence, I would place the script within the general Transjordanian sequence of the 7th–6th centuries, but not within the Edomite cursive tradition as described below.

The discernible letters of the ostracon are:

...] *r/d*[.] *h*[
...] *ʾšṡ*[
..ʿ] *dʿlʾ*[40] [.
...] *slm* [

The Cursive Script

Based principally on the Ḥorvat ʿUza ostracon and ostracon 6043 from Tell el-Kheleifeh, a number of new suggestions can be made about the nature of the extreme southern cursive script (see below, figure 1). The following evidence permits the designation "Edomite" to be retained for these texts and for the script: the appeal to Qos for blessing in the ʿUza ostracon, the two (at least) PNs with the theophoric element Qos in ostracon 6043, and provenance.

ʾAlep in the Kheleifeh ostracon apparently is drawn in three strokes: a left-leaning downstroke, an upper crossbar breaking through the downstroke to the left, and a lower crossbar that is parallel to the upper but that does not break through the downstroke. *ʾAlep* in the Ḥorvat ʿUza ostracon likewise has a left-leaning downstroke, but in the clear

---

[38] DiVito, "Inscriptions," 60.

[39] "Published and Unpublished Aramaic Ostraca," *ʿAtiqot* English Series 17 (1985) 120, no. 13, pl. XX.

[40] Possibly the Aramaic adverb *ʿēllā,* with the meanings "above" (Dan 6:3) and "concerning (it)" (A. Cowley, ed., *Aramaic Papyri of the Fifth Century B.C.* [Osnabrück: Otto Zeller, 1967] 13:3,10; 28:9). If the previous letter is *dalet,* we might restore [ʿ]*d ʿlʾ* with the sense "upwards" (e.g., Cowley, *Aramaic Papyri,* 5:5,11).

examples, the crossbars form a horizontal "V" meeting at the downstroke with the point to its left. Neither form resembles the so-called "star" *ʾalep* typical of the contemporary Aramaic cursive or the Ammonite ostracon IV from Hesban of the late 7th century.[41] The nearest parallels to the Ḥorvat ʿUza examples may be seen in the early 7th century Deir ʿAlla plaster inscription[42] and the early 6th century Ammonite ostracon from Tell el-Mazar in Jordan.[43] The contemporary cursive Hebrew form, seen, for example, in the Arad and Lachish letters, is also similar to the ʿUza examples.[44]

Bet is virtually identical in both ostraca. It has an open, rounded head and a downstroke that curves to the left with a quite distinct foot. The form is very close to the Aramaic cursive. Hesban ostracon IV and the Tell el-Mazar ostracon have similar forms, but without a pronounced foot. In the Deir ʿAlla plaster inscription *bet* is closed, as it is the Hebrew cursive.

Dalet is of the greatest significance. The curious form, which resembles a lower case "d" tilted to the right about 45°, was recognized in the Ḥorvat ʿUza ostracon by the publishers, though they failed to explain it. A comparable example was noticed by Puech in a seal from Buseirah (below II.2), and he pointed out that the *Qwsʿnl ʿbd hmlk* seal impressions from Kheleifeh (below II.7) possess the same form.[45] F. Israel and R. DiVito followed Puech's lead. Israel noticed this form in another seal.[46] DiVito seconded Puech's identification of *dalet* in the Qwsʿnl impressions and suggested this was the typical Edomite lapidary form.

---

[41]For the Aramaic see, e.g., the Saqqarah papyrus (A. Dupont-Sommer, "Un papyrus araméen d'époque saïte découvert à Saqqarah," *Semitica* 1 [1948] 43–68); several good photos are available in B. Porten, "The Identity of King Adon," *BA* 44 (1981) 36–52. On the paleography of Hesban ostracon IV, see F. M. Cross, "Ammonite Ostraca from Heshbon. Heshbon Ostraca IV–VIII," *AUSS* 13 (1975) 14–17.

[42]Hoftijzer and van der Kooij, *Aramaic Texts*; Ḥackett, *The Balaam Text from Deir ʿAllā*, 10–11.

[43]K. Yassine and J. Teixidor, "Ammonite and Aramaic Inscriptions from Tell El-Mazār in Jordan," *BASOR* 264 (1986) 47, fig. 4. This form may be slightly nearer the Aramaic "star" form. See especially the comments of Cross, "Ammonite Ostraca from Heshbon," 14.

[44]Y. Aharoni, *Arad Inscriptions* (Jerusalem: Israel Exploration Society, 1981); H. Torczyner, *The Lachish Letters. Lachish 1* (London: Oxford University Press, 1938).

[45]He writes: "Ce détail suggèrerait-il une même école de scribes à l'origine des sceaux des ministres des rois d'Edom?" ("Documents épigraphiques," 12–13, and n.9). Lemaire ("Epigraphy, Transjordanian," 564) seems to follow Puech and notes the peculiarity of *dalet*, but his suggestion that this is in order to differentiate *dalet* and *reš* is not likely, since *reš* has an open head, upright stance, and a long downstroke in the Edomite examples.

[46]"Supplementum Idumeum," 338. He did not recognize the form in the cursive, though, and suggested the form in the ʿUza ostracon might be *reš*.

He wondered whether the lapidary form might not be behind the ʿUza example.[47] The problem is now solved by the new reading of ostracon 6043 from Kheleifeh proposed above. Three examples of the curious *dalet* had not been recognized previously; the second letter in each of lines 1, 5 and 9 is *dalet.* These match the Ḥorvat ʿUza example exactly. Coincidentally, the name *ʿAdīʾel* in the first line of the Kheleifeh ostracon is known from a seal in which the *dalet,* while triangular, exhibits the same breakthrough of the lower shaft upward that is seen in our ostraca.[48] The seal has been classified variously as Ammonite or Moabite by scholars.[49] The unusual *yod* notwithstanding (another Edomite trait?), nothing in the script of this seal rules out its identification as Edomite. It is added below to the corpus of Edomite seals (II.10). In the Kheleifeh ostracon *dalet* should also be read in lines 5 and 9. It should be added that the Aramaic *dalet* of this period possesses an elongated downstroke, is open, and has a vertical stance; *dalet* in the Ammonite Tell el-Mazar ostracon is similar.[50] The Deir ʿAlla plaster inscription and Hesban ostracon IV have *dalets* similar to the Aramaic, but they are closed. The cursive Hebrew is closed but exhibits breakthrough differently than the Edomite examples: the right shaft breaks through downward, and the upper part of the loop sometimes breaks through to the right. The form of *dalet* identified in the Edomite ostraca, then, is unattested in other scripts and is apparently indicative of both the lapidary and cursive Edomite traditions.

He in the ʿUza ostracon is unique. No exact parallels are known and the publishers suggest, plausibly, that this is a feature of the Edomite cursive. The form apparently is a simplification of the archaic type that possessed three horizontal bars, which are preserved in the Hebrew and Phoenician cursive traditions. It is somewhat akin to several examples from the earlier Deir ʿAlla inscription, where the lower two horizontal bars have been replaced by a separate wavy stroke.[51] The ʿUza form is further simplified, so that all three horizontal bars are transformed into

---

[47]DiVito, "Inscriptions," 54.

[48]The best photo is available in R. Hestrin and M. Dayagi-Mendels, *Inscribed Seals, First Temple Period—Hebrew, Ammonite, Moabite, Phoenician and Aramaic—From the Collections of the Israel Museum and the Israel Department of Antiquities and Museums* (Jerusalem: Israel Museum, 1979) 146, no. 116.

[49]Hestrin and Dayagi-Mendels read the first line *lmšʿ*, "belonging to Meshaʿ," and so classify it as Moabite (*Inscribed Seals,* 146, no. 116). Herr reads *lyšʿ*, which is more likely, but classifies the seal as Ammonite (*Scripts of Ancient Northwest Semitic Seals,* 73).

[50]Yassine and Teixidor, "Ammonite and Aramaic Inscriptions," 47, fig. 4 line 1.

[51]See, for example, Hoftijzer and van der Kooij, *Aramaic Texts,* pls. 1, 9.

a continuous "S"–shaped stroke. This development is not unexpected, but the particular form is very distinctive.

Waw is identical in the two texts and closely resembles that of the contemporary cursive Aramaic, represented, for example, in the Saqqarah papyrus. The more or less "L" shaped head may be slightly more archaic than the Aramaic form, in which the head is a shallow "cup."

Zayin in the ʿUza text is somewhat effaced but the reading is almost certain. It has the form of a lower case "z" rotated to the left about 45°. This "z"-shaped form was already replaced in the Aramaic sequence in the early 7th century by a simple diagonal stroke. The earlier Deir ʿAlla inscription possesses a form very similar to the ʿUza example, and this same form, though more nearly vertical, persists in the Ammonite seal script of the 7th–6th centuries.[52] The Hebrew *zayin* is very different, with its very long horizontals, short oblique, and tick on the lower right.

The first letter of the ninth line in the Kheleifeh ostracon is probably *ḥet*. On this basis I read *ḥdqws*, Ḥadīqaws, "my joy is Qos" (above n. 36). It is unclear whether the *ḥet* of the ʿUza ostracon possesses one or two bars, but in either case the right stroke seems to descend lower than the left, as in the Kheleifeh example. The *ḥet* of registry number 10,007 from Kheleifeh appears to be similar.[53] The closest parallels to this form of *ḥet* come from the Ammonite tradition: Hesban ostracon IV and the Ammonite ostracon from Tell el-Mazar also have single bar forms where the right downstroke is as long or longer than the left. The elongated right stroke is thus perhaps not unexpected in the Edomite sphere, and it is possible that this is the typical form of *ḥet* in the cursive. Of course, it is hazardous to suggest that this is an Edomite trait based on one clear example.

Kap in both ostraca possesses a long curved downstroke. In the Ḥorvat ʿUza text it also has a distinct foot, like *bet* and *mem* in the same inscription. The head of *kap* is made with two very short strokes that almost form a solid triangle to the left of the downstroke. This is similar to the Deir ʿAlla plaster inscription and Hesban ostracon IV. The contemporary Aramaic cursive, represented in the Saqqarah papyrus, also has this form.

Lamed is not diagnostically significant. In the Ḥorvat ʿUza ostracon it possesses a very short upward tick at its bottom, while none is discernible in the Kheleifeh text.

---

[52]See, e.g., Hestrin and Dayagi–Mendels, *Inscribed Seals*, 129, no. 102; Bordreuil, *Catalogue*, 72, no. 82; 73, no. 84.

[53]Pratico, *Excavations at Tell el–Kheleifeh*, pl. 83:C.

Mem was recognized already by Rosenthal as a characteristic form in the Moabite and Edomite scripts and Naveh has emphasized the point.[54] In the Kheleifeh text the wide head is apparently formed by two attached loops, and this is certainly the form in the ʿUza ostracon. The nearest parallels to this cursive form are found again in the earlier Deir ʿAlla inscription and the Ammonite ostraca of the 7th and 6th centuries. The head of the Aramaic cursive *mem* is different: it has a single horizontal stroke that attaches to the downstroke and a short vertical stroke bisecting the horizontal, as in the Saqqarah papyrus. The ostracon from ʿAroer (above I.7) also has this "Aramaic" form, suggesting that the ostracon is not Edomite.

Nun is diagnostically less significant than *mem* and offers no sound basis for typological comparison.

Samek is different in the two ostraca. The wavy-headed form of ostracon 6043 still bears some resemblance to the more archaic form with three separate horizontal strokes above the vertical. Once again it might be compared to the form in the Deir ʿAlla inscription.[55] This form does not seem to persist into the 6th century in the cursive traditions of any of the scripts. The form represented in the Ḥorvat ʿUza ostracon is much like the contemporary Ammonite and Aramaic cursive traditions: the three strokes of the older form have been simplified into a "Z" shape, from whose lower right a downstroke descends.[56]

ʿAyin is squared and always open on the top in the ostraca. It is closed in two Edomite seals that may date to the mid–7th century (below nos. II.2,3). In the Aramaic cursive *ʿayin* opens already by the early 7th century. In the Deir ʿAlla script it is closed, as it is in the late 7th century Hesban ostracon IV. In the Ammonite ostracon from Tell el-Mazar and Hesban ostracon XI, both probably of the early 6th century, *ʿayin* is open.[57] Earlier scholars identified several closed *ʿayins* in the Kheleifeh ostracon, but the reading proposed above interprets these as *dalets*. All examples of the Edomite cursive thus possess the open *ʿayin*.

---

[54]F. Rosenthal "The Script of Ostracon 6043," *BASOR* 85 (1942) 8–9; Naveh, "The Script of Two Ostraca," 29 and n. 24.

[55]E.g., Hoftijzer and van der Kooij, *Aramaic Texts*, pl. 13, v q.

[56]For the Aramaic, see the Saqqarah papyrus; the Ammonite cursive is only known from Hesban ostracon IV. The form is also common in the Aramaic lapidary of the 7th century, e.g., the second Neirab burial stele (G. A. Cooke, *Textbook of North Semitic Inscriptions* [Oxford: Clarendon, 1903] pl. VI), and the Assur clay tablets (M. Lidzbarski, *Altaramäische Urkunden aus Assur* [Wissenschaftliche Veröffentlichungen der Deutschen Orientgesellschaft 38; Leipzig: J. C. Hinrichs, 1921] nos. 1, 3).

[57]F. M. Cross, "Heshbon Ostracon XI," *AUSS* 13 (1976) 145–48.

Pe, attested only in the Kheleifeh ostracon, is not diagnostically significant.

Qop is clear only in the Kheleifeh ostracon where it possesses an "S"-shaped head. The same form emerges in the Aramaic cursive beginning in the mid-7th century and persists through the Persian period. In the Deir ʿAlla script, the ideal form appears to have two curved strokes joining the downstroke below its top; these strokes do not meet at the top as in the older Phoenician/Aramaic tradition, where the *qop* is formed with a circle bisected by the downstroke. In the Ammonite series, a *psi*-shaped example is known from the Siran bottle.[58] In the more conservative lapidary script used in Ammonite seals, two examples have closed tops, formed with two triangular or squared sides.[59] The examples in the Edomite seals all appear to be closed as well. Thus, in the cursive script, the Edomite *qop* appears to have developed in parallel with the Aramaic cursive and to have outstripped the lapidary forms, which remain closed.

Reš in our ostraca possesses an opened, curved head that joins the vertical downstroke slightly below its top. The downstroke typically leans slightly to the left but may be nearly vertical. The Aramaic cursive has this form already by the early 7th century. The Ammonite sequence, the Deir ʿAlla inscription, Hesban ostracon IV and the Siran bottle all have forms with closed heads. *Reš* in the Ammonite seals likewise remains closed through the first half of the 6th century. The early 6th century Ammonite cursive ostracon from Tell el–Mazar, however, possesses an open *reš*. The Edomite cursive, following the Aramaic, seems to develop the open *reš* before the Ammonite does.

Šin retains its classical "W" shape, penned with two separate "checks." This form remains essentially unchanged in all the national script traditions through the end of the 7th century. During the 6th century, however, there is a transition in both the Aramaic cursive and lapidary series from the classical form to a simplified one: a large "V" with a short oblique stroke that joins the left arm on the inside of the "V." Apparently, the Edomite series never adopts this Aramaic form.

Taw is attested only in the ʿUza ostracon. The elongated downstroke, also typical of the Ammonite inscriptions, originates with the earliest Aramaic sequence. This is in sharp contrast to the squat "X" type in the Hebrew tradition.

---

[58]H. O. Thompson and F. Zayadine, "The Tell Siran Inscription," *BASOR* 212 (1973) 5–11.

[59]Hestrin and Dayagi–Mendels, *Inscribed Seals,* 130, no. 103; Bordreuil, *Catalogue,* 66, no. 73.

On the whole, the cursive script of these ostraca finds its nearest parallels in the Ammonite and other Transjordanian series. Obvious influence from the Aramaic scripts can be seen in the open forms of *bet*, *ʿayin*, and *reš*, while *waw*, *samek* (in the ʿUza ostracon), "S"-topped *qop*, and *taw* are not different from the Aramaic. On the other hand, there is nothing in the script that is parallel to the distinctive characteristics of the late 7th and early 6th-century Hebrew cursive. Those letters that are similar to contemporary Hebrew forms, *kap, lamed, nun,* and *šin,* also are common to the Transjordanian series. Unique forms of *dalet* and *he* and distinctive forms of *ḥet* and perhaps *samek* (in ostracon 6043 from Kheleifeh) set this script apart from all others, however, and clarify at least some characteristics of the extreme southern, or Edomite, cursive. The script may safely be dated to the end of the 7th or early 6th centuries.

II. Seals and Seal Impressions

The corpus of Edomite seals is meager. They are subject to the same problems of identification as the ostraca and since many also lack provenance, even that criterion is often absent. I will again focus on material readings and paleography.

1. *qwsg*[br?] / *mlkʾ*[*dm* ?][60]

This seal impression comes from Umm el–Biyara. Scholars assume that the completion of the second line is *ʾdm*, "Edom," but it could just as well be a proper name such as *mlkʾl*, Malkīʾel. The script is perfectly acceptable within the Transjordanian series, contrary to the arguments of Herr.[61] The triangular headed *qop*, much more conservative than its cursive counterpart, has a reasonable parallel in an Ammonite seal of the 7th century.[62] *Waw*, while much like the Aramaic form, is also perfectly at home in the Transjordanian scripts of the 7th century, including the Edomite cursive.

2. *lmlkl* / *bʿʿbd* / *hmlk*[63] "Belonging to *Mlklbʿ*, servant of the king"

This seal from Buseirah possesses the typical Edomite *dalet*, and Puech already recognized its similarity to *dalet* in the Qwsʿnl impressions from Kheleifeh (above n.45). The closed *bet*s and *ʿayins* certainly suggest a date in the 7th century. Note that the lapidary *he* bears no resemblance to the cursive form of the ʿUza ostracon. Lemaire has argued that the name *mlklbʿ*, which remains unexplained, should be emended to *mlkbʿl*: in this argument, an illiterate engraver misplaced the

---

[60]Bennett, "Fouilles d'Umm El–Biyara," 399–401, pl. XXIIb.

[61]*Scripts of Ancient Northwest Semitic Seals,* 162–63.

[62]Bordreuil, *Catalogue,* 66, no. 73.

[63]Puech, "Documents épigraphiques," 12–13, pl. IV.

initial *lamed* to achieve symmetry.[64] This is possible, if not probable. One would not expect such a gratuitous error, however, in the seal of a servant of the king.

3. *šmʿʾl*[65]

This seal comes from Buseirah. The conservative lapidary script—closed *ʿayin*, upright *ʾalep* with the point of the crossbars meeting to the left of the downstroke—suggests a 7th century date. Names formed from the root *šmʿ* + DN are extremely common. The same name may be intended in an Ammonite seal that reads *lšmʿl b/n plṭw*, if the first name should be read *šmʿʾl*, as Bordreuil suggests.[66]

4. *ltw*[67]

The seal was excavated at Buseirah, but whether it is Edomite is open to doubt. The name is presumably not Semitic.[68] The script belongs to the 8th–7th centuries and appears more Ammonite than anything else: the "cross"-shaped *taw* and "Y"-shaped *waw*.[69]

5. *lbʿzrʾl / ʿbdybʿl*[70] "Belonging to Bi-ʿazr-ʾel (son of) ʿAbdî-baʿl"

The seal was purchased at Petra. Driver's original reading, given above, is still to be preferred. Bordreuil has recently suggested that the second line be read *ʿbd hbʿl*, and he is followed by Israel, who adds that this seal should be classified as Ammonite rather than Edomite.[71] While the *yod* is difficult, the letter is certainly not *he*. The Ammonite classification, however, is reasonable, if not entirely certain.

6. *lytm*[72] "Belonging to Yatom"

This signet ring was excavated at Tell el-Kheleifeh. Some have suggested a connection with the Judahite king Jotham, but this is speculative. It is a well attested Semitic name meaning "orphan."[73] The script fits broadly in the 7th century, and the *taw* should be compared to that in the *ltw* seal from Buseirah (above II.4).

---

[64]A. Lemaire, "Note on an Edomite Seal Impression from Buseirah," *Levant* 7 (1975) 18–19.

[65]G. L. Harding, "Some Objects from Transjordan," *PEQ* 69 (1937) 253–55.

[66]Bordreuil, *Catalogue*, 64, no. 70.

[67]Puech, "Documents épigraphiques," 18, pl. VI-C.

[68]For other possibilities, see Puech, "Documents épigraphiques," n. 43.

[69]Herr, *Seals of Northwest Semitic Seals*, 167.

[70]G. R. Driver, "Seals from ʿAmman and Petra," *QDAP* 11 (1944) 81–82, pl. XVIII.

[71]P. Bordreuil "Les sceaux des grandes personnages," *Le Monde de la Bible* 46 (1986) 45; Israel, "Supplementum Idumeum," 338–39.

[72]Initially published by N. Glueck ("The Third Season of Excavation at Tell el-Kheleifeh," *BASOR* 79 [1940] 13–15), it has been reedited with paleographic analysis by DiVito ("Inscriptions," 53, pl. 79).

[73]Noth, *Personennamen*, 231; for the same name in a Phoenician seal, see Hestrin and Dayagi-Mendels, "Inscribed Seals," 162, no. 128.

7. *lqwsʿnl / ʿbd hmlk*[74] "Belonging to Qosʿanal, servant of the king"

As many as 22 impressions of the same seal were excavated at Tell el-Kheleifeh. All are badly worn, but taken together they yield a certain reading. DiVito's paleographic discussion is sound, and a date for the impressions in the early 6th century is acceptable. He accepts Puech's identification of the unusual *dalet* (see above). The verbal element of Qosʿanal is still unexplained.

8. *lqwś[ʾ]*[75]

This seal was excavated at ʿAroer in the Judean Negeb. Although badly preserved, the *qop* appears closed with a very peculiar head, and the *samek* seems to preserve the three bars of the classical type. The *waw* is not fully preserved and may be engraved in reverse. The Edomite ascription is possible but tentative. A 7th-century date would dovetail with the stratigraphical context.[76]

9. *lmnḥmt / ʾšt gdmlk*[77] "Belonging to Menaḥemet, wife of Gaddi-melek"

This seal was acquired in Jerusalem in the 19th century and is known only through drawings. Israel noted that it possesses the unusual *dalet* that we have characterized as Edomite. This seems a weighty diagnostic trait. The other characteristics of the script are more advanced than the other Edomite seals: the "V"-shaped *šin* and the "X"-shaped *taw* would have to be placed in the 6th century. The *mem* fits well in the Edomite/Moabite tradition.[78]

10. *lyšʿ / ʿdʾl*[79] "Belonging to Yishaʿ (son of) ʿAdiʾel"

Although its provenance is unknown, the peculiar *dalet* of this seal is exactly paralleled in the Edomite script and is a sufficiently important trait to allow the seal to be included among the Edomite group. The *yod*, rotated to the left almost 90°, is difficult. The *šin* is more in line with the emerging "V"-shaped form of the 6th century Aramaic. The open *ʿayins* also fit well in the later Edomite lapidary sequence. A date in the early 6th century would be appropriate.[80]

---

[74]Originally published by N. Glueck ("The first campaign at Tell el-Kheleifeh [Ezion-Geber]," *BASOR* 71 [1938] 15); reedited with paleographic discussion and excellent photos by DiVito ("Inscriptions," 53–55, pls. 74–78).

[75]A. Biran and R. Cohen, "Notes and News," *IEJ* 26 (1976) 139–40, pl. 28b.

[76]See also Herr, *Scripts of Ancient Northwest Semitic Seals,* 165–66.

[77]M. De Vogüé, "Intailles hébraïques," *Revue Archéologique* 17 (1868) 449; M. A. Levy, *Siegel und Gemmen* (Breslau: Verlag der Schletter'schen Buchhandlung, 1869) 44, pl. 3:12.

[78]See also Israel, "Supplementum Idumeum," 338.

[79]The best photo is available in Hestrin and Dayagi-Mendels, "Inscribed Seals," 146, no. 116.

[80]See also Herr, *Scripts of Ancient Northwest Semitic Seals,* 73.

III. Other

A few incised inscriptions are known from several sites, although they add very little to our knowledge of the script or linguistic classification of Edomite.

1. *ʿb*[81]

These two letters appear on the handle of a jar from Buseirah. Puech tentatively suggested that these letters stand for *ʿ(śryt) b(t)*, "a tenth of a *bat*," a liquid measure. The closed forms of the two letters suggest a date perhaps in the first half of the 7th century. Their squared forms have more to do with the nature of the inscription (incised by an inexperienced hand onto the handle after firing) than anything else.

2.]*k*[.]*qws*[82]

Inscribed on a bichrome jar, these letters possibly form a personal name; the final three letters give the DN Qos. The wavy headed *samek* and "S"-topped *qop*, while schematic, are attested in the cursive ostracon 6043 from Kheleifeh and could easily date to about 600 BCE.

3. *lʿmyrw*[83] "Belonging to ʿAmîrû"

Inscribed on a small jar after firing, this inscription comes from Tell el-Kheleifeh. The reading of the fourth letter is difficult because of a hole in the jar's surface.

Linguistic Classification

Prior to the discovery of the Ḥorvat ʿUza ostracon, Garr could list for Edomite only eight features of the one hundred that he used to reconstruct a dialect geography for northwest Semitic. Huehnergard questioned whether this evidence even permitted the classification of Edomite as a dialect.[84] With the Ḥorvat ʿUza ostracon, several additional phonological, morphological and syntactic features are apparent. None of these, though, suggests that Edomite was noticeably different from Hebrew.

I. Phonology

As in Phoenician, Hebrew and the other Transjordanian dialects, proto-Semitic **θ* was realized in Edomite as *š* [š], e.g., *ʾšr* "which" (Ḥorvat ʿUza 4) < **ʾaθru*.

---

[81]Puech, "Documents épigraphiques," 13–14, pl. IV-E.

[82]Puech, "Documents épigraphiques," 14–15, pl. V-A.

[83]First published by Glueck ("First Campaign," 17); see the new edition with excellent photo and paleographic discussion by DiVito ("Inscriptions," 57–8, pl. 80:A).

[84]Huehnergard, Review of Garr, 531.

On the treatment of *n + consonant, Garr cites the reading *mʿdr* < **min–ʿdr* in the ostracon from Umm el-Biyara (above I.1) as evidence for the assimilation of *nun* to a following consonant.[85] Given the material uncertainty of the reading and the difficulty in concluding that this is the preposition plus DN, this evidence should be disallowed. On the other hand, within the word, **n* did assimilate, as in *ʾt* [ʾatta], "you," < **ʾantă* (Ḥorvat ʿUza, 2).

Israel argued that final **-at* of the absolute feminine singular noun is retained in the bronze weight from Petra inscribed *ḥmšt*.[86] In his opinion, this diverges from the Hebrew, where **at* > [ā].[87] The ending **-at* was preserved also in absolute feminine singular nouns in standard Phoenician, Ammonite and Moabite, leading Israel to suggest that this is a "conservative" trait. However, it is more likely that *ḥmšt* is, as Pilcher originally suggested, the feminine numeral [B.H. ḥămēšet], "five."[88] This form, therefore, provides no data about phonology of the absolute feminine singular nominal termination **-at* in Edomite.

The deictic adverb *ʿt* [ʿat] (Ḥorvat ʿUza 3) is written without *-h* as a *mater lectionis* for the longer [ʿattā]. This is a well-known phenomenon (above n. 27).

It is unlikely that Edomite possessed case endings. The use of the *nota accusativi* (Ḥorvat ʿUza 4) suggests that the semantic function of nouns was not marked by case endings. However, this is a general phenomenon within the northwest Semitic group and not particularly useful for classification.

II. Morphology

The second person masculine singular independent pronoun is *ʾt* (Ḥorvat ʿUza 2), presumably vocalized [ʾattā] < **ʾantā*, as opposed to Aramaic, in which *ʾt* < **ʾantă*. Of course, this is an assumption; the quality (or even the existence) of the final vowel can only be surmised. It may have been vocalized [ʾatt].

The relative pronoun is *ʾšr* (Ḥorvat ʿUza 4). This is significant, since the form is shared only with Moabite and Hebrew.[89]

As evidence for the coordinating conjunction *w–* in Edomite, Garr cites ostracon 2070 (rev. 3) from Tell el–Kheleifeh.[90] This evidence

---

[85]Garr, *Dialect Geography*, 43.

[86]E. J. Pilcher, "A Bronze Weight from Petra," *PEQ* 54 (1922) 71–73.

[87]"Supplementum Idumeum," 183.

[88] Pilcher, "Bronze Weight from Petra," 71–73. In other words, *ḥămēšet šĕqālîm*, "five sheqels"; cf. Num 18:16.

[89]Garr, *Dialect Geography*, 85–86.

[90]See Glueck, "Tell el–Kheleifeh Inscriptions," 230; Garr, *Dialect Geography*, 114.

should be disallowed, because the ostracon is actually Phoenician.[91] The conjunction is attested, however, in the Ḥorvat ʿUza ostracon (2, 3, 5). Again, though, this data does not help much in terms of classification.

The *nota accusativi* is *ʾt* (Ḥorvat ʿUza 3). This is significant because *ʾt* is shared only with Moabite and Hebrew. It differs from the form found in Phoenician and Aramaic, **ʾyt*, in that it has lost the intervocalic *yod.*

As in all the northwest Semitic dialects, with the exception of standard Phoenician, the causative prefix in the Ḥorvat ʿUza ostracon is *h-*, as in *whbrktk* "I bless you," and *whrm*, "he will raise" (2,5).

The inflection of the first person suffix conjugation in the strong verb is attested, *whbrktk* (Ḥorvat ʿUza 2), and should probably be vocalized *wa-hibriktī-k/ă* as in Phoenician, Hebrew and Moabite. On the possible shortened form of the suffix and the two *i*–class vowels in the causative, see above (n. 26).

III. Syntax

The direct object pronoun of the verb is attested once as an object suffix: *whbrktk.* There is no evidence for the *nota accusativi* plus suffix, but as with the other dialects where this form is absent in the epigraphic texts, this could merely be fortuitous.

Whether the so–called "conversive perfect" is attested in the Ḥorvat ʿUza ostracon is likely but not certain. The first potential form, *whbrktk,* is actually a performative perfect, well attested in epistolography. However, *whrm* very likely is a consecutive perfect. Beit Arieh translates the latter form as a jussive without explanation.

Standard word order is evinced: verb–subject–object. In one case, the sentence is introduced by the deictic adverb *wʿt,* according to expected patterns.

Summary

Two main conclusions derive from this study. First, it is possible to say that there is a recognizable cursive Edomite script in the 7th and early 6th centuries. Although poorly represented, the texts that are known illuminate several unique features of the Edomite cursive script, including *dalet* with breakthrough at the top and *he* with its "S"-shaped schematization of the classical horizontal bars. The script cannot simply be subsumed within the Transjordanian series, nor should it be described as a portmanteau of Aramaic and Hebrew features. Second, none of the texts from the 7th or 6th centuries preserve linguistic information that suggests Edomite was an independent dialect. That is

[91]Naveh, "The Script of Two Ostraca."

not to say that it absolutely was not. It is merely to admit that based on present evidence, there are no significant linguistic differences between texts that are demonstrably Edomite and texts written in the contemporary Hebrew of Cisjordan. There may be two lexical peculiarities in the Ḥorvat ʿUza ostracon, the causative of the root *brk* and the absolute use of the preposition *ʿmd*, but these lexical items do not a dialect make.

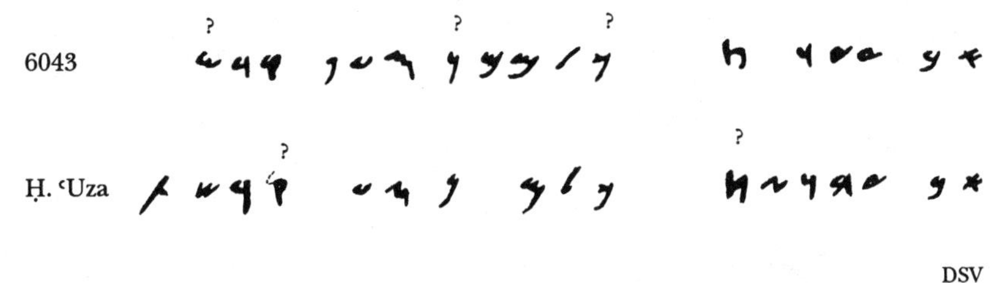

Figure 1. Ostracon 6043 from Tell el Kheleifeh and the Horvat ʿUza ostracon.

BIBLIOGRAPHY

Abel, Félix Marie. *Géographie de la Palestine.* 2 vols. 3d edition. Études bibliques. Paris: J. Gabalda, 1967.

Aharoni, Yohanan. "Three Hebrew Ostaca from Arad." *BASOR* 197 (1970): 16-42.

———. *The Land of the Bible.* Revised and enlarged edition. Philadelphia: Westminster, 1979.

———. *Arad Inscriptions.* Jerusalem: Israel Exploration Society and Massada Press, 1981.

Ahlström, Gösta W. *The History of Ancient Palestine.* Minneapolis: Fortress, 1993.

Albright, William F. "Ostracon No. 6043 from Ezion-Geber." *BASOR* 82 (1941): 11-15.

———. "The Oracles of Balaam." *JBL* 63 (1944): 207-33.

Amiran, Ruth B. K. and Dunayevsky, Immanuel. "The Assyrian Open-Court Building and its Palestinian Derivatives." *BASOR* 149 (1958): 25-32.

Archi, Alphonse. "Les dieux d'Ebla au IIIe millenaire avant J.C. et les dieux d'Ugarit." *Les Annales Archeologiques Arabes Syriennes: Revue d'Archeologie et d'Histoire* 29-30 (1980): 167-72.

———. "How a pantheon forms. The cases of Hattian-hittite Anatolia and Ebla of the 3rd millenium B.C.," in *Religionsgeschichtliche Beziehungen zwischen Kleinasien, Nordsyrien und dem Alten Testament,* 1-18. Edited by B. Jankowski *et al.* OBO 129. Göttingen: Vandenhoeck & Ruprecht, 1993.

Avigad, Nahman. *Hebrew Bullae from the Time of Jeremiah.* Jerusalem: Israel Exploration Society, 1986.

Axelsson, Lars E. *The Lord Rose Up from Seir: Studies in the History and Traditions of the Negev and Southern Judah.* ConBOT 25. Lund: Almquist & Wicksell, 1987.

Bachmann, Hans-Gerd and Hauptmann, Andreas. "Zur alten Kupfergewinnung in Fenan und Hirbet en-Nahas im Wadi Arabah in Südjordanien." *Der Anschnitt* 36 (1984): 110-23.

Baly, Denis. *The Geography of the Bible.* New York: Harper, 1957.

Banning, Edward B. and Köhler-Rollefson, Ilse. "Ethnoarchaeological Survey in the *Bēḍā* Area, Southern Jordan." *ZDPV* 102 (1986): 152-70.

Bartlett, John R. "The Edomite King List of Genesis 36:31-19 and I Chron. 1:43-50." *JTS* N.S. 16 (1965): 301-14.

———. "The Land of Seir and the Brotherhood of Edom." *JTS* N.S. 20 (1969): 1-20.

———. "Yahweh and Qaus: Response to Martin Rose (*JSOT* 4 [1977] 28-34)." *JSOT* 5 (1978): 29-38.

———. "The Conquest of Sihon's Kingdom: A Literary Re-examination." *JBL* 97 (1978): 347-51.

———. "From Edomites to Nabataeans: A Study in Continuity." *PEQ* 111 (1979): 53-66.

———. "Edom and the Fall of Jerusalem, 587 B.C." *PEQ* 114 (1982): 13-24.

———. *Edom and the Edomites.* JSOTSup 77. Sheffield: JSOT Press, 1989.

———. "From Edomites to Nabataeans: The Problem of Continuity." *Aram* 2:1&2 (1990): 25-34.

Baudissin, Wolf. "Edom," in *Realencyclopadie für protestantische Theologie und Kirche.* 24 vols. Edited by J. J. Herzog. Leipzig: J. C. Hinrichs, 1896-1913, 5:162-70.

Beit-Arieh, Itzhaq. "Tel ʿIra- A Fortified City of the Kingdom of Judah." *Qadmoniot* 18: 17-25 (Hebrew).

———. "New Data on the Relationship between Judah and Edom Toward the End of the Iron Age," in *Recent Excavations in Israel: Studies in Iron Age Archaeology,* 125-31. Edited by S. Gitin and W. G. Dever. Winona Lake, IN: ASOR and Eisenbrauns, 1989.

———. "A Small Frontier Citadel at Ḥorvat Radum in the Judean Negev." *Qadmoniot* 24 (1991): 86-89 (Hebrew).

———. "The Edomite Shrine at Ḥorvat Qitmit in the Judean Negev. Preliminary Excavation Report." *TA* 18 (1991): 93-116.

———. "A Literary Ostracon from Ḥorvat ʿUza." *TA* 20 (1993): 55-63.

———. *Ḥorvat Qitmit, an Edomite Shrine in the Judean Negev.* Forthcoming.

———. "Tel Malḥata." *Had Arkh* 101-102 (1994): 111 (Hebrew).

——— and Cresson, Bruce. "An Edomite Ostracon from Ḥorvat ʿUza." *TA* 12 (1985): 96-101.

——— and Cresson, Bruce. "Ḥorvat ʿUza: A Fortified Outpost on the Eastern Negev Border." *BA* 54 (1991): 126-135.

Bennett, Crystal M. "Fouilles d'Umm el-biyara. Rapport préliminaire." *RB* 73 (1966): 372-403.

———. "Excavations at Buseirah, Southern Jordan, 1971. Preliminary Report." *Levant* 5 (1973): 1-11.

———. "Excavations at Buseirah, Southern Jordan, 1972. Preliminary Report." *Levant* 6 (1974): 1-24.

———. "Excavations at Buseirah, Southern Jordan, 1973. Third Preliminary Report." *Levant* 7 (1975): 1-19.

———. "Excavations at Buseirah, Southern Jordan, 1974. Fourth Preliminary Report." *Levant* 9 (1977): 1-10.

———. "Some Reflections on Neo-Assyrian Influence in Transjordan," in *Archaeology in the Levant,* 165-71. Edited by P. R. S. Moorey and P. J. Parr. Warminster: Aris & Phillips, 1978.

———. "Neo-Assyrian Influence in Transjordan," in *Studies in the History and Archaeology of Jordan I,* 181-87. Edited by A. Hadidi. Amman: Department of Antiquities, 1982.

———. "Excavations at Buseirah (Biblical Bosrah)," in *Midian, Moab and Edom: The History and Archaeology of the Late Bronze Age and Iron Age Jordan and Notrhwest Arabia,* 9-17. Edited by J. F. A. Sawyer and D. J. A. Clines. JSOTSup 24. Sheffield: JSOT Press, 1983.

———. Excavations at Tawilan in Southern Jordan." *Levant* 16 (1984): 1-23.

Bienkowski, Piotr. "Umm el-Biyara, Tawilan and Buseirah in Retrospect." *Levant* 22 (1990): 91-109.

———. "The Chronology of Tawilan and the 'Dark Age' of Edom." *Aram* 2: 1&2 (1990): 35-44.

———. "The Beginning of the Iron Age in Edom: A Reply to Finkelstein." *Levant* 24 (1992): 167-69.

———. "The Beginning of the Iron Age in Southern Jordan: A Framework," in *Early Edom and Moab: The Beginning of the Iron Age in Southern Jordan,* 1-12. Edited by P. Bienkowski. SAM 7. Sheffield: J. R. Collis, 1992.

———. "The Date of Sedentary Occupation in Edom: Evidence from Umm el-Biyara, Tawilan and Buseirah," in *Early Edom and Moab: The Beginning of the Iron Age in Southern Jordan,* 99-112. Edited by P. Bienkoswki. SAM 7. Sheffield: J. R. Collis, 1992.

———. "The Architecture of Edom," in *Studies in the History and Archaeology of Jordan V,* forthcoming.

Biran, Avraham, and Cohen, Rudolph. "Notes and News: Aroer." *IEJ* 26 (1976): 138-40.

Boling, Robert G. *The Early Biblical Community in Transjordan.* SWBAS 6. Sheffield: Almond Press, 1988.

Bordreuil, Pierre. "Les sceaux des grandes personnages." *Le Monde de la Bible* 46 (1986): 46.

——— and Lemaire, André. "Nouveau sceaux hébreux, arameéns, et ammonites." *Semitica* 26 (1976): 45-63.

Borée, Wilhelm. *Die alten Ortsnamen Palästinas.* 2d edition. Hildesheim: Olms, 1968.

Borger, Riekele. *Die Inschriften Asarhaddons, Königs von Assyrien.* Beiheft AfO 9. Osnabrück: Biblio Verlag, 1956.

Bright, John. *A History of Israel.* 2d edition. Philadelphia: Westminster, 1975.

Brown, John P. "Archery in the Ancient World: 'Its Name is Life, its Work is Death.'" *BZ* 37 (1993): 26-42.

Brown, Robin M. "Ceramics from the Kerak Plateau," in *Archaeological Survey of the Kerak Plateau,* 169-280. Edited by J. M. Miller. ASOR Archaeological Reports 1. Atlanta: Scholars, 1991.

Buhl, Frants. *Geschichte der Edomiter.* Leipzig: Edelmann, 1893.

Burckhardt, Johann L. *Travels in Syria and the Holy Land.* London: J. Murray, 1822.

Caquot, André. "Le dieu ʿAthtar et les textes des Ras Shamra." *Syria* 35 (1958): 45-60.

——— and Lemaire, André. "Les textes araméens de Deir ʿAllā." *Syria* 54 (1977): 189-208.

Caskel, Werner. "Die alten semitischen Gottheiten in Arabien," in *Le antiche divinità semitiche,* 95-118. Edited by S. Moscati. Rome: Centro di studi semitici, 1958.

Cohen, Rudolph. "Excavations at Kadesh-Barnea 1976-1978." *BA* 54 (1981): 93-107.

———. *Kadesh-Barnea. A Fortress from the Time of the Judean Kingdom.* Israel Museum Catalogue 233. Jerusalem: Israel Museum, 1983.

———. "ʿEin Ḥazevah 1988-1989." *Had Arkh* 96 (1991): 38-39 (Hebrew).

Cohen, Simon. "Edom," in *Interpreter's Dictionary of the Bible.* 4 vols. Edited by G. A. Buttrick. New York: Abingdon, 1975, 2:24-26.

———. "Elat," in *Interpreter's Dictionary of the Bible.* 4 vols. Edited by G. A. Buttrick. New York: Abingdon, 1975, 2:71-72.

———. "Sela," in *Interpreter's Dictionary of the Bible.* 4 vols. Edited by G. A. Buttrick. New York: Abingdon, 1975, 4: 262-63.

Coleman, Lyman. *An Historical Book and Atlas of Biblical Geography.* Philadelphia: Lippincott, Grambo and Co., 1854.

Cooke, George A. *Textbook of North Semitic Iscriptions.* Oxford: Clarendon, 1903.

Coote, Robert B. *Early Israel: A New Horizon.* Minneapolis: Fortress, 1990.

——— and Whitelam, Keith. *The Emergence of Ancient Israel in Historical Perspective.* SWBAS 5. Sheffield: Almond Press, 1987.

Cowley, Arthur E., ed. *Aramaic Papyri of the Fifth Century B.C.* Osnabrück: Otto Zeller, 1967.

Cresson, Bruce C. "The Condemnation of Edom in Postexilic Judaism," in *The Use of the Old Testament in the New and Other Essays,* 125-48. Edited by J. M. Efird. Durham: Duke University Press, 1972.

Cross, Frank M., Jr. "Two Notes on Palestinian Inscriptions of the Persian Period." *BASOR* 193 (1969): 21-24.

———. "Ammonite Ostraca from Heshbon, Hesbon Ostraca IV-VIII." *AUSS* 13 (1975): 1-20.

———. "Heshbon Ostracon XI." *AUSS* 14 (1976): 145-48.

———. "The Epic Traditions of Early Israel: Epic Narrative and the Reconstruction of Early Israelite Institutions," in *The Poet and the Historian. Essays in Literary and Historical Biblical Criticism,* 13-39. Edited by R. E. Friedman. Chico, CA: Scholars Press, 1983.

———. "Reuben, First Born of Jacob." *ZAW* Sup 100 (1988): 46-55.

———. "A Papyrus Recording a Divine Legal Decision: The Root *rhq* in Biblical and Near Eastern Legal Usage." *EI,* forthcoming.

——— and Freedman, David Noel. *Early Hebrew Orthography.* AOS 36. New Haven: American Oriental Society, 1952.

Curtis, Edward L. and Madsen, Albert A. *A Critical and Exegetical Commentary on the Books of Chronicles.* ICC 11. New York: Charles Scribner's Sons, 1910.

Dahood, Mitchell. "Ancient Semitic Deities in Syria and Palestine," in *Le antiche divinità semitiche,* 65-94. Edited by S. Moscati. Rome: Centro di studi semitici, 1958.

Dalley, Stephanie. "The Cuneiform Tablet from Tell Tawilan." *Levant* 16 (1984): 19-22.

Dalman, Gustaf. *Arbeit und Sitte in Palästina, VI: Zeltleben, Vieh- und Milchwirtschaft, Jagd, Fischfang.* Hildesheim: Olms, (1939) 1964.

Degen, Rainer, Müller, Walter W., and Röllig, Wolfgang. *Neue Ephemeris für semitische Epigraphik.* 3 vols. Wiesbaden: O. Harrassowitz, 1972-1978.

Denizeau, Claude. *Dictionnaire des parlers arabes de Syrie, Liban et Paléstine.* Paris: G.-P. Maisonneuve, 1960.

DiVito, Robert A. "The Tell el-Kheleifeh Inscriptions," in *Nelson Glueck's 1938-1940 Excavations at Tell el-Kheleifeh: A Reappraisal,* 51-63. Edited by G. D. Pratico. ASOR Archaeological Reports 3. Atlanta: Scholars Press, 1993.

Dornemann, Rudolph H. *The Archaeology of the Transjordan in the Bronze and Iron Ages.* Milwaukee: Milwaukee Public Museum, 1983.

Dostal, Walter. *Egalität und klassengesellschaft in Südarabein. Anthropologische Untersuchungen zur socialen Evolution.* Horn-Vienna: Ferd. Berger & Sons, 1985.

Driver, Godfrey R. "Seals from ʿAmman and Petra." *QDAP* 11 (1944): 81-2 and pl. XVIII.

Dupont-Sommer. André. "Un papyrus araméen d'époque saïte découvert à Saqqarah." *Semitica* 1 (1948): 48-68.

Edelman, Diana V. "Solomon's Adversaries Hadad, Rezon and Jeroboam: A Trio of 'Bad-Guy' Characters Illustrating the Theology of Immediate Retribution," in *The Pitcher is Broken: Memorial Essays for Gösta W. Ahlström,* 166-91. Edited by L. Handy and S. W. Holloway. JSOTSup 190. Sheffield: JSOT Press, 1995.

Edens, Christopher and Bawden, Garth. "History of Taymaʿ and Hejazi Trade During the First Millenium B.C." *JESHO* 32 (1988): 48-103.

Elliger, Karl. "Ezeon-Geber," in *Biblisch-historisches Handwörterbuch.* 4 vols. Edited by B. Reiche and L. Rost. Göttingen: Vandenhoeck & Ruprecht, 1962-1979, 1:461-64.

Eph'al, Israel. *The Ancient Arabs: Nomads on the Borders of the Fertile Crescent, 9th-5th Centuries B.C.* Jerusalem: Magnes Press/Leiden: Brill, 1982.

———. "Syria-Palestine under Achaemenid Rule," in *Cambridge Ancient History IV,* 139-64. Edited by J. Boardman *et al.* 2d edition. New York: Cambridge University Press, 1988.

Ewing, William. "Elat," in *The International Standard Bible Encyclopedia.* 5 vols. Edited by J. Orr. Chicago: Howard-Severance Co., 1955, 2:923.

Finkelstein, Israel. *The Archaeology of the Israelite Settlement.* Jerusalem: Israel Exploration Society, 1988.

———. "Arabian Trade of Socio-Political Conditions in the Negev in the Twelfth-Eleventh Centuries B.C.E." *JNES* 47 (1988): 241-52.

———. "Early Arad- Urbanism of the Nomads." *ZDPV* 106 (1990): 34-50.

———. "Edom in the Iron I." *Levant* 24 (1992): 159-66.

———. "Stratigraphy, Pottery and Parallels: A Reply to Bienkowski." *Levant* 24 (1992): 171-72.

———. "*Ḥorvat Qitmit* and the Southern Trade in the Late Iron Age II." *ZPDV* 108 (1992): 156-70.

Fischer-Elfert, Hans-Werner. *Die satirische Streitschrift des Papyrus Anastasi I. Übersetzung und Kommentar.* Wiesbaden: O. Harrassowitz, 1986.

Frank, Fritz. "Aus der ʿAraba. I: Reiserberichte." *ZDPV* 57 (1934): 191-280.

Franken, H. J. "Texts from the Persian Period from Tell Deir ʿAllā." *VT* 17 (1967): 480-88.

Freedman, David Noel. "Early Israelite History in the Light of Early Israelite Poetry," in *Unity and Diversity: Essays in the History, Literature and Religion of the Ancient Near East,* 3-35. Edited by H. Goedicke and J. J. M. Roberts. Baltimore: Johns Hopkins Press, 1975.

———. "'Who is Like Thee among the Gods?' The Religion of Early Israel," in *Ancient Israelite Religion,* 315-36. Edited by P. D. Miller, P. D. Hanson, and S. D. McBride. Philadelphia: Fortress, 1987.

Fulco, William J. *The Canaanite God Rešep.* AOS 8. New Haven: American Oriental Society, 1976.

Garr, W. Randall. *Dialect Geography of Syria-Palestine, 1000-586 B.C.E.* Philadelphia: University of Pennsylvania, 1985.

Geus, C. H. J. de. *The Tribes of Israel. An investigation into some of the pressuppositions of Martin Noth's amphictyony hypothesis.* Assen and Amsterdam: van Gorcum, 1976.

———. "Idumaea." *JEOL* 26 (1980): 53-74.

Giveon, Raphael. *Les bédouins shosou des documents égyptiens.* Leiden: Brill, 1971.

Glazier-McDonald, Beth. *Malachi the Divine Messenger.* SBLDS 98. Atlanta: Scholars Press, 1987.

Glueck, Nelson. *Explorations in Eastern Palestine II.* AASOR 15. New Haven: American Schools of Oriental Research, 1935.

———. "The Boundaries of Edom." *HUCA* 11 (1936): 141-57.

———. "The First Campaign at Tell el-Kheleifeh (Ezion-Geber)." *BASOR* 71 (1938): 3-17.

———. *The Other Side of the Jordan.* New Haven: American Schools of Oriental Research, 1940.

———. "Ostraca from Elath." *BASOR* 82 (1940): 3-10.

———. "The Third Season of Excavation at Tell el-Kheleifeh." *BASOR* 79 (1940): 2-18.

———. "Ostraca from Elath." *BASOR* 82 (1941): 3-11.

———. *Deities and Dolphins.* New York: Farrer, Straus and Giroux, 1965.

———. "Tell el-Kheleifeh Inscriptions," in *Near Eastern Studies in Honor of W. F. Albright,* 225-42. Edited by H. Goedicke. Baltimore: Johns Hopkins, 1971.

Gordon, Robert L. *et al.* "Antiker Eisenbergbau und alte Eisenverhüttung im ʿAğlûn." *AfO* 33 (1986): 231-33.

Graf, David. "The Origin of the Nabateans." *Aram* 2 (1990): 45-75.

Gray, George Buchanan. *Studies in Hebrew Proper Names.* London: A. and C. Black, 1896.

Gray, John. "The Desert God ʿAttar in the Literature and Religion of Canaan." *JNES* 8 (1949): 72-83.

Gunneweg, Jan and Mommsen, H. "Instrumental neutron activation analysis and the origion of some cult objects and Edomite vessels from the Horvat Qitmit shrine." *Archaeometry* 32 (1990): 7-18.

Haak, Robert. "Prophets and History: Zephaniah." Paper presented at the W. F. Albright Institute for Archaeological Research in Jerusalem, May, 1991.

———. "Zephaniah's Oracles Against the Nations." Paper presented at the winter meeting of the Society for Biblical Research, February 2, 1992.

Hackett, Jo Ann. *The Balaam Text from Deir ʿAllā.* HSM 31. Chico, CA: Scholars Press, 1984.

Hackstein, Katharina. *Ethnizität und Situation. Ǧaraš-eine vorder-orientalische Kleinstadt.* BTAVO 94. Wiesbaden: Reichert, 1989.

Hammond. Philip. *The Nabataeans—Their History, Culture and Archaeology.* Gothenburg: P. Åströms, 1973.

Haran, Manahem. "Observations on the Historical Background of Amos 1.2-2.6." *IEJ* 18 (1968) 201-12.

Harding, G. L. "Some Objects from Transjordan." *PEQ* 69 (1937): 253-55.

Hart, Stephen. "Some Preliminary Thoughts on Settlement in Southern Edom." *Levant* 18 (1986): 51-58.

———. "Selaʿ: The Rock of Edom?" *PEQ* 118 (1986): 91-95.

———. "Five Soundings in Southern Jordan." *Levant* 19 (1987): 33-47.

———. "The Edom Survey Project 1984-1985: The Iron Age," in *Studies in the History and Archaeology of Jordan III,* 287-90. Edited by A. Hadidi. Amman: Dept. of Antiquities, 1987.

———. "Excavations at Ghrareh, 1986: Preliminary Report." *Levant* 20 (1988): 89-99.

———. "The Archaeology of the Land of Edom." Doctoral dissertation, MacQuarrie University, 1989.

———. "Iron Age Settlement in the Land of Edom," in *Early Edom and Moab: The Beginning of the Iron Age in Southern Jordan,* 93-98. Edited by P. Bienkowski. SAM 7. Sheffield: J. R. Collins, 1992.

Hartmann, Richard. "Die Namen von Petra." *ZAW* 30 (1910): 143-51.

Hauptmann, Andreas. "Die Gewinnung von Kupfer: Ein uralter Industriezweig auf der Ostseite des wadi Arabah," in *Petra: Neue Ausgrabungen und Entdeckungen,* 31-43. Edited by M. Lindner. Munich and Bad Windsheim: Delp, 1986.

———. Chronique archéologique: Feinān, 1984." *RB* 93 (1986): 236-38.

———. "Feinān 1984." *AfO* 33 (1986): 256-59.

———, Weisberger, Gerd and Knauf, Ernst Axel."Archäometallurgische und bergbauarchäologische Untersuchungen im Gebiet von Fenan, Wadi Arabah (Jordanien)." *Der Anschnitt* 37 (1985): 163-95.

——— and Weisgerber, Gerd. "Periods of Ore Exploitation and Metal Production in the Area of Feinan, Wadi ʿArabah, Jordan," in *Studies in the History and*

Archaeology of Jordan IV, 61-66. Edited by M. Zaghloul *et al.* Amman: Department of Antiquities, 1992.

Healey, John. "Were the Nabataeans Arabs?" *Aram* 1 (1989): 38-44.

Helck, Wolfgang. *Die Beziehungen Ägyptens zu Vorderasien im 3. und 2. Jahrtausend vor Chr.* 2d edition. Ägyptologische Abhandlungen 5. Weisbaden: O. Harrassowitz, 1971.

Herr, Larry G. *The Scripts of Ancient Northwest Semitic Seals.* HSM 18. Missoula, MT: Scholars Press, 1978.

———. "The Late Iron II- Persian Ceramic Horizon at Tell el-ʿUmeiri," in *Studies in the History and Archaeology of Jordan V.* Forthcoming.

Hestrin, Ruth and Diyagi-Mendels, Michal. *Inscribed Seals, First Temple Period--Hebrew, Ammonite, Moabite, Phoenician and Aramaic–From the Collections of the Israel Museum and the Israel Department of Antiquities and Museums.* Jerusalem: Israel Museum, 1979.

Hoftijzer, Jean and Kooij, G. van der. *Aramaic Texts from Deir ʿAllā.* Leiden: Brill, 1976.

Horsfield, George and Conway, Agnes. "Historical and Topographical Notes on Edom: With an Account of the First Excavations at Petra." *Geographical Journal* 76 (1930): 369-90.

Hübner, Ulrich. *Die Ammoniter. Untersuchungen zur Geschichte, Kultur und Religion eines transjordanischen Volkes im 1. Jahrtausend v. Chr.* Wiesbaden: O. Harrassowitz, 1992.

Huehnergard, John. Review of W. Randall Garr, *Dialect Geography of Syria-Palestine, 1000-586 B.C.E. JBL* 106 (1987): 529-33.

———. "Historical Phonology and the Hebrew Piel," in *Linguistics and Biblical Hebrew*, 209-29. Edited by W. Bodine. Winona Lake: Eisenbrauns, 1993.

———. "Languages (Introductory)," in *Anchor Bible Dictionary.* 6 vols. Edited by D. N. Freedman. New York: Doubleday, 1992, 4:155-70.

Huffmon, Herbert B. *Amorite Personal Names in the Mari Texts.* Baltimore: John Hopkins University Press, 1965.

Israel, Felice. "Miscellenea Idumea." *Revista biblica italiana* 27 (1979): 171-205.

———. "Supplementum Idumeum." *Revista biblica italiana* 35 (1987): 337-56.

Jamieson-Drake, David W. *Scribes and Scribal Schools in Monarchic Israel: A Socio-Archeological Approach.* SWBAS 9. Sheffield: Almond Press, 1991.

Joannès, Francis. "A propos de la tablette cunéiforme de Tell Tawilan." *Revue d'Assyriologie* 81 (1987): 165-66.

Jobling, William J. "Preliminary Report on the Archaeological Survey between Maʿan and ʿAqaba, January to February 1980." *ADAJ* 25 (1981): 105-12.

———. "The 1982 Archaeological and Epigraphic Survey of the ʿAqaba-Maʿan Area of Southern Jordan." *ADAJ* 27 (1983): 185-96.

Kammerer, Albert. *Petra et la Nabatène.* Paris: P. Geuther, 1929.

Kempinski, Aharon. "Urbanization and Metallurgy in Southern Canaan," in *L'urbanisation de la Palestine à l'âge du Bronze ancien*, 163-68. Edited by P. de Miroschedji. BAR 527. Oxford: Bar, 1989.

——— *et al.* "Excavations at Tel Masos: 1972, 1974, 1975." *EI* 15 (1981): 154-80 (Hebrew).

Killick, Alistair. "Udruh 1980, 1981, 1982 Seasons, A Preliminary Report." *ADAJ* 27 (1983): 231-43.

Kitchen, Kenneth A. "The Egyptian Evidence on Ancient Jordan," in *Early Edom and Moab: The Beginning of the Iron Age in Southern Jordan*, 21-34. Edited by P. Bienkowski. SAM 7. Sheffield: J.R. Collis, 1992.

Kletter, Raz. "The Rujm el-Malfuf buildings and the Assyrian Vassal State of Ammon." *BASOR* 284 (1991): 33-50.

Klingbeil, Gerald A. "The Onomasticon of the Aramaic Inscriptions of Syria-Palestine during the Persian Period." *JNSL* 18 (1992): 67-94.

Knapp, A. Bernard. *The History and Culture of Ancient Western Asia and Egypt.* Chicago: Dorsey, 1988.

Knauf, Ernst Axel. "Supplementa Ismaelitica 4. Hiobs Heimat." *BN* 22 (1983): 25-29.

———. "Qaus." *UF* 16 (1984): 93-95.

———. "Qaus in Aegypten." *GM* 73 (1984): 33-36.

———. "Alter und Herkunft der edomitischen Königslisten Gen 36, 31-39." *ZAW* 97 (1985): 245-53.

———. "Supplementa Ismaelitica 9. Phinon-Feinan und das westerabische Ortsnamenkontinuum." *BN* 36 (1987): 37-50.

———. "Supplementa Ismaelitica 12. Camels in Late Bronze Age and Iron Age Jordan: The Archaeological Evidence." *BN* 40 (1987): 20-23.

———. "Hiobs Heimat." *WO* 19 (1988): 65-83.

———. *Midian. Untersuchungen zur Geschichte Palästinas und Nordarabiens am Ende des 2. Jahrtausens v. Chr.* Wiesbaden: O Harrassowitz, 1988.

———. "Supplementa Ismaelitica 13. Edom und Arabien." *BN* 45 (1988): 62-81.

———. "The West Arabian Place Name Province: Its Origin and Significance." *Proceedings of the Seminar for Arabian Studies* 18 (1988): 39-49.

———. *Ismael. Untersuchungen zur Geschichte Palästinas und Nordarabiens im 1. Jahrtausends v. Chr.* 2d edition. Weisbaden: O. Harrassowitz, 1989.

———. "The Migration of the Script, and the Formation of the State in South Arabia." *Proceedings of the Seminar for Arabian Studies* 19 (1989): 79-91.

———. "Nabataean Origins," in *Arabian Studies in Honour of Mahmud Ghul,* 56-61. Edited by M. Ibrahim. Weisbaden: O. Harrassowitz, 1989.

———. "Dushara and Shaiᶜ al-Quam." *Aram* 2:1&2 (1990): 175-83.

———. "Edom und Seir," in *Neues Bibel-Lexikon,* 467-68. Edited by M. Görg and B. Lang. Zurich: Benziger, 1990.

———. "The Persian Administration of Arabia." *Transeuphrantène* 3 (1990): 201-17.

———. "War Biblisch-Hebräisch eine Sprache?" *Zeitschrift für Althebraistik* 3 (1990): 11-23.

———. "From History to Interpretation," in *The Fabric of History: Text, Artifact and Israel's Past,* 26-64. Edited by D.V. Edelman. JSOTSup 127. Sheffield: SJOT Press, 1991.

———. "Hesbon, Sihons Stadt." *ZDPV* 107 (1991): 135-44.

———. "King Solomon's Copper Supply," in *Phoenicia and the Bible,* 167-86. Edited by E. Lipiński. OLA 44. Leuven: Peeters, 1991.

———. "Toponymy of the Kerak Plateau," in *Archaeological Survey of the Kerak Plateau,* 281-90. Edited by J. M. Miller. ASOR Archaeological Reports 1. Atlanta: Scholars Press, 1991.

———. "Bedouin and Bedouin States," in *Anchor Bible Dictionary.* 6 vols. Edited by D. N. Freedman. New York: Doubleday, 1992, 1:634-38.

———. "The Cultural Impact of Secondary State Formation: The Cases of the Edomites and Moabites," in *Early Edom and Moab: The Beginning of the Iron Age in Southern Jordan,* 47-54. Edited by P. Bienkowski. SAM 7. Sheffield: J.R. Collis, 1992.

———. "Hori," in *Anchor Bible Dictionary.* 6 vols. Edited by D. N. Freedman. New York: Doubleday, 1992, 3:288.

———. "Hur," in *Anchor Bible Dictionary*. 6 vols. Edited by D. N. Freedman. New York: Doubleday, 1992, 3:334.

———. "Manahath," in *Anchor Bible Dictionary*. 6 vols. Edited by D. N. Freedman. New York: Doubleday, 1992, 4:493.

———. "Manahathites," in *Anchor Bible Dictionary*. 6 vols. Edited by D. N. Freedman. New York: Doubleday, 1992, 4:494.

———. "Menuhoth," in *Anchor Bible Dictionary*. 6 vols. Edited by D. N. Freedman. New York: Doubleday, 1992, 4:695-96.

———. "Seir," in *Anchor Bible Dictionary*. 6 vols. Edited by D. N. Freedman. New York: Doubleday, 1992, 5:1072-73.

———. "Shalma," in *Anchor Bible Dictionary*. 6 vols. Edited by D. N. Freedman. New York: Doubleday, 1992, 5:1154.

———. "Shobal," in *Anchor Bible Dictionary*. 6 vols. Edited by D. N. Freedman. New York: Doubleday, 1992, 5:1224.

———. "Teman," in *Anchor Bible Dictionary*. 6 vols. Edited by D. N. Freedman. New York: Doubleday, 1992, 6:347-48.

———. "Zur," in *Anchor Bible Dictionary*. 6 vols. Edited by D. N. Freedman. New York: Doubleday, 1992, 6:1175-76.

——— and Lenzen, Cherie J. "Edomite Copper Industry," in *Studies in the History and Archaeology of Jordan III*, 287-90. Edited by A. Hadidi. Amman: Department of Antiquities, 1987.

——— and Maáni, Sultan. "On the Phonemes of Fringe Canaanite: The Cases of Zerah-Udruh and 'Kamâšhalta.'" *UF* 19 (1987): 91-94.

Knipperberg, Renate. "Pinon," in *Biblisch-historische Handwörterbuch*. 4 vols. Edited by B. Reicke and L. Rost. Göttingen: Vandenhoeck & Ruprecht, 1962-1979, 3:1475.

Kochavi, Moshe. "Malḥata, Tel," in *Encyclopedia of Archaeological Excavations in the Holy Land*. 4 vols. Edited M. Avi-Yonah. Jerusalem: Israel Exploration Society, 1975, 3:771-75.

Koucky, Frank L. and Miller, Nathan R. "The Metal Objects from Tell el-Kheleifeh," in *Nelson Glueck's 1938-1940 Excavations at Tell el-Kheleifeh: A Reappraisal 65-70*. Edited by G. Pratico. ASOR Archaeological Reports 3. Atlanta: Scholars Press, 1993.

Kraeling, Carl H. *Gerasa. City of the Decapolis*. New Haven: American Schools of Oriental Research. 1938.

LaBianca, Øystein S. "Objective, Procedures, and Findings of Ethnoarchaeological Research in the Vicinity of Hesban in Jordan." *ADAJ* 28 (1984): 269-87.

Lagarde, Paul de. *Uebersicht über die im aramäischen, arabischen und hebräischen übliche Bildung der Nomina*. Abhandlungen der königlichen Gesellschaft der Wissenschaften zu Göttingen 35. Göttingen: Dieterich, 1889.

Lawson, John P. and Wilson, John M. *A Cyclopaedia of Biblical Geography, Biography, Natural History and General Knowledge*. 2 vols. London: A. Fullarton & Co., 1870.

Lemaire, André. "Note on an Edomite Seal from Buseirah." *Levant* 7 (1975): 18-19.

———. "L'inscription de Balaam trouvée à Deir ʿAllā: épigraphie," in *Biblical Archaeology Today: Proceedings of the International Congress on Biblical Archaeology, April, 1984*, 313-25. Edited by J. Amitai. Jerusalem: Israel Exploration Society, 1985.

———. "Hadad l'Édomite ou Hadad l'Araméen?" *BN* 43 (1988): 14-18.

———. Aramaic Literature and Hebrew Literature: Contacts and Influences in the First Millenium [sic] B.C.E." *Proceedings of the World Congress of Jewish Studies* 9 (1988): 9-24.

———. Epigraphy, Transjordanian," in *Anchor Bible Dictionary*. 6 vols. Edited by D. N. Freedman. New York: Doubleday, 1992, 2:561-68.

Levy, Moritz A. *Siegel und Gemmen*. Breslau: Verlag der Schletter'schen Buchhandlung, 1869.

Lewin, Bernhard. *A Vocabulary of Hudailian Poems*. Acta Regiae Societatis Scientarum et Litterarum Gothoburgensis Humaniora 13. Göteborg: Kungl. vetenskaps- och vitterhets-Samhället, 1978.

Lewis, Norman N. "The Frontier of Settlement in Syria." *International Affairs* 31 (Januray, 1955): 48-60.

———. "The Frontier of Settlement in Syria," in *The Economic History of the Middle East 1800-1914*, 258-68. Edited by C. Issawi. Chicago: Universtiy of Chicago Press, 1966.

Lidzbarski. Mark. *Altaramäische Urkunden aus Assur*. Wissenschaftliche Veröffentlichungen der Deutschen Orientgesellschaft 38. Leipzig: J. C. Hinrichs, 1921.

Lindner, Manfred. *Petra. Neue Ausgrabungen und Entdeckungen*. Munich and Bad Windsheim: Delp, 1986.

———. "Edom outside the Famous Excavations: Evidence from Surveys in the Greater Petra Area," in *Early Edom and Moab: The Beginning of the Iron Age in Southern Jordan*, 143-66. Edited by P. Bienkowski. SAM 7. Sheffield: J. R. Collis, 1992.

——— *et al.* "Es Sadeh—A Lithic-Early Bronze-Iron II (Edomite)-Nabataean Site in Southern Jordan. Report on the Second Exploratory Campaign 1988." *ADAJ* 34 (1990): 193-237.

Lindsay, John. "The Babylonian Kings and Edom, 605-550 B.C." *PEQ* 108 (1976): 23-39.

Lury, Joseph. *Geschichte der Edomiter im biblischen Zeitalter*. Berlin: L. Wechselmann, 1896.

MacDonald, Burton. "The Wadi el Ḥasā Archaeological Survey," in *The Answers Lie Below*, 113-28. Edited by H. O. Thompson. Lanham, MD: University Press of America, 1984.

———. *The Wadi al Hasa Archaeological Survey 1979-1983, West-Central Jordan*. Waterloo, ON: Wilfrid Laurier Universtiy Press, 1988.

———. *The Southern Ghors and Northeast ʿArabah Archaeological Survey*. Sheffield: J. R. Collis, 1992.

———. "Evidence from the Wadi el-Ḥasā and Southern Ghors and North-east Arabah Archaeological Surveys," in *Early Edom and Moab: The Beginning of the Iron Age in Southern Jordan*, 113-42. Edited by P. Bienkowski. SAM 7. Sheffield: J. R. Collis, 1992.

McGovern, Patrick E. *The Late Bronze Age and Early Iron Ages of Central Transjordan: The Baqʿah Valley Project, 1977-1981*. Philadelphia: The University of Pennsylvania Museum, 1986.

Mayes, James L. *Amos*. OTL. Philadelphia: Westminster, 1969.

Maxwell-Hyslop, Rachael. "Excavations at Tawilan in Southern Jordan, 1982. Appendix B. The Gold Jewellery." *Levant* 16 (1984): 22-23.

Mershen, Birgit and Knauf, Ernst Axel. "From Ğadar to Umm Qais." *ZDPV* 104 (1988): 128-45.

Merwe, Nikolaas van der. "The Advent of Iron in Africa," in *The Coming of the Age of Iron*, 463-506. Edited by T. A. Wertime and J. D. Muhly. New Haven and London: Yale University Press, 1980.

Meshel, Ze'ev. *Kuntillet Ajrud. A Religious Centre from the Time of the Judaean Monarchy on the Border of Sinai.* Israel Museum catalogue 175. Jerusalem: Israel Museum, 1978.

Mettinger, Tryggve N. D. "The Elusive Essence. Yahweh, El and Baal and the Distinctiveness of Israelite Faith," in *Die Hebraische Bibel und ihre zweifach Nachgeschichte. Festschrift für Rolf Rendtorff,* 393-417. Edited by E. Blum *et al.* Neukirchen-Vluyn: Neukirchener Verlag, 1990.

Meyer, Eduard. *Die Israeliten und ihre Nachbarstämme.* Halle: M. Niemeyer, 1906.

Milik, Jozef T. "Nouvelles inscriptions nabatéenes." *Syria* 35 (1958): 227-51.

———. "Notes d'épigraphie orientale: 2. A propos du dieu édomite Qôs." *Syria* 37 (1960): 95-96.

———. Communication in C. M. Bennett, "Fouilles d'Umm el-Biyara." *RB* 73 (1966): 399.

Millard, Alan R. "Assyrian Involvement in Edom," in *Early Edom and Moab: The Beginning of the Iron Age in Southern Jordan,* 35-39. Edited by P. Bienkowski. SAM 7. Sheffield: J. R. Collis, 1992.

Miller, J. Maxwell. "Moab and the Moabites," in *Studies in the Mesha Inscription and Moab,* 1-40. Edited by J. A. Dearman. Archaeological and Biblical Studies 2. Atlanta: Scholars Press, 1989.

———. "Six Khirbet el-Medeinehs in the Region East of the Dead Sea." *BASOR* 276 (1989): 25-28.

———. "The Israelite Journey through (around) Moab and Moabite Toponymy." *JBL* 108 (1989): 577-95.

———. "Early Monarchy in Moab?," in *Early Edom and Moab: The Beginning of the Iron Age in Southern Jordan,* 77-91. Edited by P. Bienkowski. SAM 7. Sheffield: J. R. Collis, 1992.

Misgav, Haggai. "Two Notes on the Ostracon from Horvat Uza." *IEJ* 40 (1990): 215-17.

Montet, Pierre. *Les nouvelles fouilles de Tanis, 1929-1932.* Publications de la Faculté des Lettres de Strasbourg II.10. Paris: Les Belles Lettres, 1933.

Moon, Cyris H. S. "A Political History of Edom in the Light of Recent Literary and Archaeological Research." Doctoral dissertation, Emory University, 1971.

Müller, Hans-Peter. "Religionsgeschichtliche Beobachtungen zu den Texten von Ebla." *ZDPV* 96 (1980): 1-19.

Musil, Alois. *Arabia Petraea II. Edom. Topographischer Reiserbericht.* 2 vol. Vienna: Alfred Hölder, 1907-1908.

———. *The northern Hejaz.* New York: Czech Academy of Sciences and Arts and Charles J. Crane, 1926.

Myers, Jacob M. "Edom and Judah in the 6th-5th c. B.C.," in *Near Eastern Studies in Honor of William Foxwell Albright,* 377-92. Edited by H. Goedicke. Baltimore: Johns Hopkins Press, 1971.

Na'aman, Nadav. "The Kingdom of Judah under Josiah." *TA* 18 (1991): 3-71.

———. "Israel, Edom and Egypt in the 10th Centruy B.C.E." *TA* 19: 71-93.

Naveh, Joseph. "The Scripts of Two Ostraca from Elath." *BASOR* 183 (1966): 27-30.

———. "The Date of the Deir ʿAllā Inscription in Aramaic Script." *IEJ* 17 (1967): 256-58.

———. *The Development of the Aramaic Script.* Israel Academy of Sciences and Humanities Proceedings Vol. 1, No. 1. Jerusalem: Israel Academy, 1970.

———. "The Aramaic Ostraca from Beer-Sheba (Seasons 1971-1976)." *TA* 6 (1979): 182-98.

———. *Early History of the Alphabet.* Jerusalem: Magnes Press, 1982.

———. "Published and Unpublished Aramaic Ostraca." *ʿAtiqot*, English Series 17 (1985): 114-21.

———. "Aramaic Script," in *Anchor Bible Dictionary*. 6 vols. Edited by D. N. Freedman. New York: Doubleday, 1992, 1:342-45.

Nissen, Hans J. *Grundzüge einer Geschichte der Frühzeit des vorderen Orients*. Darmstadt: Wissenschaftliche Buchgesellschaft, 1983.

Nöldeke, Theodor. *Neue Beiträge zur semitischen Sprachwissenschaft*. Strasbourg: Trübner, 1910.

Noth, Martin. *Die Israelitische Personennamen im Rahmen der gemeinsemitischen Namengebung*. Stuttgart: Kohlhammer,1928.

———. *The History of Israel*. 2d edition. New York: Harper & Row, 1960.

Oakeshott, Marion. "A Study of the Iron Age II Pottery of East Jordan with Special Reference to Unpublished Material from Edom." Doctoral dissertation, University of London, 1978.

———. "The Edomite Pottery," in *Midian, Moab, and Edom: The History and Archaeology of Late Bronze and Iron Age Jordan and North-West Arabia*, 53-63. Edited by J. F. A. Sawyer and D. J. A. Clines. JSOTSup 24. Sheffield: JSOT Press, 1983.

Oded, Bustanay. "Observations on Methods of Assyrian Rule in Transjordania after the Palestinian Campaign of Tiglath-Pileser III." *JNES* 29 (1970): 177-86.

———. "Egyptian References to the Edomite Deity Qaus." *AUSS* 9 (1971): 47-50.

Ogden, Jack. "The Gold Jewellery," in *Excavations at Tawilan in Southern Jordan*. Edited by C. M. Bennett and P. Bienkowski. Forthcoming.

Peckham, J. Brian. *The Development of the Late Phoenician Scripts*. Cambridge: Harvard University, 1968.

Pilcher, E. J. "A Bronze Weight from Petra." *PEQ* 54 (1922): 71-73.

Porten, Bezalel. "The Identity of King Adon." *BA* 44 (1981): 36-52.

Porter, J. Leslie. "Edom, Idumea or Idumaea" in *Smith's Dictionary of the Bible*. 4 vols. Edited by H. B. Hackett. Boston: Houghton, Mifflin & Co., 1986, 1.661-63.

Pratico, Gary D. "Nelson Glueck's 1938-1940 Excavations at Tell el-Kheleifeh: A Reappraisal." *BASOR* 259 (1985): 1-32.

———, ed. *Nelson Glueck's 1938-1940 Excavations at Tell el-Kheleifeh: A Reappraisal*. ASOR Archaeological Reports 3. Atlanta: Scholars Press, 1993.

Price, Barbara J. "Secondary State Formation: An Explanatory Model," in *The Origins of State: The Anthropology of Political Evolution*, 161-86. Edited by R. Cohen and E. R. Service. Philadelphia: Institute for the Study of Human Issues, 1978.

Priest, John. "The Covenant of Brothers." *JBL* 84 (1965): 400-406.

Pritchard, James B. *Ancient Near Eastern Texts Relating to the Old Testament*. 3d edition with supplement. Princeton, NJ: Princeton University Press, 1969.

Puech, Emile. "Documents épigraphiques de Buseirah." *Levant* 9 (1977): 11-20.

Rainey, Anson. "The Toponymics of Eretz-Israel." *BASOR* 231 (1978): 1-17.

Rast, Walter E. and Schaub, R. Thomas. "Survey of the Southern Plain of the Dead Sea, 1973." *ADAJ* 19 (1974): 5-53.

Reich, Ronny. Palaces and Residencies in the Iron Age, in *The Architecture of Ancient Israel from the Prehistoric to the Persian Periods*, 202-22. Edited by A. Kempinski and R. Reich. Jerusalem: Israel Exploration Society, 1992.

Robinson, Edward. *Comprehensive Critical and Explanatory Bible Encyclopaedia*. Toledo: B. F. Rigg & Co, 1881.

——— and Smith, E. *Biblical researches in Palestine, Mount Sinai and Arabia Petraea: a journal of travels in the years 1838 and 1852*. 3 vols. London: J. Murray, 1841.

Robinson, George L. *The Sarcaphagus of an Ancient Civilization.* Chicago: MacMillan, 1930.

Rose, Martin. "Yahweh in Israel-Qaus in Edom?" *JSOT* 4 (1977): 28-34.

Rosenthal, Franz. "The Script of Ostracon 6043." *BASOR* 85 (1942): 8-9.

Rüger, Hans Peter. "Seir," in *Biblisch-historische Handwörterbuch.* 4 vols. Edited by B. Reicke and L. Rost. Göttingen: Vandenhoeck & Ruprecht, 1962-1979, 3:1760.

Ryckmans, Jacques. "Le panthéon de l'Arabie du Sud préislamique. Etat des problèmes et brève synthèse." *RHR* 206 (1989): 151-69.

Sauer, James A. "Transjordan in the Bronze and Iron Ages: A Critique of Glueck's Synthesis." *BASOR* 263 (1986): 1-26.

Savignac, Raymond. "Le dieu nabatéen de Laʿaban et son temple." *RB* 46 (1937) 401-16.

Sayce, Archibald H. "Edom, Edomites," in *A Dictionary of the Bible.* 5 vols. Edited by J. Hastings. New York: Charles Scribner's Sons, 1911, 1:644-46.

Schoville, Keith. "A note on the oracles of Amos against Gaza, Tyre and Edom," in *Studies on Prophecy. A Collection of Twelve Papers,* 55-63. Edited by G. W. Anderson *et al.* VTSup 26. Leiden: Brill, 1974.

Schultz, Siegfried. "Petra," in *Biblisch-historische Handwörterbuch.* 4 vols. Edited by B. Reicke and L. Rost. Göttingen: Vandenhoeck & Ruprecht, 1962-1979, 3:1430.

Seetzen, Ulrich F. *Reisen durch Syrien, Palästina, Phoenicien, Transjordan-Länder, Arabia Petraea und Unter-Aegypten, herausgegeben und commentiert von Prof. Dr. Fr. Kruse.* 3 vols. Berlin: G. Reimer, 1854-1859.

Seligsohn, M. "Edom, Idumea," in *The Jewish Encyclopedia.* 12 vols. Edited by I. Singer. New York: Funk & Wagnalls, 1903, 5:40-41.

Service, Elman R. *Origins of the State and Civilization. The Process of Cultural Evolution.* New York: W. W. Norton, 1975.

Simons, Jan Jozef. *Handbook for the Study of Egyptian Topographical Lists Relating to Western Asia.* Leiden: Brill, 1937.

———. *The Geographical and Topographical Texts of the Old Testament: A Concise Commentary in XXXII Chapters.* Nederlands Instituut voor het Nabije oosten. Studia Francisci Scholten memoriae dicata 2. Leiden: Brill, 1959.

Skinner, John. *Genesis.* ICC 1. Edinburgh: T. & T. Clark, 1910.

Smith, George Adam. *The Historical Geography of the Holy Land.* 26th edition. London: Hodder & Stoughton, 1935.

Smith, W. R. S. "Animal Worship and Animal Tribes among the Arabs and in the Old Testament." *Journal of Philology* 9 (1880): 75-103.

Soden, Wolfram von. *Akkadisches Handerwörterbuch.* 3 vols. Wiesbaden: O. Harrassowitz, 1965-1981.

Stade, Bernhard. *Geschichte des Volkes Israel.* 2 vols. Berlin: G. Grote, 1887.

Starcky, Jean. "Une tablette araméenne de l'an 34 de Nabuchodonosor (AO, 21.063)." *Syria* 37 (1960): 99-115.

Stark, Jürgen K. *Personal Names in the Palmyrene Inscriptions.* Oxford: Clarendon, 1971.

Staubli, Thomas. *Das Image der Nomaden im Alten Israel und in der Ikonographie seiner sesshaften Nachbarn.* OBO 107. Fribourg: Universitätsverlag and Göttingen: Vandenhoeck & Ruprecht, 1991.

Steele, Caroline S. "Early Bronze Age Socio-Political Organization in Southwestern Jordan." *ZDPV* 106 (1990): 1-33.

Stieglitz, Richard. "Ebla and the Gods of Canaan," in *Eblaitica: Essays on the Ebla Archives and Eblaite Language.* 2 vols. Edited by C. H. Gordon and G. Rendsburg. Winona Lake, IN: Eisenbrauns, 1987, 1990, 2.79-89.

Stern, Ephraim. *Material Culture of the Land of the Bible in the Persian Period 538-332 B.C.* Warminster: Aris & Phillips, 1982.

Stolper, Matthew W. "The Neo-Babylonian Text from the Persepolis Fortification." *JNES* 43 (1984): 299-310.

Streck, Maximilian. *Assurbanipal und die letzen assyrischen Könige bis zum Untergang Niniveh's.* 3 vols. Vorderasiatische Bibliotek 7. Leipzig: J. C. Hinrichs, 1916.

Teixidor, Javier. "Bulletin d'épigraphie sémitique 1972." *Syria* 49: 419-20.

Thompson, Henry O. and Zayadine, Fawzi. "The Tell Siran Inscription." *BASOR* 212 (1973): 5-11.

Tigay, Jeffrey H. *You Shall Have No Other Gods. Israelite Religion in the Light of Hebrew Inscriptions.* HSM 31. Atlanta: Scholars Press, 1986.

Torczyner, Harry. *The Lachish Letters. Lachish 1.* London: Oxford University, 1938.

Van Seters, John. "The Conquest of Sihon's Kingdom: A Literary Examination." *JBL* 91 (1972): 182-97.

———. "Once Again: The Conquest of Sihon's Kingdom." *JBL* 99 (1980): 117-24.

Vaux, Roland de. "Téman, ville ou région d'Édom?" *RB* 76 (1969): 379-85.

Vincent, L. Hugues. "Le dieu Saint Paqeidas à Gérasa." *RB* 49 (1940): 98-129.

Vogüé, Charles Jean Melchior, marquis de. "Intailles a légendes sémitiques." *Revue archéologique* N.S. 17 (1868): 432-50, pl. XVI:40.

Vriezen, Theodor. "The Edomite Deity Qaus." *OTS* 14 (1965): 330-53.

Wallerstein, Immanuel. *The Capitalist World-Economy: Essays.* Cambridge: Cambridge University Press, 1979.

Walzer, Michael. *Interpretation and Social Criticism.* Cambridge: Harvard University Press, 1987.

Weinfeld, Moshe. "Kuntillet Ajrud inscriptions and their significance." *SEL* 1 (1984): 121-30.

Weippert, Manfred. "Edom. Studien und Materialien zur Geschichte der Edomiter auf Grund schriftlicher und archäologischer Quellen." Doctoral dissertation, University of Tübingen, 1971.

———. "Semitische Nomaden des zweiten Jahrtausends." *Biblica* 55 (1974): 265-80; 427-33.

———. "Remarks on the History of Settlement in Southern Jordan during the Early Iron Age," in *Studies in the History and Archaeology of Jordan I,* 153-62. Edited by A. Hadidi. Amman: Department of Antiquities, 1982.

———. "Edom and Israel," in *Theologische Real-Enzyklopädie.* 21 vols. Edited by G. Krause and G. Müller. Berlin and New York: W. de Gruyter, 1971-1991, 9: 291-99.

———. "Zur Syrienpolitik Tiglatpilesers III," in *Mesopotamien und seine Nachbarn II,* 395-408. Edited by H. J. Nissen and J. Renger. Berlin: Reimer, 1982.

———. "The Relations of the States East of the Jordan with the Mesopotamian Powers during the First Millenium BC," in *Studies in the History and Archaeology of Jordan III,* 97-105. Edited by A. Hadidi. Amman: Department of Antiquities, 1987.

Weippert, Manfred and Helga. "Die 'Bileam'-Inschrift von Tell Der ʿAllā." *ZDPV* 98 (1982): 77-103.

Wirth, Eugen. *Syrien. Eine geographische Landeskunde.* Darmstadt: Wissenschaftliche Buchgelsellschaft, 1971.

Worschech, Udo. "*Collared-Rim Jars* aus Moab: Anmerkungen zur Entwicklung und Verbreitung der Krüge mit 'Halswulst.'" *ZDPV* 108 (1992): 149-55.

Yassine, Khair and Teixidor, Javier. "Ammonite and Aramaic Inscriptions from Tell el-Mazar in Jordan." *BASOR* 264 (1986): 45-50.

Young, Ian. "The Dipthong *ay in Edomite (Clues in Isaiah)." *Journal of Semitic Studies* 37 (1992): 27-30.

Younker, Randall. "Israel, Judah and Ammon and the Motifs on the Baalis Seal from Tell el-ʿUmeiri." *BA* 48 (1985): 173-80.

Zayadine, Fawzi. "The Pantheon of the Nabataean Inscriptions in Egypt and the Sinai." *Aram* 2 (1990): 151-74.

Zeitler, John P. "'Edomite' Pottery from the Petra Region," in *Early Edom and Moab: The Beginning of the Iron Age in Southern Jordan,* 167-76. Edited by P. Bienkowski. SAM 7. Sheffield: J. R. Collis, 1992.

Zwickel, Wolfgang. "Das 'edomitischen' Ostrakon aus Ḫirbet Ġazza (Ḥorvat ʿUza)." *BN* 41 (1988): 36-40.

Index of Biblical References

Author Citation Index

Subject Index